A Testament of Revolution

NUMBER THIRTEEN
EASTERN EUROPEAN STUDIES

Stjepan Meštrović, General Editor

A Testament

of Revolution

BÉLA LIPTÁK

TEXAS A&M UNIVERSITY PRESS

COLLEGE STATION

The paper used in this book meets the minimum requirements
of the American National Standard for Permanence
of Paper for Printed Library Materials, z39.48-1984.
Binding materials have been chosen for durability.

∞

Library of Congress Cataloging-in-Publication Data

Lipták, Béla G.

    A testament of revolution / Béla Lipták.—1st ed.

      p. cm.—(Eastern European studies ; no. 13)

    Includes bibliographical references and index.

    ISBN 1-58544-120-1 (alk. paper)

    1. Hungary—History—Revolution, 1956—Personal narratives.

  I. Title. II. Eastern European studies (College Station, Tex.) ; no. 13.

DB957.3.L56   2001

943.905'2'092—dc21   00-012028

Dedicated to the memories of

István Angyal, János Danner,

and the heroic children of Budapest

and also written for my grandchildren,

Ivan, Katie, and Ava

Hungary conquered and in chains

has done more for freedom and justice

than any people . . . we have only

one way of being true to Hungary,

and that is never to betray,

among ourselves and everywhere,

what the Hungarian heroes died for.

—*Albert Camus*

Contents

List of Illustrations   ix

Prologue   3

CHAPTER 1   Just an Average Day   15

CHAPTER 2   Birth of MEFESZ and the Sixteen Points   25

CHAPTER 3   My Tricolor Armband   36

CHAPTER 4   Enough of Listening   46

CHAPTER 5   MEFESZ Headquarters of the Technical University   58

CHAPTER 6   Getting the Arms   66

CHAPTER 7   Hungary's Jews and Germans   77

CHAPTER 8   A Barrel of Blood   91

CHAPTER 9   Top Secret   103

CHAPTER 10   Jancsi's Murder   111

CHAPTER 11   Beginning of the End   123

CHAPTER 12   Lives on the Line   132

CHAPTER 13   Interrogation   142

CHAPTER 14   Home   151

CHAPTER 15   Escaping Hungary   159

Postscript   167

Notes   179

Index   195

Illustrations

1. Author's parents   9
2. Memi, author's brothers, and author   10
3. Map of Budapest   18
4. Katalin Stricker and Maria Wittner   51
5. Head from Stalin's statue on Budapest street   54
6. Untouched goods in broken windows of department store   61
7. Trucks bringing food to freedom fighters   62
8. Unguarded collection box   63
9. István Angyal   72
10. Soviet tank in Dohány Street   75
11. Soviet tank on observation duty   78
12. Group of fighters of Corvin Alley   83
13. Cardinal Mindszenty at news conference   99
14. Gergeley Pongrátz, Imre Mécs, and author   101
15. István Bibó in Parliament   134
16. Getting ready for the second Soviet assault   137
17. The MEFESZ office door in the center and Stocek's bust to its right   146
18. Móricz Square apartments   150
19. Hiding behind street corners   154
20. On the road to Austria   164
21. Freight cars of escaping freedom fighters   165
22. Author in 1957   169
23. Márta   170
24. With Governor Pataki and his son   174
25. Author's family   178

A Testament of Revolution

Prologue

THIS IS NOT A HISTORY BOOK. It is a memoir of one who in 1956 was a twenty-year-old student in Hungary and today is a sixty-four-year-old grandfather in the United States. In a way, this book is written by both of us. This prologue, the postscript, and some footnotes have been prepared in 2000 by my grandfather-self (Béla), while the memoir itself was written by my student-self (Öcsi) in an Austrian refugee camp in December 1956. *Béla* is a common given name in Hungary, while *Öcsi* is an equally common nickname there, meaning *little brother.* In 1956 everybody called me that. Throughout the book I use real names and describe actual events.

The memoir is presented in fifteen chapters. Before starting the memoir I have inserted a brief summary of the history of Hungary followed by a description of my own family, so when you start the first chapter, which begins on October 21, 1956, you will have a better feel of where the events are taking place and who the participants are. You should also know that this book is dedicated to two martyrs of the Revolution, one a devoted Christian, the other an agnostic Jew. After reading the paragraphs on Hungary's history, you will better understand why I mention that István Angyal was Jewish.

Hungary's History

For one thousand years Hungary occupied the oval-shaped central plain of the Danubian Basin, which was once the Roman provinces of Pannonia and Dacia, an area surrounded by the protective bulwark of the Carpathian Mountains. Hungary was a tolerant and multiethnic kingdom that served not only as a balancing power between Slavic and Germanic nations but also as the eastern bulwark of Europe. The first king of Hungary, Saint Stephen, wrote to his son: "Make the strangers welcome in this land, let them keep their languages and customs, for weak and fragile is the realm which is based on a single language or a single set of customs." Throughout the centuries Stephen's advice was respected, and eventually fourteen nationalities composed the kingdom of Hungary, with Latin being its official language until 1844.[1]

In 1222 the privileges of Hungary's nobility were set down on paper, and the beginnings of a parliament were established in the "Golden Bull," which document is junior to the English Magna Carta by only five years. During the reign of the Renaissance king Matthias Corvinus, Hungary's population equaled that of England, the court of Buda became one of the cultural centers of Europe, and the library of Buda was one of Europe's finest. After that golden age, one tragedy followed another.

In 1526 the Turks occupied central Hungary. The western parts of the country were taken by the Habsburgs, and for 150 years only the eastern parts of the country remained under Hungarian control. That part (Transylvania, today part of Romania) is where Béla Bartók collected his Hungarian folk tunes. Transylvania is also the place where the Hungarian Diet (an assembly of noblemen similar to a parliament) at Torda in 1568 proclaimed the freedom of religion for the four "received" religions (the Catholic, Calvinist, Lutheran, and Unitarian faiths). It was also in Transylvania that Francis David in 1560 laid the foundation of the Unitarian Church. After the end of Turkish occupation, the Habsburgs attempted to take over all of Hungary.

The first fight for Hungarian independence (1703–11) was led by Francis II Rákóczy (1676–1735), and the second (1848–49) by Louis

Kossuth (1802–94). Kossuth was the second foreigner ever to be invited to address the U.S. Congress (1852), and it was also Kossuth who later suggested converting the Austro-Hungarian duality, which was formed in 1867, into a Danubian Confederation, a united states of Central Europe. Kossuth in his nineties said, "Whenever a power vacuum evolved in the Carpathian Basin, the Balkans became unstable, and no outside power can permanently fill such vacuum, because all outsiders lose interest after a few years."[2]

The period between the formation of the Austro-Hungarian duality (1867) and World War I was not only a period of great progress for Hungary but also the golden age of Hungarian Jewry. There was no official anti-Semitism (although there was some popular anti-Semitism in Hungary), and Jews were treated with much more tolerance and enjoyed greater opportunities for upward mobility than elsewhere in Europe. In gratitude for being accepted, the Jews of Hungary assimilated and became Hungarian patriots. The unique mix of Hungarian and Jewish talent resulted in contributions that are relevant in science and in all the fields of scholarly and artistic endeavor.[3]

At the beginning of the twentieth century Russia started to sponsor pan-Slavic agitation and a drive for a Greater Serbia. Archduke Francis Ferdinand opposed it, and for that reason the Serbian nationalists ordered his assassination. He was murdered in 1914 in the same city (Sarajevo) where, eighty years later, the Bosnian War would begin. The retaliation against Serbia (opposed by Count Stephen Tisza of Hungary, who argued that a whole nation should not be held responsible for the acts of a few fanatics) ignited World War I.

During the war, the Czech leaders Eduard Benes and Thomas Masaryk supported the pan-Slavic ambitions of Russia and Serbia. They organized a propaganda campaign, suggesting that French dominance of Europe could be achieved only if Hungary were dismembered. Two French politicians, Georges Clemenceau and Raymond Poincaré, agreed to support the plan, while President Woodrow Wilson opposed it—he preferred borders that corresponded to ethnic frontiers. Still, the Treaty of Trianon was implemented, and Hungary was dismembered. President Wilson called this step "absurd," and the U.S. Congress refused to approve either the Treaty of Versailles (1919) or the Treaty of Trianon (1920), and in 1921 the United States signed a separate treaty with Hungary. While the prevailing mood of isolationism in the U.S. Senate played a part in this rejection, the main reason was the Senate's sense of fairness and its desire not to be tainted by the obvious injustice of Trianon.

As a result of Trianon, Hungary's territory was reduced by two-thirds, and the Hungarians became Europe's largest ethnic minority. They became foreigners in other peoples' lands without ever leaving their thousand-year-old hometowns, because the borders had been redrawn around them. Towns were separated from their suburbs, villages were split in two, and communities were cut off from their railroad stations or water supplies. From the fragments of the Hungarian kingdom, the artificial and unstable entities of Czechoslovakia, Yugoslavia, and greater Romania were created.

The chaos that followed World War I resulted in a short-lived Communist dictatorship in "mini-Hungary." This "red" dictatorship of the proletariat was directed by Béla Kun (1886–1937), whose brutality, and the fact that he was Jewish, later resulted in both "white terrorist" reprisals and the rekindling of anti-Jewish sentiments in the country. The Kun government was followed by the conservative reign of Admiral Horthy (1868–1957), who initially cooperated with Mussolini in the hopes that Il Duce would help Hungary regain her lost territories. After the suicide of premier Pál Teleki, that desire tragically led Hungary first to declare war on Serbia and the Soviet Union (June, 1941) and later to halfheartedly support the German war effort by sending some of her military forces to the eastern front only while holding her antiaircraft fire when western aircraft passed over Hungarian territory.

During World War II, Hungary became a sanctuary for Jews; she gave shelter to about a quarter million refugees from Poland and Ukraine. The Jews of Hungary would have survived the war if Germany had not occupied the country. Unfortunately, when the Germans no longer viewed Admiral Horthy as reliable—and because they wanted to deport Hungarian Jews—in March, 1944, the German army occupied Hungary, and a few months later, in October of that year, it overthrew the Horthy regime and arrested the admiral. After German occupation, over half a million Hungarian and foreign Jews were deported (as a child, Pista Angyal—one of those to whom this volume is dedicated—was one of them), but the majority of the Jews of Budapest survived. They were saved by the heroic deeds of both Hungarians, such as Colonel Koszorús, who on July 6, 1944, militarily evicted

Eichmann's supporters from the capital, and by foreigners, such as the Swedish diplomat Raul Wallenberg, who provided many safe houses and false identity papers to Jews.

At the end of World War II, Hungary was occupied by Soviet forces, but she still managed to hold reasonably free elections in 1945 and 1947. In the first election the Communist Party received only 17 percent of the vote, but after that, because of Soviet pressure, the party gained control of the ministry of the interior. First some key politicians were arrested by the secret police (the ÁVH), then democratic institutions were gradually eliminated, and by 1949 the Communist Party gained full control. The Soviets organized a secret police and appointed a puppet government, both dominated by Jewish Hungarians. This was a conscious effort on the part of the occupiers to deflect and redirect the loathing of the public from themselves to the Jews. This puppet government, headed by Mátyás Rákosi, eliminated all democratic institutions, nationalized industry, closed the private schools, confiscated the land of the farmers, arrested Cardinal József Mindszenty, and, in order to obtain housing for the Communists and their collaborators, deported most of the middle class from Budapest.

These actions destroyed not only the nation's economy but also her agriculture, which used to be one of Europe's best. To reverse this trend, the Soviets in the mid-1950s began to promote some reform-minded Communists, such as Imre Nagy, who was considered to be a friend of the farmers. In 1955 the puppet government of Hungary joined the Warsaw Treaty Organization and thereby gave the "right to the brotherly socialist states to defend Hungary," even against her own people. The situation in Poland was not any better, and in October 1956 strikes broke out in the Polish city of Poznan. The news of these strikes triggered the events in Hungary that are the subject of this book.

My Family

My grandfather, Dr. Pál Lipták, was born in 1876 as one of ten children of a poor carpenter in a small town named Békéscsaba. Thanks to the educational policy of the Hungarian kingdom and to the personal efforts of one of its cabinet ministers, Gábor Baross, all my grandfather's education was paid for by the government. In 1906 he completed his Ph.D. thesis, which laid the theoretical foundations for construction using reinforced, prestrained steel in concrete. This invention made him very rich. He owned steel mills, mines, and all kinds of other property. When I asked my father how rich grandfather was, he would reply, "He was the second highest taxpayer of Budapest." The fact that grandfather was most proud of the amount of taxes he paid shows his sense of indebtedness for his free education to Hungarian society and the nation.

When during World War I the government could no longer pay for the military supplies that were needed at the eastern front, my grandfather's plants continued shipping the supplies without getting paid. His effort was so substantial that the last king of Hungary, Charles IV (who was also the Austro-Hungarian duality's Emperor Charles I), took pains to thank him in writing. The king wrote to him a few days before the dual monarchy disintegrated.

My grandfather died in 1926, ten years before I was born. By then not much was left of his fortune, because both the war effort and the dismemberment of Hungary cost him dearly. For him the consequence of the Treaty of Trianon was that his mines no longer belonged to Hungary. Still, there was enough inheritance for my father (Béla Lipták, Sr., the second youngest of his six children) to get started.

After my grandfather died, my father, who was an athlete and a shot-put champion in his university days, quickly completed his degree. In 1928, at the age of nineteen, he purchased an eleven-hundred-acre farm in Tolna County, where he created a model farm and a textile factory. In 1932 he married a blonde beauty, the daughter of a colonel, the belle of the balls of Budapest. My mother was very religious, very sociable, always happy, singing, and joking. Her father was a military man, reserved, highly educated, while her mother was a bit conceited and somewhat domineering. Péter, my older brother, was born in 1934; I in 1936; and my younger brother, András, known as Andris, in 1940. We in our family always came up with unique nicknames. My father was called Aptyi. The regular Hungarian equivalent of *daddy* would be *apu* or *papa,* but, as always, we had to be different. My mother was called Memi, rather than the common *anyu* or *mama.* We called my maternal grandmother Nagymemi. And I got the name Öcsi, or "little brother," probably before they realized that in a little while we would have an even smaller brother.

Our early childhood was a very happy one. Our fourteen-room house

Figure 1. My parents

was always full of relatives and guests. My mother loved company and was a good hostess. Aptyi enjoyed hunting and horseback riding but basically was a workaholic. Our isolated farm (called Furkó Puszta) on the floodplains of the Danube had a bucolic quality to it. We did not need to go to the zoo to see wild animals. During the winter we would get snowed in so deeply that for weeks we were isolated from the outside world. Santa Claus came to our house on a reindeer-drawn sled. Later, I learned that behind Santa's white beard and mustache was my rather corpulent godfather, my father's younger brother, while the four reindeer were in fact horses wearing cleverly attached antlers. If, on Christmas Eve, we peeped through the keyhole of the living room, we saw angels hanging the ornaments on the tree. Later I learned that the angels were my mother, her sister, and my godmother with wings on their backs and halos attached to the wigs on their heads.

Figure 2. Memi with my brothers and me

I was probably six or so when I first heard that there was a war going on. At that time we did not go to school; the teacher came to our house, and she did not talk about such things as wars. The little I knew about the world I learned while sitting next to Nagyaptyi (my maternal grandfather), who was constantly listening to the BBC on his shortwave radio. He referred to a fellow named Hitler as "the madman." I also heard that Uncle Laci, my father's older brother, who was involved with politics, was fighting against some anti-Jewish laws.[4]

I did not know what that meant, but I did know that there were Jewish people, because Jóska Bácsi was one. The closest translation for *bácsi* is *uncle*, but *bácsi* does not refer to a blood relative, only to an older friend. We referred to most people who were older as *bácsi* or *néni*— *uncle* or *aunt*—as a sign of respect. József Litván was a friend of my father and was also a buyer of his products for the firm of Budakalászi RT. For a while he stayed in our house. I do not know for sure, but he was probably hiding.

I was about eight when one day there was a lot of commotion in the house: Memi was crying as Aptyi got his army revolver and stormed out of the house. He did not come back for a long time. Later I learned that Germany occupied Hungary and Eichmann's thugs had taken the mother of my godmother (the Jewish wife of an Austro-Hungarian general), and Aptyi went to try to get her out of the concentration camp. In the process he almost got himself shot by the SS.

Not much later, in the winter of 1944, the Russian troops entered Hungary. First Memi escaped with us, the three kids from Furkó. Aptyi stayed behind for a while, but he, too, left before the Russians got there. Only my old friend Bundi, a gigantic Saint Bernard dog, was left behind to defend our home. Bundi did his best and was killed while fighting the intruders. As the Russians kept coming from the east, we kept moving to the west, but when we reached the Austrian border, Aptyi could not cross it. He just could not leave his homeland.

So we waited and waited in this village at the border. I remember my mother getting dressed in torn peasant clothes, her face dirtied with mud and ashes. Next I remember watching as the last Hungarian gendarme patrol calmly marched through the village, their uniforms and bayonets shining, their steps in unison. And then, after a period of deafening silence, all hell broke loose as the drunk and dirty Russian troops started to arrive and the pillage began. That night I remember waking up to see my former shot-put champion father, Aptyi, lifting up a Russian soldier with one hand while taking away his gun with the other. The young soldier was not prepared for such a reception and started to cry while Aptyi took the bullets from the gun and gave it back empty. The Russian was relieved. Apparently, Russian soldiers were executed if they lost their guns, no matter the circumstances. Later on, Aptyi became friendly with this young Russian, and in exchange for one thousand cigarettes the soldier got us a stolen horse and carriage. This was important because our car was long gone, but on this carriage we could return to the city of Sopron.

There was nothing to eat. We would pick mushrooms in the woods and collect the bones of dead horses. The baby of Duduke (Memi's younger sister) died from hunger. Aptyi and I left the family in Sopron and set out on our thousand-cigarette carriage for Budapest. On the way there, when we saw a loose horse, we would tie it to the cart. By the time we arrived in the outskirts of Budapest we must have had a dozen hungry horses trailing behind the cart. At night we slept under the wagon, and I still remember the white eyes and teeth of the hungry horses as they tried to bite me. When we arrived in Budapest and were waiting in front of Nagymemi's apartment house, I was playing with the whip and accidentally hit a Russian officer. Because of that, Aptyi was arrested, and when he got out, I was surprised that he did not beat me up.

Aptyi knew that the Russians confiscated all factories, so we never went back to our farm and factory at Furkó, which my dog Bundi had tried to defend, but settled in a village named Kerepes. The rumor was that the Russians would deport the middle class from the capital in order to get apartments for their collaborators, so we did not stay in Budapest. In Kerepes, Aptyi rented some land and resumed farming. I went to the local school and got into fights because the peasant kids wore long pants and did not like my short ones or because I did not like their doubting the existence of Santa Claus, whom I had met in person.

As soon as Aptyi made some money (he traded horses in Austria and he also got paid for some textile shipments he made to Switzerland during the war), he sent us to the best school in the country, the ancient Benedictine school of Pannonhalma. I spent the years 1946 and 1947 there and then transferred to the Piarists in Budapest for my sixth grade, but I could not stay there for long, because the Communists were closing all the private and religious schools.

It was in 1948 when the Communists arrested Cardinal Mindszenty, and it was the year after that when they hanged János Meloccó, an investigative reporter, who identified the drug they used on the cardinal to obtain his false confession to treason and illegal monetary transactions. Aptyi was a Lutheran, and until that time he had never come with us to the Catholic Church in Kerepes. But after they hanged János Bácsi, who had been my mother's boyfriend and was a good friend of the family, he not only came, but he sat in the front row during the high mass every Sunday, and when he sang the national anthem, the windows shook. This was also the time when they took away Aptyi's rented farm in Kerepes and he became a laborer. We barely had enough to eat. Memi was feeding pigs and raising chickens, and Nagyaptyi, Memi's father, first stopped talking and then died.

Because my paternal grandfather was a major supporter of the Lutheran High School of Budapest, they accepted me (in spite of my being a Catholic). I was very happy there. This was not only because of my grandfather's memory but also because this was the school where such geniuses as the Nobel Prize–winning Eugene Wigner and John von Neumann had studied. It was the best high school in Europe. In

1952 the Communists also closed down this school, and as a result I continued my school hopping until I finally graduated from Eötvös High School in 1954. In spite of my good grades, I stood no chance of being admitted into any college, because I was branded a class enemy, "Category X," indicating that my parents were "enemies of the state."

Once again my long-dead paternal grandfather came to my help. In earlier years he had given some help to the man who now was the president of the Technical University of Miskolc, and when in 1954 the quota of that university was not completely full, this man got in touch with Aptyi. The president had the right to fill eight spaces without considering the category of the applicants, and I ended up as one of those eight. Needless to say, all eight of us were Category X students. We started school in September, and by October we got in trouble for organizing a Russian book-burning party. By November we were all kicked out of both the dormitory and the cafeteria of the university.

The authorities assumed that this would be the end of our college careers, as no student could continue without food and housing—but four of us did. We formed a jazz band (I played the drums), we rented the back room of a retired prostitute's apartment, and we stole food from wherever we could. One source was the North Koreans' kitchen and the other was the baker's truck. There were only a few North Koreans at the university, so their chef and waiter was the same person. Therefore, while he was serving the food in their dining room, we would jump through the kitchen window and steal what we could. I never told Aptyi about losing my dormitory and cafeteria privileges, because I knew it would break his heart and because he couldn't help, anyway. So I just studied like a maniac to make the honor roll, because if I did, I could transfer to the Technical University of Budapest. Out of the eight of us, one was taken away by the ÁVH, four dropped out of school, one stayed at Miskolc and died during the Revolution, and two, Laci Török and I, managed to transfer to Budapest.

This was a fantastic achievement and also a great lesson for me. From then on I kept my mouth shut and did not say anything about the Russians or about politics. Fortunately, thanks to the incompetence of Communist bureaucracy, the documentation of my expulsion from the dormitory in Miskolc did not follow me to Budapest. So I had a clean slate. I became involved in sports, started to discover girls, made some good friends, and in general enjoyed myself at the Technical University of Budapest. Aptyi, in the meantime, became an advisor to the collective farm in Csömör, Péter was a student at the Agricultural University of Gödöllő, and Andris was in high school. We all pretty much accepted Russian occupation and Communism as a given, as something permanent, and tried to live our lives in spite of that. That was my frame of mind on October 21, 1956, when my memoir begins, and you will hear the voice of my twenty-year-old self, Öcsi.

CHAPTER 1

Just an Average Day

If ten or so Hungarian writers had been shot at the right moment, the revolution would never have occurred.

—*Nikita Khrushchev*

I T WAS A CLOUDY SUNDAY AFTERNOON. People were walking their dogs on the mountain of Saint Gellért on the banks of the Danube in the middle of Budapest. Gellért became a saint when some one thousand years ago the Hungarians got tired of listening to the sermons of this Italian priest and threw him off these cliffs. I loved to walk on that hill and take in the panoramic view of this beautiful city.

I had no money left after I paid the entrance fee to get into the Gellért spa, but that did not bother me. I knew that tomorrow I would get my monthly scholarship of 140 forints.[1] Budapest is a city of spas; it is sitting on what used to be the bottom of the ancient Pannon Sea. In almost every city block there is a public bath, each supplied by a natural spring. Some are medicinal, as their waters contain various minerals, while others are just hot-water springs. At the Gellért there are both kinds, but this time I did not come to soak but to loosen up. I swam my usual fifty laps, glanced at the clock, and got out of the water. I had only twenty minutes to change and get to the high-jump competition. I was running as I got to the streetcar station on Béla Bartók Street.

The yellow No. 47 tram was screeching as it made the ninety-degree turn onto Freedom Bridge. (That bridge used to be named after the king of Hungary, Franz Joseph, but like everything else, it too was renamed by the Communists.) It took only three or four long steps to reach the last car and jump onto it. The ticket collector, a big-busted blonde woman, was right there on the dirty back platform. She barked at the young man standing next to me, "No standing on the stairs! Please come up to the platform!"

He moved up. I stayed on the stairs. I knew that being 187 centimeters tall (6 feet, 2 inches), I was tall enough for her to think that I was already up. I must be six inches taller than the average Hungarian. That is almost the height of one step on the stairs. I was right; the ticket collector did not bother me. I was poised for a quick jump and dash to the sports field when I reached my stop.

I was so impatient, so afraid of being late for the competition, that I decided to jump off the tram between stops, right in front of the Kinizsi sports field in the district of Ferencváros. Actually, I was pretty good at jumping off. I practiced it a lot and knew that you have to jump backward to reduce the forward speed, and when your shoes come in contact with the pavement, run like hell. The trick is to do this while facing forward and to start running during the flight, so that when you hit the pavement you are already running like crazy and will not fall on your face—which, at thirty miles an hour, is no fun at all.

I quickly changed into my slightly dirty red-and-white jumping outfit and put on my spiked and rather stinking jumping shoes in the equally smelly changing room. I liked my red athletic tricots, because they made my skinny upper body look more muscular. The jumping competition had already started. The bar was at 130 centimeters. When I checked in, the coach, Jani Bácsi, gave me an annoyed bark. "Hey, are you another one of those conceited prima donas? You don't even show up until we pass one-thirty? Or was it Ágnes?"

I acted as if I did not hear him and concentrated on bending, stretching, and loosening my muscles. I was surprised that he remembered Ágnes. Jani Bácsi did not see my fifteen-year-old (well, almost sixteen-), green-eyed little girl friend more than once or twice, when she waited for me after a training session. So how could he remember?

When I got in line, the bar was already at 140. There were two jump-ers ahead of me. The first was a spectacled, redheaded fellow. He took off his glasses and ran directly at the bar, jumping headfirst in the newly fashionable "rolling" style. He cleared. The next jumper, a tall, blond guy, used the same "scissoring" technique as I, except that he pushed off from his left foot and therefore approached the bar from the right. He also cleared. Now it was my turn. I ran at the bar from the left, kicked off when I was almost completely under it, felt a good lift . . . and then my left knee hit the bar. While I was spitting out the sand I had swallowed on landing, the judge yelled, "Number twenty-nine! Sec-ond try!" I walked back and got ready to try again.

I cleared 140 on the second try and that made me less nervous. I cleared 150 on the first try, and by a good margin. I actually got a "Not bad, number twenty-nine" from the judge. At this point, out of the fifty or so jumpers at this meet, only about half were still in the compe-tition. My best jump to date was 155. But on this day I felt particularly good and cleared 155 with no difficulty at all. At 160 I got a bit scared. The bar was high enough for my mother or Ágnes to walk under! I missed twice but cleared it on the third try. Wow! That felt good! There were only six of us left, and now a few spectators started to gather around the jumping area. It felt good to be the center of attention. Just their presence gave me more energy and confidence. Among the spec-tators was a friend, a fellow student, Attila, and a petite blonde runner, Marika, the bride of another friend, Gyuszi Perr. She was so vibrant, so full of energy. When I cleared 165 and was basking in the kudos from the crowd, she came up to me, jabbed a finger into my gut, and pro-claimed, "Just like a field frog!"

I started taking off my jumping shoes, but Jani Bácsi stopped me. "Don't you want to try for one-seventy? If you clear, you get a medal!"

But I was thinking of something else. "We have no bread at home and it's my job to bring some for dinner," I replied.

"Bread on Sunday?" mused Jani Bácsi.

"Yeah," I told him, "The Közért on Baross Square is open until six, so I have to run!"[2]

When one is twenty and has not eaten since morning, the smell of freshly baked bread is very special. The 2-kilogram (4.4-pound) loaf cost 6.80 forints. Memi had given me ten for the bread, and I had two of my own, which I had spent to get into the Gellért spa. So Memi's ten

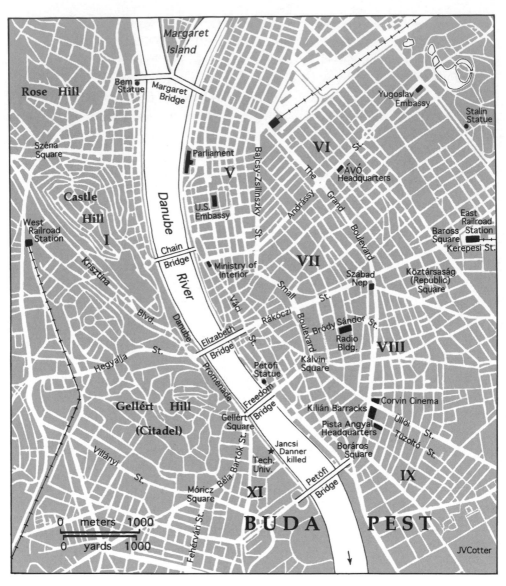

Figure 3. Map of Budapest. Drawn by John Cotter

was just enough for the bread and to call Ágnes. I was hoping we could make plans to see a popular Italian movie, *The Women of Selistye*, the next day. The movie was to start at 4:00 P.M. Her classes would be over by then. Of course I did not have money for the movie tickets either, but tomorrow would be October 22, so I would try to get my November stipend of 140 forints. God, that was a lot of money! I would be rich tomorrow![3]

It took more than an hour to get from the Közért to our house in Kerepes. I did not even notice that half the bread was gone by the time I got to our gate. I first picked at the crust, then the insides. It was warm and tasted so good. As I opened the creaking iron gate of the house, my young German shepherd, Bukucs, ran to me at full speed. She was just crazy about me. Nobody ever loved me like that. I do not know why I deserved it. Was it my smell? Was this my reward for keeping my urges for personal hygiene under control? She just rubbed her nose to my knee and could not stop licking and jumping. Was she trying to remind me that it had been some time since I went with her—only her—for a full day in the woods? Did she have the urge for another trip for mushroom picking and bird watching? Was she trying to make that point?

The light was on in the kitchen, and as I stepped through the door my younger brother, Andris, started yelling, "Öcsi ate the bread! Öcsi ate the bread!"

Andris was four years younger than I, a skinny crybaby, but he still called me Öcsi, "little brother." I got the name before he was born, when I was the little one compared to my older brother, Péter. So at that time it made sense, but the name stuck to me, as do most family nicknames.

In the corner of the kitchen my father, Aptyi, was talking excitedly with two of our neighbors. Their hats were still on and their hands held half-empty wine glasses. I heard the mispronounced name Eisenhoffer—Eisenhower—over and over again, but I was not paying much attention. Memi took the bread—in fact, confiscated it—with the declaration, "For tomorrow's sandwiches!" She gave me a bowl of steaming hot bean soup, but no bread.

Péter was reading in the next room, and Nagymemi, my maternal grandmother, was slowly moving back into her room. As always, she had her winter coat on. We did not heat the house until it got very cold, and this was only October.

"I cleared 165," I said to no one in particular.

The room fell silent for a few seconds as Aptyi looked at me proudly and Memi promptly went to the doorpost, where the heights of the family members were marked and dated, to see how high 165 centimeters was. Andris exclaimed, "My foot! You did not!" Now that was a real brotherly compliment.

After dinner—my bowl of soup—I threw my drafting board on the kitchen table and started working on the ball-bearing design that I had to hand in the next day. I already had the outlines drawn in light pencil. What was left to do was to mark over the pencil-drawn lines in black India ink. I used a razor blade to scrape out the slightest mistakes and commented to Andris, "Appearance is everything to Professor Vörös. This machine-design professor doesn't care if the balls are cubical as long as the drawing is neat."

I was still working when the neighbors started saying their good-byes. It is said that Hungarians have a tendency to say good-bye and stay, but this is a slight exaggeration. They eventually do leave. It just takes them longer than anybody else.

Memi finished cleaning up and was off to bed. Aptyi checked on the animals (we had a milk cow, a horse, a couple of goats, pigs, and a bunch of chickens) before following her to their bedroom. It was well after midnight—Andris and Péter were already snoring—when I finally rolled up my drawing and hit the bed myself. We had three rooms. We called one of them the bedroom, the others the living room and the dining room, but at night we slept in all three of them.

The next morning, Memi tried to wake me at 6:00 and again at 6:15. There was no heat in the house, and the bathroom was dreadfully cold, so who wanted to get up? The toilet did not flush. The "hot" water was cold. And everybody wanted—or needed—to get in there at the same time. I finally got out of bed and dressed quickly.

My sandals were cold for October, but I certainly was not going to wear out my beautiful new *csukas*, my shoes with the two-inch-thick synthetic rubber soles. I had spent all my earnings of the last summer (nine hundred forints) to buy my csukas. This summer's earnings were spent on an equally smart purple corduroy jacket. We received no stipends during the summer months, and I spent all my earnings this summer on that jacket. I had never had new shoes before. So on this day, October 22, I wore only the sandals along with my *jampec* (teddy-boy) pants, which were so tight below the knee that I needed to open zippers to get into them.

I did wear my new corduroy jacket. It was tailor-made. It had cost me the equivalent of ten weeks' wages. It was my first and only tailor-made jacket. It gave me broad shoulders and a muscular, dashing look. More important, it gave Ágnes an armpit to nest in whenever we walked. It was as though that warm niche was made just for her, and she loved it. She would look up from there with a mischievous twinkle in her eye while contemplating whether she should trip me or whether an unexpected shove with her little bum would do.

I left the house at 6:35. The train would leave at 6:52. I needed twenty minutes to walk to the station, so I walked with a fast pace. I passed Éva Ordassy, another beauty I was in love with (without her knowledge). She was on her way to the Teachers' College. That encounter told me that I was in trouble; she was catching the 7:02 local. I had to pick up my pace. So I started to run like a gazelle, which was not easy in sandals and with the drawing of the ball bearings and the books tucked under my arm.

It was 6:51 when I got to the top of the hill. I could see the train coming in, and I was still three hundred meters from the station. Now I ran like my life depended on it. I still had another two hundred meters to go when the train stopped in the station, one hundred when the last passenger boarded, and fifty when the train started to move again. My friend Tibi Bakonyi had noticed me running and was holding the door open for me on the last car. The train was already picking up speed when I grabbed the handle with my right hand and was yanked forward by it. I flew up onto the stairs with the drawing and books safe under my left arm. I had made it!

Though Tibi was my friend, he pretended to be uninterested in the world around him. He was constantly playing it cool. His pitch-black hair was always neatly combed. He also owned an authentic Pelikan fountain pen, a real treasure, especially for a student. Tibi's father—his name was Aladár and we called him Aladár Bácsi—had been one of the Regent's guards.[4] He had lost his right leg during the fighting in October, 1944, when the German SS occupied the palace and arrested Miklós Horthy. Now, twelve years later, Aladár Bácsi still hated the occupiers, all occupiers, including our current ones, the Russians.

That morning, my cool and aloof friend Tibi was playing tarots.

According to Tibi, tarots was the aristocrat of card games. To him, it compared rather favorably with bridge: highbrow to lowbrow. It was also the card game of the opposition—any and all types of opposition, opposition to anything. There is no such person as a conformist tarot player.

My mother's first love, János Melocco, was a tarot player. He was first a diplomat and later was the editor of a Catholic newspaper. We called him János Bácsi, and the woman who became his wife we called Dóra Néni.

When János Bácsi found out that the Communists had drugged Cardinal Mindszenty during his staged trial in order to make him "confess" to his "crimes," he tried to publish an article about it, and for that "crime" he was hanged.[5] The delicate Communist method of notifying Dóra Néni of her husband's fate was to send her a package containing his clothing with a printed form. The form stated that his hanging was a state secret, not to be discussed with anyone. There was no other explanation—nothing.[6] None was needed. We all knew that this was the way the "heroic" Soviet people performed their struggle against the reactionary, counterrevolutionary, chauvinistic enemies of the state. This was how the Communists "fought for peace."

When the train got in, in order to be on time for my first class at the Technical University, I did my usual running and streetcar jumping. I scaled the many stairs leading up to the main entrance of the university two at a time. Every time I did that, I still marveled at this majestic jewel of Hungarian architecture on the banks of the Danube. My first class was Machine Design 302, surely the most boring subject any junior of mechanical engineering ever had to endure. I turned in my ball bearing drawing and settled down next to Attila Lipcsey, who commented, "If I knew about India ink when I applied for admission to this university, I would have tried for music school." I chuckled. For my own part (being Category X and the son of a state enemy), I was grateful to be admitted anywhere.

I started reading the sports paper, which reported on the previous day's athletic competition. "Yeah!" I blurted out, "Varga took the bronze!" Professor Vörös, in the middle of his lecture, stopped in midsentence, and some two hundred heads turned toward me, so I shut up.

At lunchtime, on the way to the cafeteria, I stopped at the scholarship office and felt lucky, because my favorite administrator was there.

She was a Communist Party activist or something, but in spite of all that she still was a good woman. I told her that I was penniless and wanted to get my November scholarship early.

She chided, "But this is only the twenty-second of October!"

I pleaded, "Yes, but Ágnes and I would like to see this movie, *The Women of Selistye*. It's an Italian movie. And today is the last day they are showing it."

"I know that *The Women of Selistye* is an Italian movie," she said, seeming to imply that not all party secretaries were complete morons.

I did not debate the point, just continued pleading. "You know, Ágnes is only fifteen, though she is going to be sixteen next month. For her, seeing this movie is very important. Besides, the national economy is not going to collapse if I get my 140 forints of stipend four days early, now, will it?"

She smiled, opened the safe, and counted out the money. As she handed it over, she reminded me: "You know about the meeting in the aula at two o'clock. Be there! It is going to be a very important meeting."

I could not resist. "Another one of those very important ones? What is it this time? Are we intensifying the fight for peace or just reestablishing our eternal friendship with Mongolia?"

"No, this is important! It is about Poland and Poznan."

Of course I did not believe her. Yet her face was serious, so I just shut up and backed out of her office.

I called Ágnes from the cafeteria. She was home for lunch. I could hear her jumping up and down as we talked. She wanted to see this movie very badly, and her mouth was running at twice the speed of her brain. It made me happy that she was so excited. It was worth pleading a little to get that money. I assured her, "Yes sweetheart, I will see you at the Bástya movie house at four!"

And she in turn assured me, "You bet you will! Yes, sure, definitely, absolutely, and in addition certainly. I will be there even if mini-Gypsies are falling from the sky!"

During lunch Attila and I bumped into another friend, Gyuri Egry. His nickname was Menő, which suggested a person who was "with it," who was "going places." He told us that on the previous Saturday in the city of Szeged there had been a meeting at which an independent student organization, MEFESZ, was established. (MEFESZ was the Hungarian acronym for the League of Hungarian University and College Student Associations. Members were the associations themselves; the MEFESZ had no individual membership.) That was unbelievable news. No independent organization of any kind existed in the country. The Communists ran everything.

Menő was a close friend and classmate, also a junior in mechanical engineering and an inch or two taller than I. He had a long, always smiling horse face and walked like a camel, with his toes turned in, swaying from side to side. Yet even with that unusual gait he was a basketball player. During the past summer's military training, we both had marched, in the front row of our platoon in tennis shoes, because none of the boots were big enough for us. I suspect that the reason the Russians did not occupy Scandinavia was that the Red Army lacked the shoe sizes for the male population there.

I asked Menő, "Are you coming to this meeting at two?"

He gave me a casual "Yeah, it can't hurt."

"It *can* hurt me," I said. "If I miss the movie at four, Ágnes will never forgive me!"

"So what? You leave at half past three. End of discussion."

After lunch Attila and I decided to visit the "Gellért department." Attila did not understand why I liked to visit the Cliff Chapel, the church in one of the caves of Gellért Hill. I never told him that my mother, as a teenager, spent a whole night praying in that chapel because she had missed her curfew by a few minutes and was afraid to go home. That tells you something about my grandfather. He was a tough little Austro-Hungarian colonel who in 1915 participated in the beating of the Serbian army after a Serb nationalist killed Francis Ferdinand. After that bloody war he came home and proceeded to translate the poems of such French poets as Mallarmé, Rimbaud, and Verlaine. He was a complex fellow, to say the least.

CHAPTER 2

Birth of MEFESZ
and the Sixteen Points

ATTILA AND I SETTLED DOWN in the gallery of the aula, the large assembly hall of the Technical University. The aula was ornate, its walls covered in marble. Surrounding the hall was a corridor where stood the busts of famous former professors, university presidents, whom we called rectors. One of these busts, that of Rector Stocek, would save my life in a couple of weeks, but today I did not even notice his bust. I was just looking at the names and guessing at the origins of these highly respected and famous people.

As Attila noticed me inspecting the busts, he commented, "Did you know that many of them were Jews?" Then he added, "Just like the majority of Rákosi's government and of the ÁVH officers."[1]

"A talented people!" I said sarcastically.

That day there must have been a couple of thousand students in the aula, but none of us was really paying much attention to what was going on. One could hear this constant murmur in the hall. It was like any other meeting in the Communist world. They talked *at* us, and our only defense against that was to not listen.

Below our gallery, on the main floor of the aula, the two rectors of the dual university, László Gillemot and Tibor Cholnoky, were at the microphone. With them were some professors, the Communist Party secretary, lesser Party officials, and the leaders of the Communist Youth Organization, the DISZ. It was the DISZ that had convened the meeting. In their uniform of blue jackets, white shirts, and red neckties, the leaders of the DISZ looked like a special breed of penguins or booby birds. Their purpose for calling the meeting was to preempt the spread of MEFESZ, the new non-Communist student association. Since the recent formation of MEFESZ in the city of Szeged, suddenly the DISZ seemed to care a lot about us. They talked about special train passes for students, cheaper textbooks, and better food and housing. We did not speak up. We never did. It was their show, and we let them do all the talking.

And talk they did. I was scraping the corrosion off my "gold" ring, which had cost me thirty-six forints and must have had some copper in its heritage, because it was turning green. I was spitting on it, rubbing it, and was just beginning to make some progress when I felt Attila's elbow in my side. He was pointing down to the speakers' platform, where there was some commotion. The murmur in the aula stopped. Now there was total silence. In startled curiosity the dozing students were beginning to wake up. We were sitting up and starting to pay attention. Now you could hear a pin drop. Then, from the middle of the tumult at the microphone, a voice rose: "I represent the MEFESZ of Szeged! I want to speak!"

It was unprecedented! Extraordinary! The air was thick with tension. We did not know who had spoken, did not understand what was happening. All we could see was that the DISZ penguins were shoving a small fellow away from the microphone. He was a student like us, and he was talking, gesticulating, but we heard nothing—the blue-jacketed DISZ had pushed him all the way to the wall.

Then the Party secretary, Mrs. Orbán, came to the microphone and admonished us, "You have only one duty! Your duty is to study!" She was almost screaming. "You don't want the MEFESZ of Szeged! You don't want any ideas from Szeged!" I could not imagine why Szeged was suddenly such a bad place. I did not particularly care what she was saying but I was hypnotized by this minihero, this crazy little guy from Szeged.

My mind raced on: I do not understand him. I do not understand what he wants. Is he out of his mind? Does he not know that he will be kicked out of the university? Not only that, he will also be thrown in jail—that is, right after they beat the shit out of him. Does he not understand that we are nobodies, that our collective name is "Shut Up"? Does he not understand that he is nothing, that I am nothing, that we have no say in anything? Does he not understand that the microphone is only for the Party collaborators and nobody, but nobody, else talks into it? Does he not know that even the penguins dare only read their prepared statements? And that even then they wait until they are told that it is their turn to read?

Attila muttered my own racing thoughts when he said, "I just don't get it!"

Then we saw the members of the military department, the only people who possessed arms at the university, marching onto the speaker's platform, and we got very quiet. My throat was dry, my breath bated. All eyes were on the officers. Then suddenly, from a distance, we heard a voice. It was that of a fifth-year architecture student, a blond, very tall young man by the name of Jancsi Danner. He yelled, "Let him speak!"

My heart stopped. Nothing like this had ever happened since the Red Army had occupied Hungary. I stared at Jancsi. His ears were red, his mouth was trembling, but he did not blink; he faced the bewildered and frightened stares of two thousand students.

"God, he has lost his marbles!" I said.

In the meantime a new and angry sort of murmur was building up, replacing the previously astonished silence, and now, a few rows in front of us, Laci Zsindely, a classmate of mine, hesitantly started to clap. It was then that the miracle occurred.

First one, then two, then four or five students joined in, and suddenly this sparse clapping turned into a hurricane, a burst of thunderous applause the likes of which I had never heard. I saw Attila clapping like a madman as he shouted to me, "Applaud or I will never speak to you again!"

I had never seen anything like it. As some of the students stood up, the ovation continued, and the Party officials around the microphone became nervous, surprised, angry—and just a bit uncertain. I had never seen them uncertain. That was something new. My flesh was creeping, and I was clapping as though my life depended on it, as if I were out of my mind. And during all this my mind was racing. Is this possible? Can we actually have a say? Can we contradict them like this, directly to their faces? Is it possible that I matter, that what I think matters? Is it possible that I do not have to hold my tongue all the time? Is it possible that I am not alone?

Now, it was total chaos. The Party secretary ran to the telephone. The rest of her penguins were white as sheets. The hands of the officers of the military department had moved to the guns on their belts while the chief of DISZ kept screaming into the microphone. And then, through all the pandemonium and over the thunderous applause, we heard his voice once more: "I represent the MEFESZ of Szeged! Allow me to speak!"

Now I really felt hypnotized. I stood up and began walking toward that voice and saw Attila doing the same thing. From other directions, another twenty, then thirty, students were also starting to move toward the voice. This was all completely spontaneous. We walked without knowing who was walking with us. We were drawn toward the speaker's stand, toward the angry but scared penguins, who had encircled the boy from MEFESZ. The circle thinned as we got closer and we just started pushing the whole group toward the microphone. I saw my hand rise, reaching for one of the fat penguins. And I saw my wristwatch indicating that it was 3:40 P.M. *My God, the movie!* flashed through my mind. But then I saw the microphone. Five more meters and we would have it! I pushed with all my might. The DISZ resistance faltered. Now, Jancsi Danner grabbed the microphone and proclaimed, "I ask the representative of the students of Szeged to speak!"

There was a deafening ovation that took quite a while to taper off until there was total silence. I saw the six-foot-four Jancsi Danner reaching down to his waist as he gave the microphone to the diminutive delegate from Szeged. I just stood in the protective ring around him, and my eyes filled with tears as he started to speak in a strong voice: "Fellow students! Hungarians!"

I saw the flash of cameras. I saw strangers rushing to the telephones. Floodlights started to glare and film cameras begun to buzz. And the little fellow from Szeged was oblivious to it all as he started to speak: "Once again, the wind of freedom is blowing in from Poland. The Polish exchange students at our university are asking for our support.

Russian troops are surrounding Warsaw, but the Polish army is also encircling the Russians. The city of Poznan is also free, but surrounded. Poland is showing the way and is asking for our solidarity. We will not let them down! We, the students of Szeged, have decided to follow the Poles in establishing our independent student organization, the MEFESZ. Please join us. Please do not believe the lies. Please form your own MEFESZ!"

At that point he seemed confused. His voice faltered. And then, haltingly, without a tune, he started to mumble the words of our forbidden hymn, the hymn most hated by the Communists: our national anthem. This anthem had not been heard in public for nearly a decade; one could sing it only in church, after the mass. This anthem that stood for the things the Communists most despised: God, country, and liberty. The anthem that we call our national prayer, the anthem that a Hungarian can sing only while standing at attention.

The great chandelier of the aula trembled and the windows shook as we sang our hearts out. As we finished we were all weeping. And during those couple of minutes of singing, a miracle occurred in that great hall. We were not the same people we had been a few minutes earlier. We, these tearful kids still standing at attention in that great hall, we had been reborn. We had stopped being scared. And therefore we were free!

It was sometime around five o'clock when, by acclamation, we decided to form our own branch of the MEFESZ. The Party officials and the DISZ penguins were still near the speaker's platform, but now we had the microphone, and it was up to us to decide who would use it and we did not stop anybody from speaking. If the students liked what a speaker was saying, they would clap, if they did not, their silence spoke for them.

The first few speakers concentrated on student matters. One suggested that we should also learn English, French, and German instead of only Russian. Another proposed that the subject of Marxism-Leninism no longer be compulsory. In the meantime, people started to arrive from other universities and factories. Through some magic, which I still do not understand, by this time the whole city knew that something unusual was happening at the Technical University. The speeches became more and more passionate and fiery, the demands broader in scope and more radical.

I was completely euphoric. I was really starting to believe that I mattered, that what I thought, what we the students thought, made a difference, that our future was in our own hands. These few minutes transformed the students of this university into true patriots. If that sounds maudlin, I am sorry; I cannot help it. All I know is that it felt great and that my life suddenly had a purpose. All I wanted to do was to serve, to be part of this struggle that would make my countrymen free, proud, and happy.

But fear and self-doubt followed the euphoria. I knew that zeal and enthusiasm were no substitute for experience. I was afraid that we might do something stupid. How would we know what were the right things to do?

Almost as if he were answering me, I heard the next speaker introduce himself. "I am József Szilágyi." He was an adult evening student and a follower of the Reform Communist politician Imre Nagy. I listened to him very closely.[2]

"What you are doing is not illegal! The Hungarian Constitution gives you the right to free speech and the right to petition your government. It is not only your right, it is your duty to articulate your concerns. And it is the duty of the government to respond to your concerns!"

After Szilágyi, a writer named Péter Kuczka took the microphone. "The Party secretary of your university was lying to you. Your duty today is not to return to your studies. You have a higher duty today. The workers of Poznan are on strike. Warsaw is surrounded by tanks. Today you must show your solidarity. You must support the Polish workers. You must support those people who are fighting for all of us."

By then we started scribbling down the demands that the assembled students approved by acclamation. We wrote on regular notebook pages. The students doing the scribbling included Ede Némethy, Iván Szabó, Jancsi Danner, Bandi Nemcsik, Imi Mécs, and several others. We were trying to follow the example of the last Hungarian revolution, the example of those who, in 1848, condensed the demands of the nation into twelve concise points.

It must have been about 7:00 P.M. when a shy student with a bad stutter came to the microphone. His stammer made his already quiet voice barely audible. With tremendous effort he squeezed out: "C-c-could th-th-the R-r-russians l-l-leave?"

The response was indescribable. First there was deathly silence, and then the thousands of people in the aula rose to their feet with an ovation that seemed to go on forever. We just could not believe it! Finally! Finally somebody dared to ask the question that was on all our minds, but nobody had the courage to say it out loud. And then, mixed with the applause but slowly drowning it out, a rallying cry grew until it was deafening: "Russkis go home! Russkis go home!"

For the last hour I simply stood at the microphone with those who helped to clear the way for the student from Szeged to speak. Off to our right were the Party officials, the DISZ people, and one of the rectors of the university, Tibor Cholnoky. The officers of the military department were standing behind them. They seemed to be just as astonished as the rest of us. Finally, the Party secretary strode to the microphone. Her tone was ominous. She told us that the meeting was closed, that anybody who remained would be participating in an illegal gathering, and that the penalty for that was expulsion. After that, she abruptly marched out, followed by the DISZ and other Party officials. The representatives of the press also left; only one newspaper reporter, a redheaded young man from the paper *Szabad Ifjuság (Free Youth)* dared to stay.

To our surprise, though, the officers of the Military Department and their commander, Colonel Marián, Rector Cholnoky, and a few of the professors also remained. Maybe even more remarkable was the fact that in spite of the expulsion threat, none of the students were leaving.

Now a new speaker took the microphone: "Let us take our demands to the radio," he suggested. One of our young assistant professors, István Jankovich, was the owner of a tiny Italian car, a Topolino, and he offered to take a delegation to the radio station to find out if they would broadcast our demands. The station was just on the other side of the Danube (see fig. 3). The time must have been about nine o'clock. When they returned, they reported that the censors at the radio were willing to broadcast our demands in a news bulletin, but only if we deleted the most critical demands dealing with the Russians, Poland, free elections, freedom of the press, and the formation of a new government under Imre Nagy. Instead of bargaining with the censors, our delegation simply returned to the university.

In the meantime, trucks with workers' delegations were arriving from the factories of Budapest, and the mood in the aula was turning angrier. By ten o'clock I had already eaten all of the bread crumbs I could find in the pockets of both my trousers and my corduroy jacket. Gone, long gone, was even the memory of the boiled kale I had had for lunch when another speaker came to the microphone and suggested that we march on the radio station right away. He wanted all of us to go—all three or four thousand of us. "They refused a delegation of three. See what they do with a delegation of three thousand?"

The acclamation that followed seemed to obviate the need for any debate. It seemed that we were going to march on the radio station right away. We were collecting our things and getting ready to leave when the officers of the military department, whom we had almost forgotten and who until now stood quietly at the wall, started walking toward the microphone. Everything stopped. All eyes turned on the commander and department head, Colonel Marián.

He was a short, dark man of about thirty-five. Naturally, he was a Communist, and he was also Jewish, as were many people who were in positions of authority at that time. It seemed that just as the German occupiers picked mostly German Hungarians to run the country for them, the Russians had chosen mostly Jewish Hungarians. But Marián was a Reform Communist like Imre Nagy. He was no traitor, and certainly not a fanatic. Marián was a farmer's son from Transylvania, the part of Romania that was taken from Hungary after World War I. In Transylvania the Jews were fully integrated into Hungarian society. There, it made no difference if you were a Jewish Hungarian or a Calvinist one.

Still, as István Marián walked to the microphone I did not know what to expect. As I lowered the microphone to match his five-foot-something stature, I was silently praying to God: "Don't let him call us comrades! Anything but comrades!" Marián's first words were: "My sons!"

About half the students were female, but we still felt that he used the right address—in fact, the only possible address. He continued, "My life is not more valuable than yours. I, too, am first a Hungarian, and everything else comes only after that. But I am older and I know this regime better than you do. I will not allow you to walk into an ÁVH trap in the dark of the night. No, we will march in the daylight tomorrow and we will march after having obtained the proper permits. We will not break any laws. And if we do a good job tonight, tomorrow the whole capital will march with us. And then I will lead you!"

I was so relieved! This was what I was waiting for; this was what I needed. I needed the guidance of someone who knew what needed to be done—someone who was both smart and brave—someone I could trust. In that moment I decided that I would stick with Colonel Marián.

It was about eleven o'clock when our small group at the microphone decided to let the meeting continue without us. We asked Bandi Nemcsik to take our demands to Iván Sándor, the editor of our paper, *A Jövő Mérnöke (The Engineer of the Future)*. Iván had both the guts and the shrewdness to get the demands printed by next morning. Then we went to our rector, Tibor Cholnoky, and asked his permission to reproduce the fourteen demands using the stencil duplicators of the university. He refused. He would not dare take the responsibility for something like that.[3]

We did not know what to do. The demands and the announcement of tomorrow's demonstration had to be duplicated, but how would we do it? At that point a young blonde assistant professor of chemistry said, "Listen, I can show you where the stencil room is, and if you force the door open I can teach you how to operate it. I have been using those copiers to reproduce my homework assignments and tests."

We knew that Kati was young and beautiful. Now we learned that she was also brave. She and I became instant friends; I trusted her the same way I trusted the colonel. We called her Kati Szőke because she was so blonde—*szőke* in Hungarian means blonde—but her real name was Kati Nemes.

It took two minutes to break the lock. Kati Szőke, Ede Némethy, Jancsi Danner, and a few others and I got started on the job of reproducing the demands.

There was a telephone in the room, so I called Ágnes. It was Ágnes's half-sister, Judit, who answered my call. "No, she will not speak to you! No, I know she will not! She locked herself in her room and has been crying all evening. How could you do such a thing?" I stammered something about the meeting, about protecting the microphone and copying the demands. But as I listened to myself, it all sounded so stupid, made no sense at all. I felt terrible. I begged Judit to explain to Ágnes, I tried to convince her that this meeting today had been something special, but it was no use.

When I finally hung up, Attila asked, "What happened?"

"Nothing, nothing," I replied, but very, very quietly.

It was near midnight when the demands and the announcement of next day's demonstration were finally printed. I went back to the aula, passed out a few copies, and kept a dozen or so for myself. The meeting was still going on. All agreed that during the night we would spread the news of the demonstration. Gyuszi Perr had a motorcycle, so he and his bride Marika—the runner at the previous day's athletic competition—would take the announcement to Csepel, the largest industrial complex in Hungary. I, in turn, would alert the Agricultural University of Gödöllő, where my brother Péter was a student. I would be back by 7:00 A.M. to act as one of the MEFESZ guards at the gates of the university. Everybody had an assignment. There was not much time left for sleep that night.

It was close to 1:00 A.M. when I left the university. I caught the completely empty No. 49 tram, but there was no connection on Rákóczy Street, so I ran all the way to the East Railroad train station. The train was just starting to pull out, but I managed to jump on, dripping with sweat. The train was unheated, and I knew I would have to thank my beautiful corduroy jacket if I did not catch a cold.

Later, walking to our house, I was greeted by every dog in the village of Kerepes. What a concert! Next, Bukucs was jumping all over me. It was past 2:00 A.M. on that Tuesday, the twenty-third of October. I tried to open the creaking kitchen door quietly. Memi had left my supper on the stove, and I started eating from the stew pan. Then I heard some stirring in the bedrooms, so I quickly got a plate and continued stuffing myself with slightly improved manners. Memi appeared in her bathrobe, then Aptyi in his nighttime beret, which warmed his balding scalp. Eventually Péter and Andris also joined us. I told them about the meeting and read out loud our demands and the announcement of the demonstration.

So there I was, announcing that we demand this and we demand that. Memi's expression was one of fear—fear that her son had gone mad. Andris, who had just awakened, first thought that I was telling about a dream I had had. Aptyi's eyes were wet. He knew. During the German occupation, when he heard the Nazi salute, "Victory or death!" he would mutter under his breath, "To you, definitely death!" And now, a few years later, whenever he heard the Communist salute, "Freedom!" he always muttered, "Yes, we could use some!"

Next I handed over the stenciled copies of our announcements to Péter. He took them, but warned me: "Tomorrow there will be no demonstrations, there will be arrests!" As Péter spoke I saw a flashback, I saw the scared kid from Szeged; I heard the trembling voice of Jancsi Danner as he yelled, "Let him speak!" I also saw Colonel Marián as he slowly walked to the speaker's stand, waited for me to lower the microphone, and then started by saying, "My sons!"

So I tried to argue that Stalin was wrong when he asked, "How many divisions does the Pope have?" I was convinced that our ideals were stronger than their divisions, and I also believed that occupied colonies must eventually liberate themselves. There was no question in my mind that societies built on lies will and must self-destruct. I also quoted President Eisenhower, who, when he proclaimed the policy of self-liberation, said that only those who sacrifice for freedom and liberty deserve it. "So if we get into a jam with the communists, don't you think that the Americans will help?" I asked.

Péter only scoffed, "Sure. They would help themselves to our oil if we had any. How stupid can you get?" He believed that it was Eisenhower's predecessor, Roosevelt, who gave Hungary to Stalin in the first place. "We were his birthday gift at Yalta," he claimed. Péter felt that the rich don't give a damn about ideals, that the only thing they care about is getting richer!

I did not agree. I was convinced that rich people too have a conscience. I argued that Americans conceived the Marshall plan, and there were American volunteers fighting against Franco's fascists in Spain. "Americans, too, have a heart. They, too, like to sleep at night," I added. I also pointed out that we were not asking the Americans for anything, that tomorrow there would be no clashes with anybody; we would simply be holding a peaceful demonstration with a legal permit, and our march would be led by a communist colonel!

I went to bed at about 3:00 A.M. but was up by 5:00 to catch the 6:02 train.

CHAPTER 3

My Tricolor Armband

MY SANDALS WERE COMPLETELY SOAKED from the morning dew. To keep warmer I turned in the lapel of my corduroy jacket and turned up its collar. Around me the people on the train did not seem to know about the events of the previous night. They were mostly blue-collar workers, exhausted and half asleep. Today was only Tuesday, but they already appeared as if the whole work week were already behind them. There were no students on the train. It was too early for students. Supposedly, these poor, exhausted workers were the backbone of the "dictatorship of the proletariat," the backbone of Communism.

I arrived at the university at about seven o'clock. Jancsi Danner was already at gate four. I was six feet, two inches tall, and he must have been six-four or six-five. He was also older than I; he could have been as old as twenty-six or even twenty-seven. He slapped me on the shoulder and handed me a tricolored armband. I could not believe it: the national colors, the colors of our flag. He spoke quietly. "Go to gate number two and check the identity cards of all who enter. Only people who belong here, only students and professors can enter. No strangers should be allowed in. None!"

There was a faint smile on his lips. He had to stoop a bit as he turned to the much shorter Iván Szabó and asked, "Iván, could you get hold of a bullhorn? We might need one later."

As I headed for gate two, I was preoccupied with my armband. Throughout the Russian occupation the displaying of any national symbols, even the flag, had been carefully controlled. The average person could not even own one. And when an official flag was displayed, it had to be placed to the left of the red flag of the Communists. Any sign of patriotic feeling, any national symbol, was taken as an affront to the internationalist doctrine of the Communists. We had gotten used to it. So something like a tricolor armband was unthinkable. It was a provocation, a sign of open rebellion. And now, I had one!

I felt ten feet tall. As I walked to gate number two, near the chemistry building, I held my head high and kept peeking at my armband. I felt happy, elated, special, and honored. As I took my place at the gate, the first person to enter was Kati Szőke, the young chemistry professor who last night had helped us with the stencil copier. She stopped and stared at my armband. Her eyes were misty. When I explained that we were screening out strangers who might stir up trouble, she quietly handed me her identity card.

A little later, Gyuszi Perr arrived on his motorbike with Marika on the back seat. She reported, "We distributed the announcements at the factories of Csepel and Belojannisz and also took some to the miners of Dorog."[1]

"My brother is passing them out at the University of Gödöllő," I replied.

The traffic at the gate increased, so Gyuszi stayed to help me with the checking. The line got longer, but the people remained patient. There was a dignified pride in the air. I tried to be quick, so I did not even look up as I read one identity card after another. Then I read: *Rector*. I looked up, and there was László Gillemot, the president of the university, quietly waiting for his card. I was embarrassed and made something like a curtsy when I handed it back. But if I felt out of place checking the rector's card, his eyes reassured me. In them I saw respect, emotion, and warm reassurance. They seemed to be saying, "Don't worry. The young men of other ages were just as scared as you are. Yet they changed the world. You, too, will leave a mark; you, too, will do what the adults could not. You will mortally wound this barbaric system."

Almost an hour later there were four of us at the gate. There was no line anymore, so I felt I could leave for my mechanics class. My professor was Ádám Mutnyánszky, or Mutyi Bácsi, as we called him. It was unthinkable to miss his class. It was 7:59 A.M. He started exactly at 8:00, so I ran as fast as I could. A friend, Laci Zsindely, had kept a chair for me in one of the upper rows of the KA-51 lecture hall, which was filled to capacity with about three hundred students. I slumped down beside Laci, whom I knew from high school. He was a broad-shouldered fellow, always well dressed. He did not know it, but he was responsible for my selecting naval architecture as my major. I selected it because I wanted to be with Laci.

Professor Mutnyánszky was standing down in front. He had already started to draw the cross section of some machine element on one of the sliding blackboards. We looked down at him from the tiered, theaterlike gallery. Each chair had its own writing table, which lifted and slid aside to allow one to get in and out of the chair. The tables were carved with initials, with engravings of the names of loved ones and with less mentionable comments made by many generations of students.

Mutnyánszky was a remnant of the old pre-Communist school of professors, a born teacher, one who educated generations of engineers, inventors, and even some Nobel Prize winners. His knowledge and dedication was surpassed only by his love of teaching. He enjoyed opening young minds, passing on his own devotion to science and faith in the power of knowledge. You could hear the proverbial pin drop during his lectures; Mutyi Bácsi did not use a microphone, and we did not want to miss a single word he said.

He lectured like a priest celebrating mass: he was the high priest of science. He had two assistants. One was an assistant professor, the other a school porter. Mutyi Bácsi did not refer to any notes and did not use a textbook. He did not use a ruler either, yet his lines were as straight as a bowstring. He never ran out of board space; he had a natural instinct for spacing and proportion, no matter what the project was. And he certainly never made a mistake. When he finished drawing, he would nod to his second-in-command, the old school porter, who would take a big sponge, dip it in a bucket of water, and wash and then dry that blackboard as Mutyi Bácsi moved on to the next board.

The porter kept those blackboards neat as a pin, even though they were already old when Theodor von Kármán's generation studied there at the turn of the century or when, after the dismemberment of the kingdom, John von Neumann's generation did the same in 1925.[2] The boards were surely considered ancient by the time Edward Teller, Eugene Wigner, and Leo Szilárd (leaders in the American team that developed the atomic bomb) left this university to escape the Nazis. Yes, the boards were ancient, but they were still pitch black, so Mutnyánszky's white lines were sharp and clearly visible even from the back of that spacious hall. The professor and the porter were the same kind of people. They got along because they both took pride in what they did and because they respected each other.

But that morning Mutnyánszky was in bad form. He could not concentrate. He often lost his chain of thought and would stop, cough, look at us then back at the board, starting and stopping over and over again. Finally he put down the chalk, wiped his hands, turned away from the board, and slowly walked back to his desk. For a while he played with his glasses, then he lifted his eyes and looked at us for a long moment. His voice was choked. "Go my sons, go! This is not a day for mechanics. You have a higher duty today. Make this a proud day in the history of our much-suffering, poor nation."[3]

He left, and we stayed in the lecture hall to hold a brief meeting with the class. We told them about the meeting last night and about the demonstration planned for the afternoon. We also told them that we would march using the same formation we used during military training, which was part of our regular curriculum. That way we would all know the persons who were on our left and right, so no strangers could infiltrate our group and cause trouble. We did not want to give the secret police any opportunities or excuses to interfere. We decided to march silently, ten to a row, arm in arm. We would carry no signs. We agreed that Gyuri Egry (the Menő) would lead the class, and I would be the liaison with Colonel Marián.

At about nine o'clock the class left the lecture hall to practice the marching formation in front of the chemistry building, and I went to find Colonel Marián. As I walked toward the military department, I saw Iván Sándor, the editor of *The Future Engineer.* He had just arrived from the printer and was carrying a great pile of copies of the new edition. The ink was still wet. Our demands were printed on the front page. So I grabbed some, took half of them to my class, and then decided to take the rest over to the universities on the Pest side of the Danube.

All eyes turned toward me as I jumped on the streetcar with my tricolored armband and with the freshly printed newspapers under my arm. An older woman stood up from her seat, walked over, and stood next to me, as though she wanted to protect me. Then a mailman came over and whispered in my ear, "I heard it from my daughter. I know everything. Be careful!" Even as he spoke, he kept looking around to see if there would be any reprisal for his daring act of talking to me.

As I left the streetcar, it seemed that the rest of the capital was still oblivious to what was happening at the universities. I visited three colleges. In each, meetings were in progress. I passed out the paper with our demands and explained the plans for the afternoon march. At the Marxism-Leninism University, the DISZ penguins were still in control. At the Academy of Dramatic Arts, a stranger affixed a Polish emblem to my lapel. As I was rushing on to Eötvös University, a tall woman stopped me on the street, hugged me, kissed the Polish insignia, and started to speak to me in Polish.[4] I smiled at her, pointed to my armband, and, since I had nothing else to offer, gave her a copy of *The Future Engineer*.

By eleven o'clock, as I reached Eötvös University, Radio Budapest was already announcing the news about our march of solidarity with the Poles. Now the whole city was aware of our plans. People stared at me. An old man even crossed himself, as though he were either seeking divine protection or witnessing a miracle. In the meeting hall of this university, the head table was covered with red felt. When I finished reading our demands, I pointed at that covering: "Don't you have a more appropriate cover?" On my way out, as I was still squeezing through the crowd, I saw the red felt being replaced by the Hungarian tricolor.

In the corridor I noticed a telephone. I dialed Ágnes. Judit answered again. Of course she had heard the news on the radio; she knew why I had missed my date with Ágnes. I asked, "So does she forgive me?" There was only silence. "Just remind her that we're doing important things. Very important! But, to me, not more important than her! Please tell her that."

As I returned to the Technical University, I could feel that the atmosphere of the city had changed. Now everyone knew what my armband meant. I felt an outpouring of love and encouragement. It was a strange experience. It was as if overnight I had become a very important person. Strangers looked up to me; they trusted me. I would have liked to remind them that I was only a kid and that they should not expect much from me. But my other self took over, and when people stopped me I made such speeches as: "Come with us to the Bem statue! This is *our* country! It is up to *us* to make it free!"[5]

As I handed out the copies of our paper, some started to read the demands out loud. Others were just staring at the floor. As the streetcar reached my university and I was jumping off, I saw an elderly woman crying quietly while the mustachioed conductor gave me a military salute.

The university was like a disturbed beehive. Thousands of students were assembling within the gates, and new groups were arriving. A loudspeaker had been placed on the roof of the machine laboratory building; Jancsi Danner and Iván Szabó were using it, identifying and greeting the new arrivals. They announced the arrival of the students from the Veterinary College, now from the School of Horticulture, the School of Agricultural Engineering, or from the Petőfi Military Academy.

For hours, my class, the juniors of mechanical engineering, had been waiting in formation in front of gate number two near the chemistry building. We had obtained an immense national flag, which was to be carried by the six-foot, eight-inch Laci Gabányi, a member of the national basketball team. Because gate two was the closest to Saint Gellért Square, our class was to lead the march. Gabányi's gigantic flag would give the starting signal to the students on the other side of the Danube, who had gathered on the Pest side at the Petőfi statue.[6] In short, we were ready and waiting, waiting, waiting.

There must have been ten—maybe even fifteen—thousand people assembled on the university grounds. Several trench-coated figures had also appeared just outside the gates but did not enter. These people were taking photographs and were making periodic phone calls on the public phone at the street corner, reporting what they observed. We knew who they were. It was because of them that some of us had decided to use only our nicknames. Mine, of course, was Öcsi. Yet some people, such as Jancsi Danner, did not do that; he would not hide his identity.

At noon we were still waiting, and I was getting very hungry. Then again, I had been hungry for most of the past decade. It was my normal state. I had been hungry since the day of "liberation," as the Communists called the end of World War II, or since the day of the "collapse," as the Nazis called it. (For the average Hungarian it was neither. It was getting out of the frying pan and into the fire.) At any rate, the sandwich Memi prepared for me that morning was only a memory by now. As I searched my pockets for crumbs, I found my 140-forint stipend, so I vowed to get something at the very first food stand I came across. That turned out to be a long wait.

The minutes dragged on. In the front row Gyuri Egry, the Menő, was on my left, and another friend, Nándi Kiefer, on my right. Our patience was wearing thin. Finally, at 12:50 or so, came an announcement on the radio: "The minister of interior, László Piros, has forbidden the march!"

A few minutes later Colonel Marián appeared on the roof of the machine laboratory and using the loudspeaker asked, "Will you obey the minister's orders?" The answer was a thunderous "NO!" I was pushing myself through the crowd, but by the time I reached Colonel Marián, a delegation had already left for the ministry of the interior. Jancsi Danner headed the delegation. They went by car, a small Skoda, driven by Imre Majoross. The Skoda belonged to the university.[7]

When I got back to my class of junior mechanical engineers, I could tell that the number of trench-coated people outside the gates had multiplied. They were still taking their photographs, still making their phone calls. Now, for the first time, I felt tension in the air. It was Menő who tried to break that tension by telling one of his typical jokes: "So what did the sadist say to the masochist when he begged for a kick?" Grinning, he waited a long time before finally revealing the answer: "He said no!"

Nobody laughed. He tried again. "Who is an absolute nun?" There was no answer. Nobody paid any attention to him. This never happened before, but he did not give up; he gave the answer anyway: "The nun whose mother was also a nun." Again, nobody laughed; nothing, not even a giggle. So Menő gave up, and we waited in that tense silence. We just waited and waited.

Still more people were arriving. The university grounds were becoming very crowded. It was not until about 2:30 P.M. that we saw some commotion on the roof of the machine laboratory building. We saw the tall figure of Jancsi Danner with a short, dark-haired police officer. The officer grabbed the bullhorn and said: "I am Sándor Kopácsi, the police chief of Budapest. I bring you good news. Your march has been permitted!"

He tried to say something else, but our cheering drowned him out. When our shouts finally subsided, Colonel Marián took the loud-speaker. "Our silent solidarity march will start at gate number two. We will march north, up to General Bem's Square on the west bank of the Danube. There we will take part in a commemoration of Polish-Hungarian friendship directed by the Writers' Union. The march will start immediately."

Laci Gabányi raised the enormous national flag. Gate two opened, and, arm in arm, shoulder to shoulder, we burst out onto Saint Gellért's Square. We walked silently. It felt like a dream. My heart was in my mouth. A shiver ran down my spine. I had never experienced anything like the feeling I had then and there.

As we approached the square, all traffic came to a standstill. The streetcars and buses screeched to a halt. The pedestrians froze in place with wide-eyed, astonished faces. They were more than amazed; they were as if watching a miracle. The broom dropped from the hands of a sanitation worker; she crossed herself and started to kneel as our flag passed in front of her. A tall, mustachioed man took off his hat and stood at attention. A young traffic cop at first reached for his flat cap to remove it as a sign of respect—but he caught himself and pretended to be just wiping the nonexistent perspiration from his brow. As he did that, he was also wiping his eyes. A tormented and humiliated nation was stirring in front of my eyes. People were straightening their backs. They were regaining their self-respect. Some did it boldly; others secretively. It was a good, a proud, feeling to be Hungarian that day.

As we marched through the square, an ocean of people followed. And from across the Danube, at the Petőfi statue on the Pest side, the students saw us and also started to march. They, too, marched silently. The effect of all these people marching was overpowering. The sidewalks were full. People were marching with us on both sides of our columns. It was more than just a demonstration; it was a dream, a miracle. An entire nation was marching with us. I walked in a state of hypnotic trance.

I imagined that in our solemn parade there marched Saint Stephen, the founder of our nation, with his heavy golden crown. And next to him walked our other great king, Matthias Corvinus, with his fabulous books. And there were the freedom fighters of the past: Prince Rákóczy with his rugged *kuruc* soldiers; Louis Kossuth with his bloodied but unbowed redcaps.[8] And now I saw more-recently departed patriots: Imre Madách, the philosopher; Endre Ady, the poet; Béla Bartók, the composer; Ferenc Molnár, the playwright; and on and on. I felt that the collective soul of this nation was there marching with us. Then from my right I heard the voice of the Menő: "This moment made life worth living." I did not reply. I could not speak.

On our right, we first passed the Freedom Bridge, then the Elizabeth Bridge, and finally the Széchenyi Chain Bridge, the first chain bridge of its kind in all of Europe. People stared at us in open-mouthed wonder, with disbelief in their eyes, their hats in their hands, their teary eyes full of amazement. I saw a lady in a white smock in one of the windows on Döbrentei Square. She had cut the Communist crest out of our national flag and was waving this flag with the hole in its center. In that instant we all knew that that flag had to and would become the symbol of our revolution. For just a short moment we forgot that this was a silent march, and we cheered that lady waving the flag in the window.

Then I saw Professor Jankovits's little Topolino parked on the sidewalk. Jancsi Danner, Iván Szabó, and others were writing something, using the roof of the car as if it were a desk. The Menő yelled out to them: "What are you doing?"

"We have just converted the fourteen points into sixteen!" came the answer.[9]

As we arrived at the statue of the Polish general József Bem, its base was already covered with flowers and wreaths of laurels. The president of the Writers' Union, Péter Veres, was speaking. After that we heard Petőfi's poem:

Up, Hungarians! Freedom forever!
Now's the moment, now or never!
Shall we be slaves? Shall we be free?
That is no choice: we must be free!

The poem was followed by the reading of the newly born sixteen points. After the reading, a delegation once again left for the radio station, hoping to broadcast our demands, while another delegation, with Sándor Széll, left to deliver our demands to Imre Nagy.

At the end of the commemoration, some of the classes returned to the university. We, the junior class of mechanical engineering, decided to march on to the parliament. We felt that our work was incomplete, that we could not go home like that. We had to obtain some concrete result; we had to obtain a response from the government. Our march was still silent and dignified. We were maintaining our arm-in-arm formation and our mood was happy, optimistic, as we reached the Bridge of Saint Margaret, which would take us to the Pest side, where the parliament was.

CHAPTER 4

Enough of Listening

I T WAS EIGHT O'CLOCK IN THE EVENING. We were on
Saint Stephen's Avenue, on the Pest side of the bridge. People
living in the surrounding buildings had opened their windows
and placed their radios there. Therefore we could hear the hated
voice of the general secretary of the Communist Party, Ernő Gerő: "We
condemn those who organize nationalist demonstrations and who
strive to spread the poison of chauvinism among our youth," he was
saying. Our mood changed. Menő turned to me: "The dirty, lying skunk!
This quisling fears all patriots, and with good reasons, too!" Now our
march was no longer silent. I heard Laci Zsindely's voice from far back:
"Down with Gerő!"[1] The slogan spread, and then new ones, like "Hungarians, come with us!" took over. The one slogan that spread the quick-
est was "Russians go home." The walls of the avenue echoed with this
rallying cry.

On Alkotmány Street I saw a pub. I had not eaten since the morning, so I ran in: "Give me something to eat, a roll, anything." The mustachioed bartender gave me a French roll. I pulled out my still intact

140 forints, two twenties and a one-hundred-forint bill, and handed him one of the twenties. He took it, looked at my tricolored armband, hesitated for a second, and then returned the twenty saying, "I will close down the pub and join you!"

By the time we arrived at the parliament, there must have been a quarter of a million people on the square in front of it. We heard a lot of yelling as people demanded that the illumination of the red star on the dome of the building be turned off. When the light finally went out, a thunderous ovation rose to the sky. A moment later all the lights in the immense Kossuth Square went off. Now it was total darkness. This was a less than subtle hint by the Communists implying that it was time for us to go home.

Now, somewhere far, far away, at the other end of the square, somebody put a match to a rolled-up issue of the party paper, the *Szabad Nép (Free People)*. Others followed this example, and within a few minutes thousands of flickering torches illuminated the plaza. It was a serene and unforgettable sight. As we stood hypnotized by the flickering of thousands of flames, a deep voice somewhere in the back started singing the national anthem. The quarter-, perhaps half-, million people in this gigantic square stood to attention as the hymn spread, filled the square, and then rose to the sky. As our voices blended in this prayer for our homeland, our souls filled with a new unity and determination. The paper torches were still burning when Kossuth's favorite song began to thunder through the plaza:

Louis Kossuth sent the message,
That his army is a wreckage,
If he needs us, we are coming,
The enemy can start packing,
Long live Hungary!

Finally, from the balcony of the Parliament, Ferenc Erdei announced that Imre Nagy, one of the remaining few Communist leaders who was still respected in Hungary, was going to speak.[2] There was no sound amplification, so we could barely hear what he was saying. But we all heard the first word he said, "Comrades!" That was the ultimate insult. We did not want to hear any more. We did not want to listen to any more speeches. Enough of listening, enough of talking, it was time to make our own decisions. It was time for action. (Later it was reported that he said, "My friends, there are no more comrades!" In any case, what mattered at the time was what we *thought* he said.)

It was about nine o'clock. Our junior class of mechanical engineering was still in one group when Gyuszi Perr found us. He arrived on his motorbike with the little blonde athlete Marika on the back seat. The news he brought was that in Hero's Square people were trying to topple Stalin's twenty-four-foot-tall bronze monument.[3] At the radio station, the ÁVH had been reinforced, and the station's director, Valéria Benke, was holding our delegation captive. The situation was very tense there. Trucks were arriving, bringing workers from Csepel to the radio station. They were in a fighting mood.

We held a brief meeting. Some suggested that we go to the radio station; others wanted to help topple Stalin's statue. Gyuri Egry said, "We should do something that others are not doing. Let us go to the Szikra publishing house and print a strike proclamation." We agreed on that. So, Gyuszi Perr went back to the station, and we, the whole junior class of mechanical engineering, still in a disciplined, orderly formation, marched to the Szikra publishing house.

The workers at the printshop offered no resistance. They asked only for a written statement that we had requisitioned their facility, and from that point on, their questions involved only the text, letter sizes, margins, and the like. It felt too easy. In about an hour the strike proclamation was printed. We were about to leave with the still-wet leaflets when Gyuszi Perr—with Marika still on the back seat of his motorbike—arrived once more. This time Gyuszi was unnerved, shaken. His report explained why: "At the radio station, the ÁVH first used tear-gas grenades but later started shooting with live ammunition. People have been killed. There is chaos at the station. Also, Stalin's statue has been knocked down in the park. The trucks of Csepel are dragging it through the city."

It must have been about eleven o'clock when we decided to break up. The majority of our class of two or three hundred was starving and tired, so they went home. I joined the group that was headed for the radio station. It must have been about midnight when we got there.

The radio building was on Bródy Street. We were still several blocks away when the rattle of gunfire became audible. As we got closer, we could also smell the gunpowder. I was frightened, my heart was pounding, but I could not turn back. As we reached the corner of Museum Boulevard (which we called the Small Boulevard) and Bródy Street, I saw three Hungarian tanks. People were surrounding them, talking to the officers. It was obvious that these soldiers were not going to shoot at other Hungarians.

As we turned into Bródy Street, it seemed empty. There was smoke in the air. People nestled in the doorways. My corduroy jacket rubbed against the wall as I ran toward the radio building. I passed some abandoned Red Cross ambulances in the middle of the street, then stopped at the next doorway. "What are these ambulances doing here?" I asked.

"The ÁVH task force arrived in them. These bastards, the ÁVH reinforcements were wearing the white coats of doctors over their uniforms. They were also bringing more ammunition to the ÁVH thugs inside. The demonstrators overpowered them and took their arms." The voice was familiar. I leaned closer. It was Zsuzsa, the bride of my friend Gábor Illés. "Don't tell Gábor!"—she pleaded when she recognized me. She had a submachine gun in her hand.[4]

"Where did you get that?" I asked.

"From them," she replied, and she pointed to a young soldier standing next to her. He was an enlisted man. I could tell that he was from the Great Plains region of Hungary, because in the middle of all this madness he held out his hand for a handshake and politely introduced himself.

"How did you get here?" I asked.

"Our unit was sent to reinforce the ÁVH, but when our commander saw what was going on, he refused the order. Some of my mates gave their arms to the people, like her. Others, like me—we joined them." He spoke slowly, precisely, without a single unnecessary word, without overstatement, without theatrics. He spoke like all farmers do anywhere in the world. And he spoke with the accent of the region of Szeged.

Now I noticed a group of demonstrators marching toward the radio building. They were not running, were not clutching against the wall (as I did), but were marching in the middle of the street. They marched behind a giant of a man with a large Hungarian flag. The man must have been a blacksmith, someone whose work made him very strong, because he was able to hold the immense flag in one hand. They must have been a hundred yards from the building when the ÁVH started firing. In that narrow street the echoes of the explosions were amplified, and the resulting racket was almost unbearable. Yet I saw no bullets hitting the pavement. They must have been shooting into the air. The demonstrators froze to a standstill but did not run, and once the shooting was over, they started slowly to move again.

Suddenly, I heard another burst of firing. This time the bullets struck the pavement like lumps of ice in an ice storm. When a bullet hit the pavement it made a high-pitched *phing* sound. When it hit flesh, it made a much deeper *thud* sound. The wounded were screaming, those demonstrators who were not seriously wounded were running away, but the blacksmith still stood, took another step forward, and then slowly, like a falling oak tree, started to topple to the ground, still holding, lifting, the flag.

Next to me, I heard the enlisted man talking to Zsuzsa: "No, you first release this. Yes. Now you look through that." And now came a deafening burst. A window shattered on the radio building. Now the pavement was sparking in front of our doorway. "Only people with guns, please!" the enlisted man said. I patted Zsuzsa's back and started running away from the radio station, close to the wall, in the direction I had come from.

As I got to the corner of Museum Avenue, I saw a truck with a crowd around it. "What's happening?" I asked. The man next to me was well informed: "They are from the Soroksár Street arms factory. You know, the one that is officially called the United Lamp Factory. They brought rifles and ammunition." I pushed my way to the truck to get hold of a rifle and some bullets. The rifle was slippery; they must have been stored in grease. My first reaction was *Oh God, this rifle will mess up my beautiful corduroy jacket.* So I moved over to a garbage can and started rubbing the grease off the rifle with old newspapers.

As I was rubbing away, I heard somebody call out, "Öcsi!"

I looked up. It was my older brother, Péter. "What are you doing here?" I asked.

"Oh, we came in from the Agricultural University of Gödöllő."

"So you changed your mind?"

"No, not at all. This is madness. The ÁVH will butcher you all. You don't stand a chance with that ancient rifle. All it is good for is to mess up your jacket! Besides, if the ÁVH cannot handle you, the Russians will."

"OK, OK. So, you still feel that way. By the way, I just talked with

Figure 4. Katalin Stricker and Maria Wittner in 1956. For having been a freedom fighter, Stricker was hanged in 1958. Photo by Leslie A. Toth

Zsuzsa, Gábor Illés's bride. She is fighting at the radio building. She just learned how to use a submachine gun."

At that point a truck pulled up next to us and a young man yelled out, "This truck is from Újpest (one of the newer districts of Pest), and we are on our way to the Károly Barracks in Budaörs to get more arms. If you want to help, get on." As I started climbing onto the truck, Péter yelled at me to stay. It felt good that he was worried about me, but my mind was made up. It was made up when that blacksmith with the big flag fell.

"See you soon!" I called out to Péter as the truck took off.

There were two wooden benches on the truck. I wiped the seat with my handkerchief to protect my favorite jacket. On my bench there were two other young men; on the opposite side of the truck were three boys and two girls. I was the only student on this truck. The others, from the way they dressed, the way they talked, I could tell that they were all factory workers. We all were holding on to the same grimy rifles.

The second boy on my right was in the process of loading his gun. It never occurred to me to do that. I got the rifle only because that appeared to be the ticket to taking part, to being there, but it never occurred to me that I could use it. As far as I was concerned, my bullets were just fine in the pocket of my corduroy jacket.

The truck was heading for the Petőfi Bridge. From Museum Boulevard it turned onto the deserted Üllői Street. We must have been doing close to sixty miles an hour. The boy on my bench had finished loading his gun, and the butts of our rifles were all resting in front of us on the truck's floor. Suddenly—we must have run over a brick or something—I felt a big bump. Our rifles all jumped into the air, and as they fell back, the loaded one went off. The boy next to me fell forward, blood streaming from his right ear.

I grabbed him as the truck came to a screeching halt. Because I was a student and because I was wearing the tricolored armband, the others automatically expected me to decide what we should do. The Haynal Clinic was only a few hundred yards from us, and when we got there the night watchman opened the door and called for emergency help. In a few minutes the wounded boy was taken away on a stretcher, and we were back on the truck. The right side of my spotless favorite jacket was bloodied now.

We should have turned right on Ferenc Boulevard (Grand Boulevard on the map) to reach the Petőfi Bridge, but there was a long row of Russian tanks coming from that direction. So we stayed on Üllői Street, then turned left on Hungária Boulevard. A big crowd was at the HÉV railroad station near Baross Square. They told us that the director of the Ruggyanta rubber factory refused to take part in the general strike—refused to shut down the plant. We drove to the main gate of the plant. "Where is the emergency loudspeaker?" I asked the confused gatekeeper. He looked at my armband and without the slightest hesitation flipped a switch and pointed to a microphone. I spoke into the mike: "A general strike been declared in Budapest. This factory will shut down immediately!" I repeated this twice, and as we left, the porter said, "The shut-down procedure takes some time, you know; these are chemical processes, you know!"

Earlier we learned that Sándor Kopácsi, the police chief, had instructed the precinct police chiefs not to resist the requisition of arms. So our next stop was the police station on Baross Square. It seemed that they were expecting us. The policeman on guard duty even helped load their spare guns onto our truck. Back on Baross Square, we distributed the guns, and as the young people got their weapons, they automatically climbed up onto our truck until it was completely full; there was absolutely no room left. So I continued on foot.

It must have been about 2:00 A.M. on this Wednesday, October 24, when I suddenly remembered Ágnes. It was an impossible hour, but I had to go there immediately and let her know that I was safe. It was a long walk. The apartment house was dark, the door was locked, and the mailboxes were on the inside. I did not dare call at that hour, so I slipped a note under the front door and left.

As I reached the corner of Rákóczy Street and the Grand Boulevard, I could hear intense gunfire at the main offices of the Communist Party paper, *Szabad Nép.* The massive bulk of Stalin's bronze statue was resting in the middle of the road. As the firing intensified, I decided to seek protection behind the twenty-four-foot metal casting of Stalin's body. As I hit the pavement, a voice next to me remarked, "This is the first time that our beloved leader did something for me!" The speaker was a skinny little guy with a blue beret and a massive hammer in his hand. He continued: "I was trying to take home a piece of Stalin as a souvenir when the fighting broke out. There is a large ÁVH contingent inside the *Szabad Nép* building, but the Hungarians have already occupied the ground floor." This was the first time that I heard somebody implying that the ÁVH thugs were not Hungarians. I had always thought of them as traitors or collaborators, but never as disowned outcasts.

On my way back to the radio building, I saw Russian tanks approaching on Museum Boulevard. They were not firing. An officer was standing in the open hatchway of the first tank. The boulevard was empty. People were hiding in the doorways. "Don't show your gun!" I heard from one of the doorways as I jumped into the semidarkness. The tanks roared by, and I continued on my way, back to the university. It was about 5:00 A.M. when I crossed the Freedom Bridge back to Buda and reached Saint Gellért Square. The scene I found there was surreal.

The square was full of people. Some were fully dressed, while others were in their nightgowns or pajamas. They were in the process of building barricades. Some were carrying old bedsprings; others brought chairs or bricks. One group was digging up the cobblestones of the

Figure 5. A hated symbol, Stalin's head, on the street in Budapest. Photo by Rolf Gillhausen, courtesy 1956 Institute of Hungary, Budapest

pavement, using crowbars and other, less likely, tools. They intended to block the bridge so that the Russian tanks could not come over from the Pest side. When they saw my rifle, the armband, and the blood on my jacket, they respectfully gave way. A policeman, twice my age, asked, "What do we do now?"

Without thinking and without hesitation I answered, "We push them out of the city!"

At that point, three trucks arrived from the direction of Móricz Square. "Let us help the people on the Pest side!" shouted a young man from the first truck. Unarmed people started climbing onto the trucks. I saw two elderly ladies in their dressing gowns—they were probably sisters—carrying a heavy cobblestone. I gave them a hand as they struggled to lift it onto the truck. "Just in case you might need it," one said, "Just in case, you know!" I jumped onto the second truck.

As we turned onto the bridge, I looked back. The people on the square had come to a standstill. They were watching our trucks. Some were crying, some took off their hats, and a nun was on her knees, praying. We were about halfway across when the tanks at the Pest bridgehead started firing. The first truck was hit and burst into flame. Our driver tried to make a U-turn and crashed into a pole. The cobblestone flew forward; people were falling and jumping off. It was chaos. We were all running back; nobody made it to the Pest side.

I got back to the university at about nine o'clock in the morning. It was hard to believe that twenty-four hours earlier I was checking identity cards at these gates. Ages had passed during those hours. Now, everything was empty; not a soul was to be seen. As I walked through the main aula, I could hear the echo of my footsteps.

The door of the DISZ office opened. It was Jancsi Danner with a submachine gun on his shoulder. He was just as dirty and tired as I. "We must be the first ones. I just got back from the Corvin Cinema. We beat back the Russians there. They lost some tanks," he said.

"This place looks abandoned. Let's check the military department," I suggested.

As we were walking over, I notice that the sole of my sandal was coming off. Jancsi's shoes were big and rugged; they would last longer than mine. He was from Szeged, very tall, dark blond with grayish blue eyes. He took life seriously. He was about to get married to a girl named Gabi—short for Gabriella. I was different. I used to think of life as an opportunity to have fun, but now I was not sure. Now I felt that these solemn Jancsi types might just have a point.

As we looked up at the windows of the military department, we saw no movement or light inside. The main door was open, so we entered. As Jancsi opened the door of Colonel Marián's office, there was some movement in the background, and a voice asked, "Who is that?"

"It's János Danner and . . ." Jancsi looked at me, and I finished his sentence: "Öcsi." I still did not dare to use my real name.

The colonel and two of his officers stepped out from the back of the room. They were in the process of putting away their pistols. "Why didn't we see you from the outside?" I asked.

"We have been crawling under the windows on all fours," replied a lieutenant.

Marián's eyes were bloodshot and the corner of his mouth was twitching as he said, "We came back here after the march and have been here ever since. I expect to be arrested any minute."

We tried to cheer them up. We told them that the regular army and the police were on our side. We told them about the general strike, the heavy fighting at the radio station and at the Kilián Barracks, but their gloom did not lift.

"Have you eaten?" Jancsi asked them. They shook their heads, so we went to the cafeteria and got a pitcher of stale coffee, apples, and some bread. They still looked paralyzed. They still bent down before passing in front of the window. At that point I thought of Memi and Aptyi. They had to be worried, so I decided that it was time for me to go home and reassure them. So I left.

My mother's younger sister, Duduke, lived at 1 Béla Bartók Street. Their apartment house used to belong to my grandmother's family; now, of course, it belonged to the state. It was built when Budapest was the elegant capital of the dual monarchy. The marble stairway was wide enough to carry up a grand piano. The mahogany banister was supported by richly decorated wrought iron. The turns were so sweeping, so gentle, that one could slide from the fourth floor all the way to the street level on it. As a child I tested that many times. The stone was carved, the ceilings were tall, and the building radiated the confidence, pride, and defiance of a thousand-year-old kingdom.

That building would still be standing when the Red Empire had already faded into a bad memory. It would prove that a European city cannot be pushed into Asia. The buildings would not allow that. The spirit of that one building was more powerful than all the secret police of that slave empire. The soul of such a city can never be conquered.

After I rang the bell, Uncle Feri opened the door. Even in the semi-darkness of the hallway, he was dumbstruck at the sight of me. The vestibule was full of Feri Bácsi's hunting memorabilia; antlers and tusks, hunting knives and horns covered the walls. In his time he chased big game in the Carpathian Mountains, hunted for fox in Transylvania and for partridge near the Adriatic, without ever leaving Hungarian soil. Today, because of such artificial new states as Czechoslovakia and Yugoslavia, he needed a visa to visit his birthplace, Kassa (today Kosice). Today he was a different man; today the main challenge of his life was to find his dentures in the morning.

As we entered the living room, I left my rifle and the bloodied corduroy jacket in the foyer. Duduke was in the process of changing the baby. It would have been her third child if one had not starved to death at the end of the war because she had had no milk. Péter and I tried to help. I will never forget: I was trying to steal some milk for the baby by creeping on my belly, with a saucepan in hand, among a herd of kicking cows guarded by Russian soldiers. That was scary for a nine-year-old.

Now, in Duduke's apartment, the radio was on. It said that the deadline for laying down our arms had been extended until 2:00 P.M. We could hear the explosions through the window. They seemed to come from the direction of the Kilián Barracks. I did not know what to do. Duduke left the room for no obvious reason, and a few minutes after her return, my father's older sister showed up. She did not explain how she knew that I was at Duduke's. She just said, "You must be hungry!" With that she handed me some of my favorite sausage. The sausage tasted funny. The more I ate, the sleepier I got. Later I learned that her doctor husband, Uncle Tivadar, had injected some barbiturates into the sausage.

It was midafternoon when I woke up. I felt woozy and had a splitting headache. As I put on my jacket in the vestibule, I had a blurry sense that I was missing something, but I did not remember what it was, and since I did not see anything else, I left as I was.

On the way home I saw that the curfew was ineffective. Russian tanks were stationed at the main intersections, but the rest of the city was controlled by the freedom fighters. The ÁVH resistance had subsided, but one could still hear some sporadic firing. The general strike seemed to be in full force. I again went to Ágnes's house. Her family was not home. According to the superintendent, they probably had gone to Lake Balaton.

Kerepes was about fifteen miles from Budapest. By the time I got home, it was dark. As I opened the gate, Bukucs was all over me. He kept bouncing in total ecstasy. The family was in the kitchen listening to Radio Free Europe. When I entered, there was a lot of crying and excitement followed by endless questions. Hours later, Aptyi finally called it a day. As we left the kitchen, he turned to me and said, "Remember that we are all alone. We can only lose and I do not want to lose you!"

CHAPTER 5

MEFESZ Headquarters
of the Technical University

I
T WAS THURSDAY MORNING, October 25. The radio had just announced that Ernő Gerő was no longer the secretary of the Communist Party and that Imre Nagy had been named the new prime minister. At breakfast, Aptyi explained, "The Russians are in a difficult spot. They have been claiming to be anti-imperialists in order to make inroads in the former colonies of the West. Now, if they crush us, they can no longer claim to be an anticolonial power; if they don't, they show weakness. Therefore, you and your friends must make it easy for them to withdraw their tanks. You must reassure them that the new Hungary will be a neutral and friendly neighbor." He was talking to me as if I were the new government.

At that point Memi interjected, "Couldn't somebody else reassure the Russians, instead of our Öcsi?"

"But we, the students, started it, we have a responsibility to lead!" I interrupted.

"And where would you lead, if they let you?" asked Péter.

In answering Péter I spoke about not wanting to exchange the communist zoo for the capitalist jungle, not wanting to turn back history nor to concentrate on revenge. Yet I emphasized that we did want justice. At a minimum, we wanted repentance from the traitors and we wanted the courts to decide the fate of those whose hands were bloody. On the issue of property rights I spoke against all forms of state ownership, because it breeds bureaucracy and corruption. I suggested that the homes, land, and small businesses should be returned to their rightful owners and that larger industry or collective farms could be given to their employees if the workers wanted that, or if they did not, could be privatized. I spoke about equal opportunity for all, while protecting the dignity of the less fortunate and the poor. I ended up saying: "And most of all, we want liberty! We want our new society to be free and democratic."

Now, there was silence in the kitchen. Memi blew her nose, Aptyi cleared his throat, and we, Péter and I, slipped our sandwiches into our pockets; it was time to go.

Because of the strike, there were no trains. The only way to get to Budapest was by hitchhiking. Péter decided to come with me. Andris, at sixteen, would have been too young to join us, but I did not see him. As we waited on the side of the road, a horse-drawn lorry passed by. It was collecting food for the people of Budapest. The lorry was in front of the Rapavys' house.

"No way! It is against the religion of Jóska Bácsi to give anything to anybody without getting paid!" I said jokingly. József Rapavy was known to be as miserly as only a Hungarian farmer can be. A moment later I saw him coming out of his house carrying a gargantuan sack of potatoes on his broad shoulders. My mouth must have fallen open, because he gave me an angry look, ran back into the house, and reappeared with a slab of bacon. "There!" he said triumphantly. "This is my fight, too, you know!"

After some walking, finally a truck slowed down and we climbed up. All the traffic was headed into the city, and all the trucks were loaded with young people. There was little question why they were coming. The fighting in Budapest had subsided, but we were still far from a full victory. There still were a few ÁVH pockets left, and the Russian tanks, while they were no longer firing, were still stationed at the major intersections. So we did not really know where we stood, and volunteers were probably still needed.

We got off the truck at the Eastern railroad station because Péter was taking a train to the Agricultural University of Keszthely. After we parted, I walked through Baross Square. It was swarming with armed young people. I was on my way back to the Technical University but made a detour to check on Ágnes. Gábor, her brother, opened the door. "She is still down at Lake Balaton," he said. I also learned from Gábor that the police chief of Budapest, Sándor Kopácsi, and his regular police had joined the revolution, the radio station had been captured, the twelve hundred soldiers of Kilián Barracks, now commanded by General Maléter, had repulsed the Russian tanks, and a major demonstration was being planned on that day at about noon in front of the parliament.[1]

In front of the Emke restaurant, near the National Theater, dozens of people were swarming over the carcass of Stalin's statue. Using welding torches, hammers, and a variety of saws, they chipped off pieces of the fallen tyrant's statue. Behind the statue, on the Grand Boulevard, one could see the remains of burnt-out Russian tanks.

As I walked on Rákóczi Street, I noticed that most of the store windows had bullet holes, and some had no glass at all. Yet the goods were untouched. In one window I saw a small, handwritten note: "Protect the honor of the Revolution! Show the World that we fight for FREEDOM, not to steal!" I stood and stared at the sign for a long time; I was proud of my people. In the windowless display case all the goods were still there.

As I walked toward Museum Boulevard, I saw a small, freckled teenager with black-ringed eyes and a big rifle. He stood in front of a watch store.

"Are you guarding them?" I pointed at the watches behind the broken window. He first looked me in the eyes, then at my tricolored armband, and said, "You should know better. Guards are not needed here!"

A woman listening nearby added, "Besides, now, all of this is ours anyway! Not just the watches, but this wreck of a house, this street, this devastated city, everything. You don't steal what is yours, you don't steal from your family! This store belongs to my family; this is a Hungarian store!"

A few houses down the street, I saw a horse-drawn lorry. People were lined up, waiting while the driver filled their baskets and shop-

Figure 6. The windows of the department store are broken, but the goods are untouched. Courtesy 1956 Institute of Hungary, Budapest

ping bags with potatoes. He was like any street vendor except for one difference: there was no payment; the distribution was free and anonymous. He was handing out the gifts from the surrounding villages. This took place on several street corners.

At the corner, the body of a young man was lying on the pavement. He was on his back. His face was white, serene, almost happy. His body was covered with a flag and flowers. He had no gun; somebody probably felt that he no longer needed one and took his. He was the first corpse I had ever seen in such close proximity. I stood there for a long time. I wondered if my dead face would also be so proud and reassuring. There was a large, handwritten sign on his chest. It read: "They did not die in vain."

There was a crowd in front of the Astoria restaurant on the corner of Kossuth Street and the Small Boulevard. They were surrounding some Russian tanks. The tank hatches were open, and the commander had climbed out and was talking with the people in the crowd. This officer had obviously been stationed in Hungary for some time, because he spoke some Hungarian: "Russian people, Hungarian people, friends people," he said. There was a rose in the barrel of his cannon, and a

Figure 7. Trucks brought food from the villages to the freedom fighters in the capital. Courtesy 1956 Institute of Hungary, Budapest

Hungarian flag fluttered over his tank. (His unit later followed the demonstrators to the parliament, and when the ÁVH opened fire on the marchers, his tanks returned fire on the ÁVH. Hundreds of unarmed Hungarians died that day in front of the parliament. The demonstrators went there to demand the withdrawal of the Russian tanks from the capital. They also expected to greet Imre Nagy, their new prime minister, who at Communist Party headquarters was still a virtual prisoner of the Hungarian secret police.)[2]

On the next corner I saw the burnt-out Ady movie theater. Apparently the Russian tank commander on that corner was not as friendly as the one on the Kossuth Street corner. When the firefighters' truck arrived to put out a fire in the movie house, the tank opened fire on that truck too. Now both the building and the fire truck were smoldering. "Madness!" I mumbled to myself, "Madness!"

On Kossuth Street I saw a large wooden box, placed there by the Writers' Union. A sign above the crate read, "Please give to the casualties of the Revolution!" The container was full of paper money. The box was unguarded. In terms of my standards, a fortune was already in that box.

A dazed, elderly women stood in front of the box; her eyes were red, she could barely stand. She was picking up some red one-hundred-forint bills. Then I saw that instead of taking out more, she was putting some back. "It does not need to be oak, he can rest in pine too," she was murmuring to herself. I just stood there and thought of Memi. I reached into my pocket and took out my 140 forints. I dropped in the red hundred and one of the blue twenties. I kept the other twenty-forint bill, just in case Ágnes came back from the lake and she still wanted to see *The Women of Selistye.*

When I arrived at the university, the doors were open, the gates were unguarded, and the buildings were empty. Only Jancsi Danner and Pali Zádor were in the headquarters office of the newly formed MEFESZ. Previously, that office had belonged to the Communist Party and was the gathering place of the DISZ penguins. Now it was our MEFESZ office. The tables were covered by copies of our sixteen demands and by other

Figure 8. The sign above the unguarded collection box reads, "The purity of our revolution makes it possible to use this method of collecting for the families of our martyrs." Courtesy 1956 Institute of Hungary, Budapest

proclamations. Pali was writing; Jancsi was on the phone. "Yes, we will fully cooperate with the police. Yes, we will organize regular patrols throughout the eleventh district," he was saying.

"Who was that?" I asked when he put down the phone.

"Sándor Kopácsi, the chief of police."

Now the phone rang in the inner office. I picked it up. I could tell that it was a long-distance call, because the connection was bad, barely audible: "I am calling from the MEFESZ office of the University of Forestry and Mining in Sopron. I would like to reach the MEFESZ headquarters of the Technical University," said the distant voice.

"You did," I replied.

"So, what do we do next?" the voice asked.

"The general strike continues until the Russians leave. You should disarm the ÁVH, organize an armed student battalion, organize joint patrols with the police, use the radio to keep the public informed, and stay in touch with us."

"We will do that," said the voice and hung up.

The telephone kept ringing all afternoon. About five, Kati Szőke and Sándor Varga arrived. Then came the university's two drivers, Imre Majoross and Gyurka Vereczkey. They reported that the garage was intact and the cars were safe. Later on, in the evening, we decided to invite Colonel Marián from the military department to settle in the inner room of our offices. He accepted.

During the night we talked and talked, and talked some more. By the time I went to sleep, we were all on a first-name basis (which in Hungary, under normal circumstances, might take a decade). Colonel Marián became Pista (the nickname for István). We felt like brothers and sisters. It was a warm, marvelous feeling. We had developed such a strong bond and I felt such love and respect, such trust and admiration for them that I had never known before. Our bond was based on more than our willingness to give our lives for Hungary's liberty. It was our conviction that we were changing the world and that it would be a happier place when we were finished.

During the night I learned a lot about Pista and Jancsi. The colonel was born in Transylvania. He was a talented and ambitious young Jewish officer who joined the Communist Party because of his desire for social justice. Now, in his early thirties, he found himself at a crossroads. He had to make a choice, and he chose his country. It was not an easy decision. He also had a family to worry about, and he knew how Moscow treated "traitors."

Jancsi, twenty-seven, had grown up in Szeged as the son of a rich shopkeeper. There, he had organized demonstrations against the outlawing of religious education in the schools. As a consequence, he was placed under police surveillance. He was well organized, level-headed, but also a romantic. He was both a refined cosmopolitan and a lover of ancient Hungarian folk culture. "There is a lot of accumulated background in how one holds a tea cup," he said, "yet social order is more than that, and Christianity is more than social order."

He talked a lot about historic roles. "The role is more than the individual playing it; the role is given, the actor is replaceable! Not you but your role determines destiny, you cannot be late for meeting your fate!" Jancsi was old for his age; Jancsi was too serious for a twenty-seven-year-old. Only his bride, Gabriella, understood him completely. Her eyes sparkled whenever she looked at him.

At the invitation of a medical student, Ili Tóth, I slept on a narrow leather bed in the medical emergency room in the basement of the university. The bed could not have been less comfortable. It was one of those narrow contraptions on wheels, used to roll the patients into the operating room. For me, it was also way too short. The leather sloped to the center and my head rested on the aluminum frame, yet I slept like a baby. I was so happy!

CHAPTER 6

Getting the Arms

O N THIS FRIDAY MORNING I must have entered the MEFESZ office with my usual grin, because Pista (Colonel Marián) winked at me. He was in the middle of some discussion. The full-bosomed young professor Kati Szőke offered me a French roll. The big bear Gyurka Vereczkey mockingly bowed, implying that I must be too refined for early rising. As a peace offering, I gave him half of my roll and proceeded to join the group around Pista. I felt completely at ease in this warm, friendly atmosphere, where the well-focused yet frenzied activity never stopped.

Pista stood at the window. His eyes were bloodshot; he must have been up all night. He was lighting one cigarette after another while talking to three students, Sándor Varga, Imi Mécs, and Jancsi Danner. He was constantly moving, and the students moved with him like planets around the sun. Outside this inner core were his officers, a captain and a lieutenant. They followed this inner group on an outer orbit. Beyond the officers' ring were the messengers. They too circled the core. The smoke rose, the identities of the participants changed, but this slow waltz, this hypnotic dance, went on from morning to night, day after day. There was something harrowing yet also splendid in this whirling and swirling activity, in this process that just might give birth to a new world, a better society.

After swallowing my half of the roll, I moved to the core of this human whirlpool. Pista immediately turned to me: "Öcsi, you go to Kopácsi's headquarters and bring us his spare guns. Take one of the trucks from the university garage. Vereczkey will be your driver. From now on you and he are a team. Tell Kopácsi that we need arms. I soon expect a couple of thousand students here. I also invited the cadets of the Petőfi Academy, so we need lots of small arms. Oh yes, and tell him that I am forming a national guard division here."

"It's done, Pista, but now go, take a nap. You must! Your hands are shaking. Please!" I pled, but the process was unstoppable; a new face, a new problem, and the swirling dance continued around the red-eyed little colonel.

Gyurka Vereczkey heard what Pista said. He bowed deeply and opened the door for me. From then on, whenever there were people around, Gyurka stayed behind me. He also let me speak first, but when we were alone, all the theatrics ended, and he treated me as if he were my older brother. He was about five years older than I. Five years is a lot when you are twenty. He was smart, experienced, and brave, and I loved and respected him.

Gyurka was to graduate from medical school, but the Communists kicked him out. "Politics, you know," he said, but I did not know, and he did not tell me any more.[1] He got this driver's job through the influence of Endre Sík, the father-in-law of his sister. The story of the Sík family is a typical Jewish-Hungarian story. One brother, Sándor Sík, was Hungary's best-known Catholic poet, a converted Jew and an anticommunist. The other brother, Endre Sík, was a Communist and a Russian collaborator. He was Hungary's ambassador to Moscow, and after the Revolution he became Hungary's foreign minister. Gyurka's brother-in-law Igor Sík was Endre's son. He was born in Moscow and spoke fluent Russian, yet, as I was to learn later, he was a Hungarian patriot.

We got the truck from the garage on Budafoki Street. As we made the turn at the corner of Bertalan and Bartók Streets, I saw a crowd. Because it was our job to maintain order in this district, I asked Gyurka to stop. Some twenty people were listening to a man who was sitting on his bicycle with one foot on the ground for support. As we got closer, I began to hear fragments of his repulsive oration: "We the real Hungarians . . . Jewish ÁVH renegades . . . they are the inner enemy." When we got even closer, it became obvious that he was trying to incite his listeners against Jewish-Hungarians. This was the first (and only!) anti-Semitic incident I witnessed during the Revolution. I knew that I had to be firm and decisive, but I had no idea how to do that. The people saw my tricolored armband, so they opened a path. As I walked toward the cyclist, I sensed that the people expected me to take care of this situation. I also knew that we could not tolerate such disgusting provocation.

"I guess I have to arrest him," I whispered to Gyurka, but I had no idea how one went about that. And once arrested, what should I do with him? Should we take him back to the university? Where would we put him there? I had no answers for any of these questions, but I did know that the honor of the Revolution was at stake and that it was my duty to act. Now the cyclist had noticed me, so he shut up. The people were all looking at me; I had only a second or two to decide what to do. At that instant I saw the movement of the bearlike figure of Gyurka, who seemed even bigger in his quilted driver's parka. He was passing me on my right. He did not speak, just lifted his arm and smacked the man backhanded in the face. The man's mouth was open as he fell over his bike. Gyurka did not even look at him. Instead, he cast his eyes on the people gathered around and said, "Now you know how it's done. Next time you do it yourself!"

"You don't waste too many words, do you?" I complimented him as we walked back to the truck.

"I despise these hatemongers. Look at what they did to the Sík family. They scared one brother into becoming a Catholic poet and the other into becoming a Communist traitor, while their kids don't even know who they are. These racist fanatics did that not only to the Síks but to most Jewish-Hungarians!"

"It turns my stomach!" I replied. "Although I never thought that much about it. I have never seen a thug like your punching bag here. The only Jew in our family was the mother of my godmother. I was eight when Eichmann's thugs took her away after the Germans occupied Hungary in 1944. My father tried to free her, but failed. Nobody else even tried. Nobody ever explained to me why there was so little resistance to the deportations."

"Why? How much resistance have you seen to the Communist's deportations a few years ago? This lack of resistance has nothing to do with the Jews. This has to do with human nature; people are simply scared; all people are always scared. In times of trouble, they look the other way to save their own skin!" Gyurka added.

I also remembered that in Sopron, in the fall of 1944, my grandfather took a long walk every afternoon. He was always wearing his much-decorated army uniform. By that time he was retired, but if he was not, he would have refused to take the oath of loyalty to the Nazi government installed by the occupying Germans. During his long walks he would stop every person who was wearing a yellow star and ask for the time. He did not need this information; his gold pocket watch kept the best time in the city. What he needed was to let them know that they were not outcasts but fellow Hungarians. It was his way of trying to protect his countrymen from the heinous humiliation of being marked as outcasts. Gyurka smiled; I could tell that he liked my grandfather, and I know I liked Gyurka.

On our way to the police headquarters on Deák Square, I tried to fix my disintegrating sandal. The sole by now had completely separated, and I was using a piece of wire to reattach it. By the time I was done, we had arrived. Gyurka stayed with the truck, and I entered the building. It was almost empty.

Sándor Kopácsi, the police chief of the capital, was alone in his office. In many ways, he reminded me of Colonel Marián; he was also dark, short, and young. On the other hand, he seemed to be a stronger leader, a tougher person. His handshake was firm, and while talking he looked me straight in the eye. I felt completely at ease. My eyes wandered around the big office and settled on a portrait of Louis Kossuth. This was unusual. In the offices of Communist leaders one expected to see the portraits of Stalin and his Hungarian henchman Rákosi, but not Hungarian patriots. I wondered when that Kossuth portrait got on the wall. He seems to read my mind: "In my village, every family had a portrait of Kossuth and another one of the Blessed Virgin. They were like husband and wife, the two sides of the same coin. A home wasn't a home without them. Well, I am a son of my village I would not feel at home without Kossuth. It would be only an office—it would not be *my* office without him."

He told me about the previous day, when the survivors of the blood-bath at the parliament had marched on his headquarters: "Even their flags were bloody. Their leader was a kid like you, a worker in an open shirt, named István Angyal. He asked for the release of all political prisoners and for cooperation with the regular police. He had a bad cold and was coughing all the time. Ibolya, my wife, gave him hot tea and some medication. He told me that he was an Auschwitz survivor. I gave him a pistol. You know, you all should have at least a pistol! Do you have one?" he asked.

I shook my head. Since my rifle had disappeared when I left Duduke's apartment on Wednesday, I had not had a gun. Now he handed me one. It was a silvery, tiny little pistol, not much larger than a big cigarette lighter. "A lady's pistol. I got it in Prague," he said. I slipped it into my pocket and forgot it. I told him about Colonel Marián's plan to arm a couple thousand students and to form a national guard regiment that could defend the triangle made by the Freedom and Petőfi Bridges and Móricz Square. He got on the phone, and while he was talking, a dark and attractive lady walked in. "I am Ibolya Kopácsi," she said and offered me some crackling cake. I introduced myself only as Öcsi. The offer of the cake was perfectly timed, as the half of a bun I had gotten from Kati Szőke was less than a breakfast, and now it was past noon. I took two. She smiled a warm, motherly smile and said, "Take one more."

I looked out the window and saw that the police officers were already loading some handguns onto our truck. Now Kopácsi got off the phone: "My people will give you our spare guns, but we don't have too many in this building. Tomorrow, you can get a few thousand guns for your students from the Zrinyi Military Academy. They will be waiting for you in the morning. Bring a receipt from Colonel Marián. Be careful, because Russian tanks are still stationed at the bridgeheads!"

I left with the same warm feeling toward the Kopácsis that I had for our own group at the university. I trusted them fully. I do not know why, but I was positive that they deserved my trust. I felt so lucky to be working with such decent and brave people. I was proud to be part of the effort; I was proud to be Hungarian.

On the way out of Kopácsi's office, I called Ágnes. The phone rang and rang, but nobody picked it up. When I got back to the truck, I saw that we had received some fifty guns. Gyurka was ready to go. On the way back, we stopped at his apartment, just to say hello to his family. His sister was so beautiful that I could not take my eyes off her. She was the ex-wife of Igor Sík, the son of Hungary's ambassador to Moscow. She smiled at me, and that embarrassed me.

After that, we stopped at the Péterfy Street hospital, because Kopácsi had asked us to check if they had any shortages of medical supplies. It turned out that they were low on blood. I asked them to call us at the university if their blood shortage got critical.

As we were about to leave, I saw a young man in an open shirt carrying a large kettle of coffee to a truck, which was parked next to ours. A Red Cross flag covered his truck. Inside I saw some food and bandages. Just to say something, I asked, "You plan to stay up late?" pointing at the coffee. He looked at me, coughed, blew his nose, and said, "This is for the boys at the Tüzoltó Street garage." I had the strange feeling that I knew this guy. "Did you get a pistol from Kopácsi yesterday?" I asked. Now he was surprised: "How do you know about that?" I showed him my little pistol and said, "When he gave me one today, he also mentioned you and your cold. It was your cough that made me wonder."

He held out his hand: "István Angyal," he said. His handshake was firm, his eyes penetrating. "My name is Öcsi; I'm taking some guns from Kopácsi to the Technical University."

"Was there much fighting in Buda?" he asked.

"No, nothing like in your district! But we are getting ready, just in case!"

"Well, we are at 36 Tüzoltó Street. Maybe I will see you again?" he said while lifting the coffee kettle onto his truck. I waved, got into our truck, and told Gyurka, "Kopácsi said that this guy was in Auschwitz, and now he is leading the Tüzoltó Street freedom fighters. He is yet another reason why that cyclist deserved your punch."

We passed some scary but passive Russian tanks at the Pest side of Freedom Bridge. It was dark by the time we got back to the university and unloaded the guns in the gymnasium. I gave myself a submachine gun. From that point on, that gun became a permanent part of my wardrobe, together with my not completely beautiful but still smart corduroy jacket and my strange wired sandals. By now there were about

Figure 9. István Angyal, who survived Auschwitz, was hanged. Courtesy 1956 Institute of Hungary, Budapest

as many students at the university as the number of guns we had obtained. So in a few minutes everybody was armed. After that, Jancsi Danner organized our regular armed patrols. He scheduled twelve patrols a day, one every two hours.

There were heaps of food in the gym sent by the nearby villages. A lorry was unloading a dozen millstone-sized, home-baked country breads. The smell of the fresh bread, the sight of the circular, gigantic loaves, made the gym feel like home. There were also boxes of fruit, cheese, and cookies, cans of milk, and even a wine basket. We sat down, Gyurka and I, on some gymnastics mats and had a gourmand dinner of fresh bread, cheese, and watermelon. Pinned to the cheese, I found a slip of paper with a message in childish handwriting. It read, "We love you!"

Somehow, the bicyclist that morning and now the watermelon reminded me of Petik Bácsi, my father's melon farmer. He cultivated ten acres of our rented land until forced collectivization put an end to our farming. He lived in a hut dug in the middle of the field. He lived in that hut with his family from spring to fall. He worked from sunrise to sunset, every day except Saturday. On that day he dressed up in his black suit and spent most of his time reading the Bible. While reading, he also sang. The tunes were different from any other I ever heard. On Saturdays, the otherwise reserved Petik Bácsi became talkative.

He explained to me that he was a Sabbatarian and a Székely. The Székelys (also known as Szeklers or Siculi) are probably of Turkic, possibly Avar, stock. They settled in Transylvania possibly even before the Hungarians, but in any case by the eleventh century they had adopted the Hungarian language. Under the Hungarian Crown all Szeklers were regarded as of noble birth and were exempt from taxation. They formed one of the three privileged nations of Transylvania, the others being the Hungarians (Magyars) and the Saxons. They enjoyed full autonomy under the Hungarian Crown. Some Székely-Sabbatarians believed that they were descendents of the Kabar tribe, one of the ten Hungarian tribes that settled the Danubian basin in 996 A.D. The Kabars were of Turkic stock and of Jewish religion. Today, Transylvania is part of Romania, and the autonomy of all Transylvanian Hungarians, including the half million or so Szeklers, has been taken away, and their ancient culture is threatened by systematic forced assimilation.

When I told Gyurka about Petik Bácsi, he interrupted, "I bet that cyclist didn't get here in nine-ninety-six A.D.!"

"Yeah! I wouldn't be surprised if he called his mother 'Mutter,'" I added in agreement.

When I finally got back to the MEFESZ office, Kati Szőke hugged me. This I did not mind at all, but it made me blush all the same. There was silence in the room as I gave my report to Pista. Everybody was listening. Pista wrote out an advance receipt for so many rifles, submachine guns, pistols, light and heavy machine guns, but used a pencil to write in the numbers so that I could ink them over with the actual numbers when we picked them up.

With that, I was done for the day. Pista was not. His eyes were even more bloodshot than they had been in the morning. This was Friday night, and he probably had not had a good night's sleep since our historic meeting on Monday. The swirling went on endlessly around him. Now, the discussion was about sending delegations to the minister of defense and to the parliament, where Imre Nagy resided.

They also debated the conditions under which we might disarm. Jancsi Danner felt that our minimum condition should be the disbanding of the ÁVH and the withdrawal of all Russian troops from Hungarian soil. I agreed with Jancsi. Iván Szabó argued that our government had no control over the Russians; therefore, the Hungarian authorities should not be asked to promise something they could not deliver. The debate was passionate. All the while, the debaters were going through their usual swirling dance routine. Pista could barely stand up. His shaking fingers were yellow from nicotine, but his brain was still in gear. He hit the nail on the head: "The Russians claim that they were invited into the Hungarian capital by our government. If they needed a Hungarian invitation to enter, then the Hungarian government can also ask them to leave."

It was about 2:00 A.M. when Ili Tóth (the medic who last night had invited me to sleep in the medical emergency room) declared, "Öcsike! Time for bed!"—and although she was the younger, I still obeyed her. This lovely girl had that particular look in her eyes, but I made no advances. Besides being both inexperienced and a chicken, there was also Ágnes (with whom I had maintained my inexperience for a year, now). I was also completely exhausted. So I just climbed up on that miserable single bed on wheels and slept like a baby.

On Saturday morning we took our truck and first, from Buda, inspected the Russian tanks stationed on the Pest side of the bridges. They seemed to be stationed at every bridge except the Chain Bridge. On the Buda side, there were none. "We'll use the Chain Bridge on our return trip, when we are loaded with weapons!" suggested Gyurka, and I agreed. On our way to the Zrinyi Barracks, we heard machine-gun fire from Üllői Street.

"That could be Mr. Coffee Man himself!" I said, referring to István Angyal, whom we had met the day before at the hospital, when he was bringing coffee to his people in a container. "Would you like to visit him?" asked Gyurka, and I admitted that I would, but not now.

At the Zrinyi Barracks they took us to the president of their Revolutionary Council, a captain.[2] In just a few days every factory, office, and village had elected their own Revolutionary Councils. Nobody planned or suggested this; it occurred as naturally as leaves grow on trees. These councils were the first leaves of democracy. Aptyi was elected to the Revolutionary Council in the village of Kerepes.

The captain studied the list Colonel Marián had given me. "We have no machine guns, neither light nor heavy, but we do have hand grenades and flamethrowers. You want some of those?" he asked.

"Sure." I said without much thinking. He also made a quick calculation of weights and suggested that we had better bring a second truck for the next round, because it would take five or six loads to deliver everything that Colonel Marián had asked for.

Our first load was forty crates of stick and egg grenades, plus some flamethrowers. It was a heavy load. The springs and the tires of the truck were both compressed. The truck was sitting down on its back wheels. As we passed Dohány Street, we saw Russian tanks.

Gyurka aimed for the Széchenyi Chain Bridge. We were already on Roosevelt Square when we noticed that the Russians had dug in at the head of the bridge. That was why we had not seen them from the other side when we planned our return route. Gyurka laid down in my lap and floored the gas. I sank down too so that all the Russians could see was a truck racing toward the bridge without a driver. Now I heard a big bang, followed by three enormous crashing sounds in quick succession. The truck was still speeding ahead; Gyurka and I were both down on the floor. But there was no blood; I felt no pain.

Figure 10. A Soviet tank in Dohány Street where the people are still hiding behind the street corner, but the new flag (without the Communist insignia) is already waving. Photo by Leslie A. Toth

Now I heard Gyurka's voice: "They did not smash the windshield!" We were at about the middle of the bridge. As we looked around, there seemed to be no damage at all.

"So, what were those explosions?" I asked.

"I think I know," grinned Gyurka. "When I saw the Russians, I got scared and took my eyes off the road. So instead of driving on the road, we drove over their trenches, which made our crates jump. The crates taking off and falling back probably caused the big boom and those crashing sounds."

As Gyurka was parking at the university, I saw the lanky Jancsi Danner staring at the demolished crates on our truck. He came over and hugged me. It was unusual for him to show emotion; he must have thought that we had been through a lot. I hugged him back and said, "It was nothing, just rough driving." His fiancée, Gabi, was standing next to him. She was a tall girl but barely reached the shoulders of Jancsi's six-foot-four frame.

While we were away, Pista had obtained a dozen Hungarian tanks. They came with their crews from Pilisvörösvár to stay at our university. He had also gotten some anti-aircraft guns, which were now parked next to the tanks behind the library. Jancsi did not know where they came from.

We took the grenades to the gymnasium and the flamethrowers to the basement of the library. By the time we had unloaded, our second truck, driven by Imre Majoross, the other driver of the university, had also arrived. As we started on our second trip, I asked Gyurka to drop me off at the Pest side of Petőfi Bridge and pick me up there when they were returning with the next load of arms, at about 4:00 P.M. I wanted to visit István Angyal.

CHAPTER 7

Hungary's Jews and Germans

AI HEADED TOWARD THE GARAGE at 36 Tüzoltó Street, the headquarters of István Angyal, I heard gunfire from that direction. So I approached the area from the back, through Mester and Viola Streets. As I turned into the strangely quiet and completely deserted Viola Street, I could see a Russian tank at the intersection with Üllői Street.

I also noticed a strange sight: a self-propelled aluminum wastebasket on the corner of Viola and Tüzoltó Streets. It seemed to be moving by itself, slowly crossing Viola Street. I stared at it, hypnotized. Now the tank at the intersection started to fire at the rubbish bin, and at that very instant somebody pulled me into a doorway. "Are you out of your mind?" yelled a balding, bespectacled man. "Nobody walks on Viola Street, particularly not with a tricolored armband and a submachine gun!"

"OK, OK, but what made the garbage can move?" I asked.

"They are pulling it on a string. That is the only way to send things across the street!" he explained.

"So, how do I get to the garage on Tüzoltó Street?"

Figure 11. A Soviet tank on observation duty at the street corner while life is returning to normal. Photo by Leslie A. Toth

"They have knocked out the walls between the basements. That is the only safe way to get there. I'll show you." And without another word, he started moving. We descended into his basement. It was dark and dirty. I tried to be careful, protecting my once beautiful corduroy jacket, but that was hopeless. We were crawling through coal cellars and holes in basement walls. After a good half an hour, I could smell gasoline; we had to be in the basement of a garage.

As we climbed the stairs, I saw a number of parked cars, including the truck with the Red Cross flag, and a couple dozen young people, including some soldiers in uniform. Most of them were working on an ad hoc assembly line. They were converting milk bottles into Molotov cocktails. As they filled the flasks with gasoline, some of the fluid spilled out. This was why I smelled gas in the basement. Before putting the cork back, they inserted a thick piece of cloth into the jar. This wick soaked up gasoline and could be lit before the bottle was thrown.[1]

In the garage the radio was on. I heard the announcement: "A new national government has been formed, headed by Imre Nagy!" There was cheering on the assembly line. István Angyal was sitting in the corner. He was reading a leaflet.

"Must be very interesting!" I said to him.

"It's a poem—but what are you doing here?" He looked surprised but happy to see me.

"Oh, just checking to make sure you are taking your cough syrup. My secondary purpose is to buy the patent on your self-propelled garbage can."

He laughed and told me to sit down. The bespectacled bald fellow looked at us respectfully. István Angyal was a twenty-eight-year-old construction foreman; he was shorter than I, wore a white smock; his hair was brown and his teeth were a bit crooked.

"So what makes me interesting?" he asked.

"It must be the coffee! Anybody who braves tank fire to bring coffee to his men must be at least unique!"

"We also have women!" he corrected me, grinning, and askcd, "Speaking of coffee, can I get you some?"

"Sure, and also some bread, if you have any. I am meeting our truck at the Petőfi Bridge at four o'clock and camc to this coffee house for lunch."

While sipping my coffee, I told Pista (the familiar form of István), that the chief of police, Sándor Kopácsi, thought that we looked alike.

"Now, that is an insult! I don't wire my sandals, like some people!" he said, looking at my disintegrating footgear.

"Kopácsi also told me that you were deported to Auschwitz," I continued.

"Yes. His wife got me onto the subject. I was sixteen at the time and the only one in my family who survived. So we had something in common with Kopácsi's wife."

"Why do you say that you have only something in common if both of your families were deported to Auschwitz?" I ask, as I detect a bit of sarcasm in his voice.

"You are too young to understand all that; besides, it's three o'clock and you will miss your truck!"

"Not if you walk with me. Then you can explain what you mean by that *something* while you are showing me the way."

"OK, I'll take you to Mester Street; the rest of the way is easy," he said, folding up his poem.

As we climbed down into the dark basement, he began: "You see, being a Hungarian Jew is not the same as being a Hungarian of Slavic, Germanic, or Latin origin. They blend in and assimilate much easier; we dress differently and we form ghettos. In short, we just stand out.

"I don't know where Kopácsi's wife was born, but in Magyarbán-hegyes, where I was born, we were the only Jews. I knew that I am a Sephardic Jew but knew nothing about Israel. I had never been to a synagogue. I danced the Csárdás and sang the Hungarian folk songs. My father made shoelaces, and before he got divorced from my mother he called me 'the little Magyar' because I preferred boots to shoes and because I memorized all of Petőfi's poems. And then, on a May morning in 1944, Eichmann and his SS came and deported the four of us: my mother, Tibor, Teréz, and me. They shot Tibor because he refused to get into the freight car, they hanged my mother because she tried to escape, and Teréz died in the gas chambers. Only I survived."[2]

We were in the middle of a coal cellar. Pista stopped, grabbed a shovel, and threw it furiously into the coal pile. "They not only killed my family, they also wanted to destroy my soul. According to the Germans, I was not a Hungarian! They did not want me to belong here! They did not want me to be who I am! Ever since, I have been trying to prove them wrong, to show that I am not any less a Hungarian patriot than the next guy. And I am not the only one who feels that way. Did you know that József Gáli, one of our leaders today, was also in Auschwitz?

"You see, Öcsi," he called me by my nickname for the first time, "some terrible things happened here when you were a child. First, the general population allowed the Germans to deport their Jewish compatriots. Then, when the Jewish survivors returned, a few of them wanted to take revenge and decided to work for the Russians. Therefore, the Jews in Rákosi's government, the Jews heading the ÁVH, the police, and the military, became the representatives of the regime. Because of these few traitors, the hatred for Stalinism fell on all the Jews."

We were now climbing out of a basement on Mester Street. Pista was still very excited. Every time he said something, he seemed dissatisfied with himself for not having said it clearer or for not having covered the topic more thoroughly. I could tell that he could go on for hours; He continued: "Mind you, I myself am a communist, not a party member, but still a communist. I don't blame anybody who wants to im-

prove the lot of the poor and the underprivileged. What I hate is tyranny and foreign domination, not communism. And you should know
that if instead of the Jews, the stamp collectors or the Unitarians decided to collaborate with the Russians, the result would have been the
same. The same barbaric madness would have evolved, except that today the Unitarians and not the Jews would receive part of the blame
for it."

"So when you said that you had *something* in common with Kopácsi's
wife, you meant that you too survived Auschwitz—but that is all?"

Pista's eyes flashed like lightning: "Well, I don't know what her family
did, nor do I know how her husband became the chief of police, or
why, but I am positive that we, the overwhelming majority of Hungarian Jews, are not Russian collaborators but patriotic Hungarians. We
probably differ from Kopácsi's wife because we feel the most ashamed
that the Rákosis and the ÁVH murderers are Jewish, and one day, I
hope, one day . . . " his lips were trembling, his eyes were moist, and I
felt guilty and ashamed without knowing precisely why. So I put my
arms on his shoulders and we walked silently, side by side, for a while
before I said: "You know, there is another guy I really respect; he is a
German-Hungarian, a blond giant; his name is Jancsi Danner. He
fought a few blocks from you at the Corvin Theater. They knocked out
four or five Russian tanks. He does not articulate things like you do,
but he, too, is trying to prove the obvious: that he is Hungarian."

By then we had walked almost all the way to the Petőfi Bridge. I
could see Gyurka's truck waiting, so I hugged Pista and ran. This time
both of our trucks were loaded with submachine guns. By six o'clock
we had unloaded them, and by nine we had made another round and
then returned for a last trip, with only one truck. It was midnight by
the time everything was neatly stored in the gymnasium. Next to the
pile of guns were piles of fresh food that had arrived from the villages
during the day. So we all sat down and stuffed ourselves.

In the MEFESZ office Kati Szőke and Tibor Vígh were sitting in the
corner. They seemed to be in a very serious mood; they must have been
discussing the purpose of life or something. It was obvious that they
did not need me. Colonel Marián was writing, and Sándor Varga was
on the telephone, so I reported to Jancsi Danner: "We unloaded six
truckloads of weapons into the gymnasium. I also met István Angyal,
the leader at Tüzoltó Utca."

"Good job! I heard of Angyal's group when I was fighting with the group at the Corvin Cinema. They were the first ones with the Molotov cocktails. What is it like there?"

"The Russian tanks are at the main intersections on Üllői Street, some firing at anything that moves, others just sitting there, but in either case they don't make much difference. The district is ours. The ÁVH has disappeared. We are in full control. How was your day?"

"Met a bunch of generals at the Hungarian military headquarters and later some politicians in parliament. They wanted us to disarm, but I'm sure they will settle for integrating our forces with the police. We, in turn, demanded that they disband the ÁVH and remove the Russians at least from the capital. There will be more meetings tomorrow. I trust Imre Nagy, but he is naïve and isolated by the ÁVH. After the meetings I did a couple of patrol tours. The district is quiet, the stores are untouched, the people are glad to see our patrols, and Gabi is glad to see me, when on my rounds I get to her house."

"You are lucky with Gabi. I don't seem to be able to get in touch with Ágnes. I guess they left the city."

"Well, maybe it's all for the better. Your appearance is not exactly dashing at the moment, you know!" I looked at my dirty hands, my feet with the wired sandals, and my bloody corduroy jacket. They were pretty shocking. The jacket was so dirty that it could just about stand up on its own. It was also crumpled from sleeping in it and was covered by all kinds of dirt, including a recently acquired layer of coal dust. On its right side was a large blotch of blood; on the back, where my gun rested, was a big oil stain.

"Well, I see your point," I admitted, and I went to the men's room to try to improve my appearance. When I got back to the office, Jancsi was snoring on the sofa, so I quietly lay down on the rug, and in a moment his snoring solo was converted into a duet.

When I awoke, it was a beautiful Sunday morning, October 28. It was the ringing of the telephone that woke me. Attila Szigethy, the president of the Revolutionary Council of the city of Győr, was calling: "I just want you to know that the local Russian commander here has declared our cause to be a just one and has ordered his troops to cooperate with us." That was great news! In the MEFESZ office we were floating on air. It had been only five days since our march to the Bem statue, and now victory was in the air. The ÁVH had disintegrated, a

Figure 12. One group of the legendary fighters of Corvin Alley. Photo by
Leslie A. Toth

formal cease-fire had been declared, and Imre Nagy was finally in the
parliament. It was all too good to be true.

I was so happy! I wanted to share it with Ágnes. Her mother picked
up the telephone: "No, she stayed down at Lake Balaton. . . . No, I'm
leaving, too. . . . No, we have no phone there. . . . Yes, the Russians are
still surrounding the city. . . . Yes, I will tell her." She gave her answers
in her rapid-fire style. I did not think she was mad at me; she just hated
talking on the phone.

Kati Szőke was watching me with sympathy. "No Ágnes?" she asked.
I nodded while she handed me a typewritten permit that allowed me to
enter the university at any time. Pista asked her to set up some entrance controls; our numbers had grown, and we already had about a
hundred people milling around—thousands were expected. "So, don't
feel down! Your permit number is three; that's not bad for a twenty-
year-old! And Ágnes will come around too!"

This permit was just a slip of paper. A few days later we printed a
more formal version of it. On that more formal listing my number
slipped to forty-seven. Another change were the dozen or so officers of

the ÁVH in the KA-51 lecture hall. Some got there by being picked up by our patrols; others came in on their own, seeking protection. We gave them food and let them play chess; eventually, when there was a functioning justice system, we planned to hand them over to the courts.

Pista's eyes were still bloodshot. He must have worked through most of the night. Now he was drinking his third coffee and was just as optimistic as the rest of us. He declared, "We have won! The Revolution is over, the ÁVH is beaten, and the power is in the hands of the Revolutionary Councils. In a few days we will take over the government, and if the Russians attack us, that will no longer be called a revolution, it will be a war between two socialist states. This is not just my view; I am quoting the commander of the Kilián Barracks, the next defense minister of Hungary, General Pál Maléter."

Next, Pista showed us the defense plans he had worked out the previous night. It detailed the defense strategy for our first national guard battalion, which we named after the poet Sándor Petőfi. Our task was to defend the triangle between Móricz Square and the two bridges, Freedom and Petőfi.

I was about to find something to eat for breakfast in the gym when Pista turned to me: "Öcsi, would you take this plan to the freedom fighters on Széna Square and ask for their comments?" So, instead of eating breakfast, I rode with Gyurka to the headquarters of the already legendary János Szabó. I knew that he was from Transylvania, about fifty, a truck driver, and the husband of Margit Lipták, the director of my university's nursery.

I also heard that he was a most clever guerilla leader. A couple of days before, he had taken a dozen dinner plates, spray-painted them black, and placed them in front of an advancing Russian tank column. Seeing the fake mines in front of them, the column turned right into a steep street where there were no plates. That street climbed up toward Castle Hill. After the first bend, the tanks came to a steep section, where Szabó Bácsi had poured oil on the cobblestones, but by then it was too late for the tanks to turn back.[3] The caterpillar tracks of the tanks started to slip on the oil, they got stuck, and Molotov cocktails started to fly from the windows and rooftops. That was the end of that tank column.

The "headquarters" of Szabó Bácsi at Széna Square was at the workers' hostel of the construction firm that was building the subway. The place was swarming with armed youngsters, all working-class boys and girls. In the center of this commotion stood a tall, slightly graying man with a gigantic, dark mustache and a red beret pulled down to his eyes. I felt a little embarrassed, because while I was talking, my stomach decided to rumble. I tried to be very official, very military. I reported on the plans of our Petőfi battalion and I talked about Colonel Marián and his defense triangle while Szabó Bácsi just looked at me with a twinkle in his eyes. So I redoubled my efforts to sound even more military. I told him which were his bridges and which were ours and how we were to alert each other if we saw advancing Russian troops and things like that.

He still had not said anything, but suddenly he placed his arm on my shoulder and walked with me into the kitchen. The smell of bacon and eggs was making me dizzy, but I bravely continued my speech about defense triangles and bridges. Finally, he interrupted: "Three or four?"

I repeated in desperation, "No, no! You defend only two bridges, yours are the Chain and the Margaret Bridges."

"I don't mean bridges, I mean eggs!" he said, still grinning, and then he turned to the lady at the stove: "Give this hungry warrior four eggs and a lot of bacon!"

He watched me while I ate. His eyes were warm; they reminded me of Aptyi's. He swallowed when I did and he nodded when I wiped the grease from my plate with the crust of the bread. Only when I was done did he look at Pista's plans. On the map he marked in the locations of his lookouts. He wrote down two telephone numbers at which he could be reached and also listed the firearms they had. He then turned to me: "At last count, I had about a hundred sons here, but if things get rough, I'm sure they will bring their brothers and sisters. So we can stage a decent welcoming party for the Russians!" He was constantly kidding and always referred to his fighters, including the girls, as his sons.

Uncle Szabó was the first authentic popular leader I had ever met. His aura was such that when he entered a room, all activity stopped and people spontaneously looked up. He was playful and close-tongued, merry and serene; he radiated confidence and displayed composure. In short, I was so impressed with him that if Pista had not needed me at the university, I would gladly have become one of Szabó Bácsi's "sons."

On our way back to the university, we watched the streets of Budapest. There was no fighting. People were in their Sunday best and were pouring out of the churches. In the stores, the goods were untouched behind the broken windows. On the corners, trucks and horse-drawn wagons distributed the produce brought in from the villages. We saw an unguarded collection box for the victims of the fighting. It was overflowing with paper money. The streets were patrolled by youngsters wearing tricolored armbands. The city was at peace. The Russian tanks were still at the main intersections, but they were passive; they were probably getting ready to leave. In short, it was a lovely noon on this Sunday when we arrived back at the Technical University.

Colonel Marián was happy with the information we brought. He planned to call up János Szabó, but before doing that, he gave me a new assignment: we had to go to the Völgy Street military laboratory and obtain a loudspeaker car and a short-wave radio transmitter from them. Pista's bloodshot eyes looked worried as he warned me that the laboratory had not yet been visited by freedom fighters and that it was full of very "reliable" officers who worked on military secrets. By "reliable," he meant loyal Communists, possibly even members of the ÁVH. Therefore, he felt that we should be prepared for armed resistance. "In other words, be very careful. If they fire, do not shoot back, just leave!" he said.

As I got into our car, I saw the tall figure of Jancsi Danner climbing out of an armored car. "Whose car is that, Jancsi?" I asked him.

"It belongs to the prime minister, Imre Nagy. I was meeting with him and he sent me back in it from a meeting because I guess he is worried about my safety or something." Jancsi was smiling; he could not conceive that anybody would want to harm him.

Völgy Street is up in the Buda Hills, the district where the wealthy used to have their graceful and luxurious bungalows before the Communist takeover. These villas were all nationalized and given to the new privileged class, the Communist bosses. The military laboratory was in a three-story, ornate palace ringed by a tall brick wall. The tops of the walls were covered with broken glass. Next to the iron door I saw a bell pull. The street was empty except for two little girls in front of the next villa who were playing with horse chestnuts. Gyurka stopped the car a few yards from the gate and pulled out his pistol, and I, too, took out my polished lady's pistol. When we reached the gate, I pulled the bell wire.

The pleasant sound of a real bell came from some distance. As we stood on the two sides of the gate, partially protected by the brick wall, my hand was shaking and my throat was dry. It seemed that a long time had passed when finally we heard footsteps, then the key turned and the door slowly opened.

With my pistol drawn, I stepped into the doorway and declared, "In the name of the Revolution, I seize this laboratory!"

The graying officer who had opened the door looked startled. He held out his hand for a handshake, and when I finally and rather clumsily managed to put my little pistol away, we shook hands. "Colonel Kovács," he said.

"Öcsi," I replied.

He also shook hands with Gyurka and then led us into a large conference room. The conference table was the size of two Ping-Pong tables, and a dozen officers were sitting around it. Colonel Kovács directed us to the head of the table, and when we were seated, he made a formal welcoming speech.

He explained that the laboratory had formed its own Revolutionary Council, had kicked out their Russian superiors and the ÁVH general who headed the laboratory, and for days had been waiting to make formal contact with us. He welcomed us as the representatives of all freedom fighters. He assured us that they, too, wanted a free and democratic Hungary and that both their skills and their equipment were at our disposal. While he talked, Gyurka's right hand was resting on his pistol. Mine had disappeared in the side pocket of my corduroy jacket.

I told them that we would like to borrow a short-wave radio transmitter in order to make direct contact with the Russian tank crews stationed on the streets of Budapest. I also asked for a loudspeaker van. They agreed to provide both. Because I did not know how to drive, they also gave us a driver who would take the van back to our garage. One of the officers handed me a slip of paper listing the short-wave frequencies used by the Russians. Another explained how to use the loudspeaker car, either by talking into the microphone or by switching to tapes or radio broadcasts. They also gave me an organization chart that listed their names, ranks, areas of competence, and telephone numbers.

We were ready to leave when Colonel Kovács asked if we needed anything else, such as clothing or boots. I did not understand what he was driving at. I told him that our Petőfi battalion was only a temporary national guard unit, so we did not need uniforms. On our way out, he pointed at my wired sandals and said, "You cannot win a revolution if you get pneumonia!" So I finally got his point. Some officers ran to their supply storage and in a minute returned with a variety of shoes and boots and a pile of clothing.

The conference room was converted into a dressing room. I felt embarrassed, because these officers were twice my age and were now looking at my dirty feet and at the pathetic remains of my socks. They stood around and assisted while I tried on some of the soft leather beauties. I left the laboratory in black riding boots and in a rubberized trench coat over my jacket. My boots were so polished that a fly could not land on them without slipping and falling on its behind.

The change in my appearance must have been substantial, because the student guard in front of the MEFESZ office of the university stopped me and asked for my identification papers. This had never occurred before, so I decided to get rid of the officer's trench coat but kept the black riding boots.

Pista was very happy with the van and the radio equipment we got. He asked some electrical engineering students to help with the technical part of the radio broadcasts and asked Gyurka to get Igor Sík to direct the Russian-language broadcasts. Igor had grown up in Moscow when his father was Hungary's ambassador, so his Russian was perfect. Since Igor was Gyurka's brother-in-law, this was a natural assignment for him. While Gyurka was hunting for Igor, I joined Jancsi Danner for a patrol tour of our district.

It was getting late. The streetlights were dark, and no buses or streetcars were running. The people felt safer if they saw our regular patrols. I felt funny walking next to Jancsi, because at six foot two I still felt like a midget. We started out, just the two of us, on the embankment of the Danube, walking toward Petőfi Bridge. The city was quiet; there was practically no traffic. We met no one as we walked toward the bridge. Jancsi was the quiet type. He would probably cover this three-mile triangular loop without saying a word. Therefore I had to get him started. "So what do you think of my new boots? "

"Nice, really nice," he said, but I could tell that he was totally uninterested in my boots.

"Did I tell you about Pista Angyal?" I tried again.

"Only that you met him. What kind of a guy is he?"

"Well, he is a six-foot midget with crooked teeth. He is brave and smart, about your age, but already divorced. So watch out with Gabi!" Jancsi did not laugh. He did not appreciate my kind of humor at all.

"I am not interested in his teeth or height," he said. "Tell me what he stands for, what kind of a man is he on the inside."

"Well, he is a Hungarian patriot if I ever saw one. He is a selfless idealist; he thinks that he is a communist, but to him that word simply means justice and the protection of the weak. He also hates dictatorship. He told me that in his toilet, he hung Stalin's portrait upside down. His family was killed in Auschwitz. I told him that you seem to be his German equivalent."

"What do you mean?" Jancsi blurted, startled.

"Oh, nothing much. My Father told me once that the first-generation Hungarians are the most patriotic," I replied.

"I'm not first—or second—generation; the Danner store of Szeged is over a hundred years old!" said Jancsi, with his voice raised.

"OK, OK, so I am wrong. I just had that feeling that you both are trying to prove something. Sorry if I said something wrong. So why did you leave Szeged?"

"Well, my parents were divorced," he started, but I interrupted.

"So were Angyal's!"

"Stop this comparison foolishness! I stayed with my father in Szeged. Got in trouble with the police in 1948 when the Communists outlawed religious education in the schools. Did Angyal do that too?"

"No. Actually, I don't think he is religious at all."

"Good, because I am. I know that there is a Creator, I know that our lives have a purpose. I do not know what that purpose is. It might be to protect the survival of life on this planet or it might be to test whether free will makes the human soul improve or degenerate? All I know is that the atheists are wrong, that there is more to life than seventy or eighty years of selfishness, comfort, security, and animal functions. I also know that what is occurring in Hungary today is much more than an attempt by a small nation to gain her freedom. What we are demonstrating is the power of the human spirit. The human spirit itself is being reborn in Hungary. Our fight is a confrontation between ideals and tanks."

I had never seen Jancsi this electrified, this carried away. He was saying things that he probably had never articulated, not even to himself. So I kept quiet, and he went on.

"I feel it in my bones that our sun, the sun of liberty and freedom, the sun of human dignity is rising throughout the world. I feel that a new renaissance, a spiritual renewal, is coming. I feel that mankind will find its higher purpose. It might take some time and some sacrifice, but it will occur. We will be saved. Mankind will not commit physical or spiritual suicide. Our role in this revival is to take the first step. We can not escape it. We are showing a cynical and faithless world what the human spirit can do. Some might laugh at us for facing tanks unarmed, but they are wrong. Tanks cannot kill ideals; they cannot conquer the human spirit. Even if we fail, our ideals will outlast their tanks. Our ideals will be reborn. So don't worry. What has to come will come anyway. It is our destiny to show the way, to take that first step."

It was close to midnight when we got back to the university. I hugged Jancsi before going down to the emergency room to sleep on my narrow and uncomfortable bed-on-wheels. Jancsi looked a bit embarrassed for having opened up, for having allowed me to see into his heart, to take a peek under his veil of discipline and self-control. I was grateful; he had articulated some of my own feelings. It took a long time for me to go to sleep. I felt as the fishermen must have felt at the Sea of Galilee when they began to understand their roles and responsibilities. It must have been both frightening and uplifting.

Chapter 8

A Barrel of Blood

O N MONDAY, OCTOBER 29, it was hard to believe that my high-jump competition had been just a week ago on Sunday and that my main concern at that time had been to get my stipend of 140 forints needed to take Ágnes to the movies. So much had changed since then, both outside and inside, that it felt like a century had passed during these days.

In the MEFESZ office we had developed a daily routine. We started the day together, listening to the news on both Radio Budapest and Radio Free Europe. After that, Pista usually gave us the first assignments of the day. But this Monday morning was different. Today the news was terrible. We learned that Israel had attacked Egypt and that war had broken out in the Suez Canal. I did not understand why this was so bad for us, but Pista explained.

"For years, Nasser of Egypt, a Soviet ally, has denied the use of the Suez Canal to Israel. In July of this year Nasser also nationalized the canal and kicked out its previous owners, the British. So now the Israelis and the Brits are trying to take it back. These bastards timed their attack on Nasser to coincide with a time when the Russians are busy and preoccupied (in Hungary) so they will not be able to also defend Nasser. Instead of helping us, they plan to use the blood of Hungarians to grab the canal. They probably have already told the Russians that if they let them have the canal, they can do whatever they feel like in Hungary. It is Yalta all over again. Unbelievable! Simply unbelievable!"[1]

Pista's hands were shaking, his neck was red, he was out of control. We were dumbfounded but could not fully believe that the Israelis and the English could sink so low to do something like that.

Now the radio began explaining President Eisenhower's desire to roll back the Communist empire, as well as his "Policy of Self-Liberation," which was one to assist the Soviet satellite countries in liberating themselves. Our depressed mood was beginning to improve. According to the radio, Eisenhower promised that if the enslaved peoples would throw off their occupiers, the West would help them. Pista was shaking his head. He did not believe a word of what the radio said. He did not trust Eisenhower. He said that if Eisenhower really cared about us, if he really meant to help enslaved people, the Brits would not be bombing the Suez Canal today. Kati Szőke was about to cry; she had her hand in front of her mouth. The expression on Gyurka's face was one of total disgust and revulsion. But Jancsi Danner was still an optimist. He said, "Eisenhower will not allow the Brits to stab us in the back. He is an honorable man. In a week or so, there is an election in America. The nation of Washington and Lincoln, the people of liberty and justice, will not let oil and a stolen canal stand between the deeds and the ideals of their government. No, we have no reason to despair. The ÁVH has been abolished, some of the Russian tanks are already pulling out, Imre Nagy has reestablished the democratic multiparty system, and the hero of the Kilián Barracks, Pál Maléter, is our minister of defense. No! Don't despair! Forget the Suez Canal and concentrate on what we have to do here."[2]

While we were discussing the Suez Canal on this cloudy Monday morning, thousands of students were pouring through the gates of the university. Our little contingent in the MEFESZ office was overwhelmed by the task of organizing them into the Petőfi battalion. There was a lot to do; we had to distribute the arms, establish a system of communications, and arrange living accommodations. Because of this frantic activity, even Pista forgot the bad news, and we all threw ourselves at the many practical tasks. Almost the whole junior class of mechanical engineering was there. It was such a pleasure to once again see my classmates: Gyuri Egry (Csámpi the Menő), Laci Zsindely, Attila Lipcsey—everybody.

My first task that day was to accompany a redheaded Western reporter and his cameraman, who wanted to inspect our battalion. My ability to communicate with them was rather limited, as he spoke only English, while my knowledge of that language was limited to three words: *yes, no,* and *camel. Camel* I knew because there was a picture of that misdesigned horse on my father's favorite, usually empty, cigarette pack.

The reporter was very disappointed in me. It was obvious that he wanted to report on sensation, to make the front page in some tabloid. He was looking for corpses, blood, torture chambers, destruction, or at least some Nazis or ÁVH goons hanging from trees. "If it bleeds, it leads," he kept repeating while I showed him our well-organized national guard unit. In the gymnasium some eight hundred guns had already been handed out. The students stood quietly in line as they signed for the guns they received. Next to the crates of guns were piles of food, sent in as gifts from the villages.

When the reporter learned that we had some ÁVH prisoners in the KA-51 lecture hall, his eyes lit up, but when he saw that these prisoners were neither scared nor in chains, he lost interest. There was a chess game going on between an ÁVH officer (who wanted to be safe and therefore came in voluntarily) and a mailman (whom we arrested because we found stolen watches in his pocket). They would both face the same judge once we had a functioning legal system.

At that point the redheaded reporter had enough of us. He left. A few days later I saw him once more, but in a hospital bed with a head wound. On one side of his head the red hair was shaved off; the other side was soaked with blood. Obviously, he had found what he was looking for.

On my way back to the MEFESZ office, I checked on the situation at the gates. In front of the main entrance was a horse-drawn lorry. An old farmer dressed in his Sunday best climbed down from the driver's seat and asked me, "Are you the university students?"

"Yes we are."

"Well, you see, I brought this load of produce to the capital, thought that you might need it."

"Oh, we have no money for that, Uncle," I said, but as soon as I said that, I knew that it was the wrong thing to say.

His eyes narrowed, his neck got red, and his voice was choked and full of emotion as he replied, "Don't say such a thing! How could you think that I would take your money? You think that you can give your lives free of charge and we in my village would take money for our produce?" I must have looked scared, because he lowered his voice as he continued: "You see, we don't know how to write demands, and even the rifles feel strange in our hands, but we do want to take part. So please, take what I brought." I could tell that this was a very long speech for him. Under normal conditions, he probably would not have spoken that much in a week. So now he was out of breath and also needed to blow his nose. As his face was half covered by the monogrammed white handkerchief, he quietly added, "We, too, want to be free, you know!"

In the afternoon we participated in a large meeting of all the representatives of armed groups at police headquarters. Most leaders of the various freedom fighter groups were there. The topic was the organization of the new national guard. Pista sent me to represent our Petőfi battalion. Sándor Kopácsi greeted me like an old friend. He was impressed by my new boots. They, Kopácsi and his wife, were so nice that I almost thought of them as family. Naturally, I sat next to Pista Angyal. He was still in his white smock. His wheezing was better, and he seemed optimistic.

"So, how is your research progressing? How do Jewish- and German-Hungarians compare?" he asked me with a big grin. "Have you reached any conclusions yet?"

"Sure thing. Jewish-Hungarians like to drink a lot of coffee in their coal cellars, while German-Hungarians grow tall and prefer religion. So, how is your self-propelled garbage can doing?"

"Well, our friendly neighborhood tanks have left the intersections. Now we can actually walk the streets."

The meeting went smoothly. We agreed on the need to register all members of the national guard and to issue membership certificates. It was agreed that Kopácsi would be our commander and that he would sign all our documents. We made a quick head count of the different groups of freedom fighters: it seemed that the national guard was already some ten thousand strong and still growing. After the meeting, Pista Angyal went on to another meeting in the parliament, Gyurka went home to visit his family, and I walked over to Ágnes's apartment house to see if she was back from Lake Balaton.

She was not there, but her brother Gábor and her half-sister Judit were. They were in a strange mood and seemed to be packing. "What is going on?" I asked.

"It's all over!" said Gábor. "Haven't you heard? Israel attacked Egypt. This is the green light the Russians have been waiting for. I tell you, it is all over now. And I will not be a Russian slave again. I just can't take that. If they attack again, I am leaving."

"Me too!" said Judit. "My Father was Jewish, but right now I hate Israel. How can they do such a thing? What do you think will happen now?"

Judit was seventeen; I was twenty, so it was my job to reassure her. "Don't worry. The Russians are leaving. Eisenhower will put a stop to that nonsense at the Suez Canal. I just came from a meeting of the armed forces. Our national guard is ten thousand strong, and we are not threatening the Russians or anybody else, but we will defend our country. So, instead of packing, you should be signing up."[3]

Then Judit pulled out a small yellow envelope and handed it to me. She did not say where it came from; she did not need to. I grabbed the envelope and ran out. I was already on the street when I opened it. My hands were shaking; I smelled that familiar scent that Ágnes said was only her soap. My eyes caressed the familiar childish handwriting as I read the message, which went something like this: "It would feel better if I was the most important part of your life. It is hard to accept that I am not. If it was another woman, I would fight, but I cannot fight your love for our country. Actually, with time, I might even learn to respect it. Now, all I can do is to forgive you. Don't worry about the movie, do what you have to do. When the Russians are gone and we are free, I will be waiting for you here at the lake. Be very careful and make sure that I will see you. Please don't get hurt. I could not take that! Love, Ágnes."

Back at the university, it was total chaos. There were some fifty people in the MEFESZ office, and they each wanted to talk with Colonel Marián. The guards at the door were completely useless; they did not screen the people but merely checked their identity papers and let them in. It was near midnight by the time this madness ended and we settled down to talk about correcting the situation. Pista was dazed, exhausted. Kati, Jancsi, Sándor Varga, and I formulated the plans.

Because at the university we now had a couple of thousand armed students, plus the cadets of the Petőfi Military Academy and some regular army units, it was essential that we establish some system of structured communication. To prevent the repetition of today's chaos, we agreed that the students staying in each lecture hall would elect a representative and that these representatives would in turn pick a representative for the whole building. Only the building representatives and people reporting emergencies would be allowed into the MEFESZ office. We also decided that only three people would be admitted at any one time and that each morning we would distribute a general news bulletin to all building representatives. Before going to bed, we printed an announcement of these decisions.

On Tuesday morning, October 30, I had to get up early, because my bed-on-wheels in the medical emergency room had to serve its intended purpose. At daybreak, one of our brilliant warriors had nothing better to do than to try to clean his loaded submachine gun and managed to shoot off one of his own toes. So now he resided in my bed. Since my bed was gone and I had to be in a vertical position anyway, I grabbed a box of pushpins and some copies of the announcement we had reproduced the previous night and made a tour of the main building.

The main building had four stories in the shape of the capital letter E. On each floor the corridor ran in the center, and the offices and lecture-hall doors opened on both of its sides. On this morning students were sleeping everywhere, including the corridors, offices, laboratories, and lecture halls. I pinned our announcement to the doors and bulletin boards and completed my tour of the building in about an hour.

When I got back to the MEFESZ office, Pista and the others had already finished listening to the morning news. "It was a mixed bag," said Jancsi. "The good news is that Imre Nagy has abolished the one-party system and has formed a new cabinet. The bad news is that in spite of all that, Radio Free Europe is still calling him a Communist. They are also saying that he is not to be trusted. I don't understand how a radio program can editorialize like that. I don't understand why they hate him so. It is very strange how they talk. I have no idea what these people are trying to do, or who tells them that this is what they should say."

"So, is there some good news?" I asked Jancsi, because I was not particularly interested in what Radio Free Europe had to say. I did not care about their views about Imre Nagy. I knew who he was, and nothing else mattered. So Jancsi switched the topic:

"The good news is that there is no fighting anywhere in Hungary. People are cleaning up and are preparing to return to work. Israel is still bombing the Suez Canal, but the Russians have now formally agreed to pull their troops out of Hungary. They have also initiated a major airlift to remove all the Russian families from Hungary. They claim to be using some two hundred airplanes in that effort. To streamline the airlift operation, they have occupied all three airports of Budapest. Pista thinks that this streamlining business is just an excuse, and their real goal is to neutralize the Hungarian air force."[4]

Overall, our mood was still pretty optimistic. Gyurka told me that Igor Sík had started to monitor the radio transmissions of the Russian military, and twice a day he was transmitting our own broadcast to them. Pista decided that I should spend the day in the MEFESZ office with Kati, because everybody else had meetings to attend either in the parliament or at army headquarters. So I tried to maintain some semblance of order in the office. I was making snap decisions on car assignments, living quarters, and food distribution. I even sent out a patrol to protect two ÁVH officers from getting lynched. In short, I did anything and everything that needed to be done.

By the evening, when the others got back from their meetings, the MEFESZ office was operating smoothly. Their meetings had gone well also, so we were all happy and relaxed. Pista gave me my assignments for the next day, and after that, for the first time in a week, I went to bed before midnight.

In the morning of Wednesday, October 31, the radio was on in the MEFESZ office. The announcer of Free Radio Kossuth was speaking. I will never forget what he said, and I will never forget how he said it: "We have lied to you in the morning, we have lied to you at night, we have lied to you all day and on every wavelength!" He said this in a trembling, honest voice, promising that they would never do that again. Listening to those words, we all felt awed. We knew that this pledge of a free and honest media was the key to our better future. Kati was so moved that she had to run out of the office. The rest of us just stood there and stared. We could not speak.

From the radio we also learned that a Hungarian army unit had freed the imprisoned and tortured Cardinal József Mindszenty. The cardinal was beaten, drugged, thrown into women's cells, and in spite of all that, his statement started with "I hate nobody, there is no anger in my heart." But there was plenty of bad news too: the French and British, instead of stopping the Israeli attack on Egypt, had joined in the bombing of the Suez Canal. I left the MEFESZ office with mixed feelings.

My first assignment of the day was to attend a meeting of the Revolutionary Workers' Council of Greater Budapest. The meeting was held at the Belojannis Factory. As Gyurka was driving, I watched the streets. No Russian tanks were to be seen anywhere; the fighting was over. The mood of the people was happy, optimistic. They were repairing the broken windows and cleaning up the rubble. Some were listening to the radios that shop owners had placed in the windows. At the factory gate the guards seemed impressed by my letter of credence, which stated that I was a representative of the Technical University. It was still both surprising and overwhelming to feel the respect that people were displaying toward all university students.

The guards directed us to the head table in a gigantic meeting hall. As the leaders introduced themselves, I heard the names of Fazekas, Báli, and Rácz, while I still introduced myself just as Öcsi. They asked me to say a few words, so I said, "I bring you respectful greetings from the students of the Technical University. The Russian troops are leaving, the ÁVH is disbanded, and Hungary is on her way to becoming a free and neutral democracy. We ask you to correct what needs to be corrected at your factories, we ask you to express your broader concerns to our new government, but most of all, we ask you to return to work, resume production, restart the factories of Hungary, of your Hungary."

The meeting was solemn, orderly. The delegates overwhelmingly supported the motion that Hungary should leave the Warsaw Pact and should declare her neutrality.[5] They voted to entrust the direction of all factories to their elected Revolutionary Workers' Councils. They authorized the councils to dismiss and replace all incompetent Communist managers, all Russian advisers, and to resume production. As to the ownership of industry, there seemed to be surprisingly wide agreement: they were against state ownership, but they did not want

Figure 13. Cardinal Mindszenty at his first news conference in the cardinal's residence in Buda after being liberated from Communist jail. Photo by Leslie A. Toth

to return the factories to their private owners, either. They favored employee ownership for most industries.

After the meeting, we were supposed to go directly to the Kilián Barracks, but I asked Gyurka to make a detour. The Péterfy Street Hospital had called the day before to say that their supply of type AB blood was very low. In the meantime, I called the Hungarian Red Cross and learned that AB blood was available only in Vienna, and they were unwilling to deliver it. So I wanted to see how urgent the situation was.

In the hospital parking lot, Gyurka and I witnessed a surrealistic scene, one that was so unbelievable that only real life could produce it. A horse-drawn wagon, carrying a smallish barrel, had just arrived. A pipe-smoking, mustachioed peasant was sitting in the dickey seat and was explaining to an official of the hospital, "The radio said that you needed blood, so I got you some." He was saying this with a proud twinkle in his eye.

"You want to give blood?" asked the doctor.

"Well, I already gave. It's in the barrel with that of all the men in our village," he said, pointing to the dressing on his wrist.

The doctor was dumbfounded, stuttering: "The barr——— . . . the barrel, that big, dirty barrel?" he asked.

"Its not dirty!" said the mustachioed farmer defensively. "We heated the knife before cutting our wrists, and we cleaned the barrel with sulfur. This is perfectly good, clean blood!"

Inside, they told me that since the fighting had ended they were not using that much blood, but even at the present rate, they would be out of it by Friday or, at the latest, Saturday. Gyurka started counting: "Today is Wednesday, and we need two days to make the trip to Vienna and back. So that kind of decides what we will do tomorrow!"

We arrived a bit late for the meeting at the Kilián Barracks. It seemed that most of the freedom-fighter units of the capital were represented. The hall was full, and there seemed to be tension in the air. At the head table, a six-foot-eight-inch giant of a tank commander was arguing with a very angry young man with a big mustache. The mustachioed fighter was screaming, and the officer was trying to pacify him. Later, I learned that the officer was the legendary commander of the Kilián Barracks, General Pál Maléter, and the angry young man was a commander of the Corvin Cinema freedom fighters, Gergely Pongrátz. His nickname, appropriately, was "The Mustache."[6]

Colonel Marián was sitting in front, but I could not get close to him, so when I saw Pista Angyal, I settled down next to him. The meeting dealt with the coordination between the fighting units and with electing our national leadership. After the argument about General Maléter's earlier arrest of some of The Mustache's fighters, which was settled with a handshake, the meeting proceeded smoothly. Colonel Marián was elected into the top leadership of the national guard while General Béla Király and Police Chief Sándor Kopácsi were elected to head the guard. Pista Angyal was also nominated into the leadership, but he declined the honor. Instead, he recommended his cocommander, a fellow named Olaf, whose nomination was accepted.[7]

Pista Angyal was still in his white (well, not that white any more) smock. His cold or allergy seemed to have improved a bit, but he looked tired. After the meeting we exchanged a few words: "So, how is your coffee supply?" I started in my usual teasing style and added, "What are you up to?" pointing at the toolbox at his feet.

Figure 14. Meeting at the grave of Imre Nagy in 1990: from the left are Gergely Pongrátz, a leader of the Corvin Alley freedom fighters; Imre Mécs; and myself.

"Well, we got a report that the cable to the radio antenna of Lakihegy has been damaged or sabotaged. I will try to fix it. And how are you succeeding in protecting the beauty of your corduroy jacket these days?"

"I will be going to Vienna to show off my jacket and to get some blood, unless Colonel Marián gives me some other job to do."

"Say hello to the Austrian girls for me," Pista said as we got into our respective trucks.

On the way back to the university, we spotted a crowd in front of the Communist Party headquarters. We stopped. Armed freedom fighters were everywhere, yet there seemed to be no fighting. The square was full of Western camera crews. They were filming something from all directions. I even saw one crew on the roof. There was a crowd at the entrance of the building.

"What is going on?" I asked the man next to me.

"They executed some ÁVH officers, and the western reporters are filming the bodies," he answered.

"Well, I know that these reporters love blood and violence, but what has happened?"

"It seems they got lynched by a mob of former political prisoners who recognized them as their own torturers, or something like that. The national guard did not get here in time to stop them."

"Too bad," I replied.

As I got closer, I saw four or five bodies on the ground at the wall and one hanging by his feet from a tree. It was an ugly sight. A circle had formed around this uniformed, heavyset corpse, which reminded me of Mussolini's end. Paper money had fallen out of his pockets. Half-crazed people spat at the lifeless body while the cameras kept rolling. "Terrible," I said, just to myself, but the person next to me continued the sentence that I had started. "This the whole world will see! This every magazine will print! This will be the symbol of our revolution and not the untouched goods behind the broken store windows, not the unguarded paper money in the collection boxes, and certainly not the unarmed children facing the tanks. Whoever did this should be hanged right next to this ÁVH goon!"

Now the national guard arrived, and they began to clear the square. I felt sick, helpless, outraged, and humiliated. Gyurka was trying to calm me down. He said that all mobs anywhere are the same. He reminded me of the redheaded reporter who kept repeating, "If it bleeds, it leads," but I just could not accept this. I felt as if my sister had been raped, I felt that the honor of the Revolution had been disgraced, and I felt that we had been robbed of our most cherished possession: our honor.

CHAPTER 9

Top Secret

EARLY ON THIS THURSDAY, the first day of November, I went to pick up my national guard certificate. The red-white-and-green tricolor was printed diagonally across it, and its serial number was 8260. It was signed by Sándor Kopácsi. I was proud, very proud, to have it.

As I entered the MEFESZ office I heard raised voices. An intense debate was raging inside about the recent decisions of Prime Minister Imre Nagy to terminate Hungary's membership in the Warsaw Pact military alliance and to declare Hungary's neutrality. We all knew that these were decisive steps. Tibor Vígh believed that they would provoke the Soviets into attacking us. He believed that "their ego cannot allow for such a precedent to prevail."

Colonel Marián disagreed and argued that the Western powers have no legal basis to interfere in a dispute among members of the Warsaw Pact but could come to our defense if we were a neutral nation and asked for their help against an armed aggression. "In other words," he said, "Imre Nagy had no choice! He had to take these steps, because these steps were required in order to remove the legal obstacles from our receiving Western military help."

I did not know who was right and I did not understand the mentality of the Western leaders, but I did know that Hungarian public sentiment was behind Imre Nagy. I did know that Hungarians did not want to belong to any military bloc, that we wanted to be neutral. As the debate continued, the radio reported on a speech made by the new head of the Communist Party, János Kádár, who said, "Our glorious Hungarian Revolution is victorious. We have secured freedom and independence for Hungary. I am proud that the Communists fought in the front lines in this just Revolution. I will defend our achievement to my last breath, if necessary. I will fight for them with my bare hands."[1]

This made me feel good—not because I trusted this guy who still called himself a Communist. No! But because, if the chief of the Communist Party talked like this, and if there were peace and tranquility in the country, under such conditions the Russians could not possibly attack. "Can the Russians still attack after this?" I asked Gyurka. "Rule number one is that you never believe anything that a Communist says! You don't even believe the opposite of what they say. This Kádár, whose real name is Csermanek—just as the real name of our UN representative was not Koós, but Konduktorov, who is not even a Hungarian citizen—will say and do anything that his bosses in Moscow order him to say. Kádár learned the advisability of obedience when in jail—his communist comrades pulled out his nails. Believe me, he remembers that. Today he is with us because we are winning; tomorrow he will stab us in the back if a new order comes from Moscow. Just don't be so naïve!" Gyurka lectured.

Usually Pista just told me what my next job was, but this morning he gave me a typed and signed formal order. It read: "I authorize Béla Lipták to collect the weapons and ammunition in the interior ministry building and to bring them back to the university." This was the first and only time my full name was used on any of my orders during the Revolution. He also told me that we should take two trucks and that I should get the key from Sándor Kopácsi.

I assembled a couple dozen students, and when the trucks were ready we first went to the police headquarters to get the key to the building. Kopácsi greeted me like an old friend. He warned that this ministry was in fact the headquarters of the ÁVH and that no freedom fighters had entered that building yet. Therefore, he did not know what we would find there. Next, he handed me a gigantic antique key, probably hand made in the last century, and added, "If there is armed resistance, just turn around and come back."

The wooden door of the interior ministry building was at least twenty feet tall, was reinforced by iron belts and plates, and must have weighed several tons. I was tall, but the keyhole was still up at my eye level, and the door handle was even higher. This building used to be an Austro-Hungarian palace. It seemed that the aristocrats of the past wanted one to feel small when entering their palaces. I slipped the half-pound key into the lock.[2] It turned smoothly, and I heard a tiny click as the door was ready to be opened. The ten-ton giant of a door was so well balanced that I could open it with one finger. Even under those conditions I felt respect for the craftsman who created that masterpiece.

Behind the door was a dark corridor. I had an eerie feeling that I was not alone in it. While searching for the light switch, I stumbled over a metallic object that turned out to be a machine gun. It was facing the door. Once we found the light switch and could see, it became obvious that the ÁVH defenders had retreated to the upper floors of the building, because only the heaviest weapons were left on the ground floor. The rest they must have taken with them. We had no floor map. As we slowly penetrated the building, I never knew if the steps I was hearing were those of my fellow students or those of the retreating ÁVH officers.

I did not know why the freedom fighters who had fought and beat the secret police had not occupied this building. I did not know how the siege had ended or who had locked the door. All Kopácsi told me was that we should be careful. So I tried to be. As we searched the ground floor, we found weapons in almost every office. I saw large quantities of used cartridge cases next to the windows, indicating that the fighting must have gone on for some time. The many personal belongings left behind suggested that the ÁVH retreated in a hurry. While my colleagues were collecting and carrying the weapons from the ground floor onto the trucks, I proceeded to the next elevation. In Hungary, the first floor is called the ground floor, and therefore I proceeded up to the "first floor."

As in many major nineteenth-century buildings in Budapest, the stair hall was large and elegant. Next to the stairs was a perpetual-motion lift, a nonstop elevator, called a "pater-noster" because it goes on and on in a similarly nonstop manner as the continuous prayer of monks. I had never been in one before. I hesitated a bit as I stepped into a cubicle. Once the pater-noster was started, these cubicles formed a continuous belt, traveling upward on the left side and down on the right. Now, though, the pater-noster was still stationary, so it was easy to step into the cubicle. I pushed the up button, and the contraption started with a yank. I was traveling upward from the lit stair hall into the darkness, from our safe ground floor up into the unknown. The dark first floor was already approaching. Should I jump out, or should I stay and travel higher? The darkness was scary, yet the higher floors were even scarier, so in the last split second, I jumped out.

It was a strange feeling. Vertically, I was only a few feet from my friends below, yet I was totally alone and isolated. It was dark, and I had no idea where the light switches were. I heard some soft music coming from the right. So I kept one hand on the wall as I moved slowly toward the music. I felt a picture frame, then a door. The door was locked. I continued, but still found no light switch, no window. It was dark and quiet. The next door was open. My right hand was still sliding on the wall as I entered the room. Now, furniture blocked my way; I could not follow the wall anymore.

I felt a coat hanger and after that a desk. The desk was covered with papers and books; I touched a telephone and finally located a circular metallic object to one side. That could have been a lamp base, but there seemed to be no switch on it. An adjustable stem rose from the base, which did lead to a lampshade, and on the side of the shade I finally found the switch. I turned it, and after what felt like an eternity of darkness, I could see.

I was in the office of a secretary. Open on the desk was a schedule book full of names, telephone numbers, and notations. They all ended yesterday, on October 31. Today's page was empty. To the side of the desk was a calendar on the wall. One date was circled in red, and "Pista" was written above the circle. There was a leather-covered door behind the desk, and the pictures of the Hungarian Communist Party bosses were hanging over it. I had never seen a leather-covered door before. This one was soft to the touch, and it opened without creaking. Inside, the radio was tuned to a foreign station playing a French chanson.

On the floor next to a chair was a highly decorated officer's jacket.

A pillow on the leather sofa indicated that somebody had slept there. The telephone on the big mahogany desk was off the hook, the receiver dangling in midair. The liquor cabinet was open. A half-empty bottle of French cognac was on the desk, but there were no glasses. I could see some file cabinets behind an open door; one of the drawers was pulled out, and paper folders lay on the floor. As I kicked at one of them a document slipped out. It had a big red stamp on it: "TOP SECRET."

Next to the file cabinets was a bookshelf full of what seemed to be large photograph albums. They were of different colors. I picked out a thick blue one. The label read: "Case of Class I Agent X. Y." (The actual name I have forgotten.) Below the row of blue folders was a section of black-colored albums. At random, I also picked out one of these. The label on it read: "Domestic Agents—7." I took a couple more albums and settled down in the big and inviting leather easy chair in front of the low glass table with the intention of reading them. As I did, I noticed a newspaper basket full of colorful magazines next to the chair. I picked one up and in a moment forgot not only the spy albums, but also where I was and why I was there, because I was seeing things I had never seen before.

The magazines were from Holland, France, and the United States. They were printed on shining, glossy paper, and they were full of sharp, colorful photographs. There were beautiful, partially dressed women on their covers. As I opened them, I could barely believe my eyes. The women were doing unimaginable things. One was standing on a fire escape of a skyscraper with nothing on except high heels and a feathery hat. As she was descending, she was giving a goodbye kiss to a young man in the upper window, while another man was already caressing her from the stairs below. As I turned the pages, my blood pressure rose and I got dizzy.

I saw women in leather outfits that left nothing to the imagination; I saw whips, chains, and strange devices that I had never seen before. I saw a woman reclining on a silver plate among the appetizers on a buffet table. Next to her was a plate of oysters. And I saw all kinds of people doing the unspeakable. I saw waitresses on billiard tables, secretaries on desks, sailors in nunneries; I saw German shepherds of both the two and the four-legged kinds, doing it. Some of the close-up pictures I did not even understand. So I was turning the pictures upside down and sideways when I heard a distant cry: "Öcsi! Where are you?"

As if waking from a nap, I was dazed for a moment. When I finally came to my senses, I grabbed the agent albums and in total embarrassment raced to the pater-noster. As my cabin on the continuous elevator descended to the ground floor, I heard the excited murmur of the students below. Now I also saw their worried faces. "What happened? Where have you been?" asked Gyurka.

"Oh, I just checked out the next floor. If you are done here, you can start collecting the guns on that floor. I will just take these albums to the truck," I replied.

While the students worked on the first floor, I proceeded to the next. Now I was a bit more comfortable in searching for the light switches and less jittery when I heard the sounds of dripping faucets or creaking windows or doors. Now I heard the telephone ringing in a distant office of the second floor. As I proceeded toward the sound, the offices grew larger, more elegant. Now I was standing on soft Persian rugs when I finally picked up the gold-plated telephone on this enormous mahogany desk.

"This is captain so and so, reporting from Kistarcsa," said a deep, military voice.[3]

"Well, this is Öcsi from the Technical University," I replied.

"I would like to receive new orders for my unit," the man said.

"Listen, I am here only to collect the weapons left behind by the ÁVH. I don't give orders to ÁVH captains."

"Well, I would still like to ask for your advice on what to do," said the captain.

"All I know is that we have some fifty ÁVH officers under detention at the university. I know that they are safe there. So, if you want to, you can join them."

I heard a "Thank you" and then a click. Only then did I realize that I was probably talking to the head of the political prison camp at Kistarcsa.

As I had expected, the porno magazines delayed the collection of guns on the first floor. Gyurka, who was in his late twenties and therefore more experienced than the rest of us, finally just collected all the magazines and promised to distribute them among the students who collected the most guns by the end of the day.

It was getting dark by the time we started collecting the guns on the fourth floor. As a blond architecture student was rushing to become one of the best performers, he managed to destroy the pater-noster. He jumped into the moving cabin while carrying four or five guns, and as his cubicle descended, the muzzle of a rifle got caught between the sinking ceiling of the cabin and the floor as the cabin descended. Fortunately, we managed to fish him out safely, but a fuse was blown or the motor burned out. In any case, the system broke down. So from then on we had no elevator. We had to carry the guns down the stairs. It was exhausting.

When we finally reached the attic, I felt that my legs were made of rubber. I could barely stand up. In the dimly lit loft, the panic of the escaping ÁVH officers became obvious. The floor was covered with uniforms, torn-off rank tabs, identity cards with the photographs removed, eye glasses and other personal belongings, and, of course, guns and ammunition everywhere. I was thinking that this must have been the end of the road for them; this must have been where they made their last stand against the advancing freedom fighters. But I was wrong.

In the back of the loft, we found the copying machine on which they printed their new, fake identity cards. Dozens of discarded ÁVH cards covered the floor, and stacks of blank, unused, regular police cards stood nearby. Only the photographs were missing from the ÁVH cards. They must have reused the photos as they changed their identities. I went down on all fours to collect a few dozen of the old ÁVH cards and the new but unfinished police ID cards. As I collected the cards, I noticed a door behind the copy machine. It led to a corridor that in turn led to the attic of the next building. So that was the escape route these skunks had used. That was where the owners of the porno magazines and the gold-plated telephone had disappeared. "They went directly to Russian headquarters," said Gyurka.

We loaded three trucks with the guns collected in that building. It was about 10:00 P.M. when I finally locked that colossal door and returned to the university. I left the albums and the fake IDs in the truck, planning to look at them during our trip to Vienna. They would make good reading during the long drive. But our plans changed. As I arrived to report to Colonel Marián, I found the MEFESZ office in total chaos.

Pista's door was closed. Kati was in tears. Jancsi Danner was nowhere. "What has happened?" I asked Kati.

"Pista had a nervous breakdown. His wife got an anonymous telephone call. She was told that Pista will be hanged. So she came in to take Pista home. It was a terrible scene. She was wailing that the Russians will return, that the tanks will come again, that she does not want to be a widow, that Pista will be her murderer if he does not come home. When she left, Pista collapsed. He has locked himself in his office. He doesn't answer the phone. Right now, Jancsi Danner and Sándor Varga are substituting for him at a meeting in the ministry of defense. Imre Majoross drove them there. I am scared. I fear the worst."

"So what can we do? What can I do?"

"Well, one thing you could do is to get Pista some medication, some sedative or tranquilizer from the Tétényi Clinic."

"Well, Gyurka just left. He wanted to visit his family before we leave for Vienna. So I will have to go on foot. I'll be back as soon as I can."

My legs were so weak that I could barely stand, but I set out for the hospital anyway. It was a dark night and I was so exhausted.

CHAPTER 10

Jancsi's Murder

WAS THIS THURSDAY NIGHT OR FRIDAY MORN-
ING? In any case, it must have been about midnight.
The streets were dark, deserted, and the echo of my foot
steps reverberated in the night. I felt a bit scared, a bit
forlorn, and very, very tired. I had to walk only a couple of miles, but it
seemed to take an eternity. When I finally got to the hospital, the windows were dark and the door was locked. It took me some ten minutes
and a lot of banging before they even let me in. It had to have been
about 1:00 A.M. when I started walking back to the university.

I moved like a sleepwalker on Bartók Street. My legs were hurting
from climbing a million stairs at ÁVH headquarters. I was faint from
hunger. I did not even remember when I had eaten last. Drinking I did
remember, because I tasted the French cognac while researching the
porno magazines in the ÁVH general's office, but it had not quenched
my thirst. The submachine gun was pulling on my shoulder, and my
legs were weak, rubbery. The city was quiet and dark.

I heard some shots in the night! They came from the Pest side of

Freedom Bridge. I was near the Buda side of the bridge, approaching Saint Gellért Square. Suddenly I was fully awake. I could hear the approach of racing automobiles. Two cars were tearing over the bridge, the first small and gray, the second large and black. As the first car got off the bridge and turned left toward the university, it was racing at such a speed that its right wheels lifted off the pavement. There were four people in the car, and in that instant I realized that the car was our own Skoda. Imre Majoross was at the wheel, and Jancsi Danner was sitting next to him in the front.

Now, new shots rang out. I could see the muzzle flash of the submachine gun of a figure leaning out the window of the second car, a Russian Pobjeda, the type used by high Hungarian Party officials. The blasts were deafening, but I could still hear the whistle of the bullets. They seemed to pass right next to my ear. I was startled, frozen with fear, yet this picture, this split-second image, is permanently etched in my memory: Imre, the driver, is leaning forward onto the wheel; Jancsi is sitting up straight. A submachine gun is hanging on Jancsi's shoulder; he has not even bothered to take it off. The people in the back seat are bending down and forward as low as possible.

The driver of the Pobjeda was a blonde woman in ÁVH uniform. There were two ÁVH officers in the car. One was sitting in the passenger's seat in the front, the other in the back seat. They were both firing through their open windows on the right side of the car. The Skoda was racing toward the main entrance of the university with the Pobjeda right behind. I saw the two cars just for a moment, then they disappeared behind the chemistry building.

For a few seconds I could not move. I was paralyzed by fear. Then I heard firing once more. It was coming from the direction of the main entrance. I started running in that direction. While I was running, I knew what I needed to do. I was concentrating on looking at the ground to make sure that I did not fall in the darkness. I turned right after the chemistry building. The main entrance was about two hundred, possibly three hundred, yards from me. I could cover that distance in about twenty or thirty seconds. In an unconscious act I took the submachine gun off my shoulder. I had no idea what I would do next, yet I was running as fast as I could. The gun was in my hands, pointing forward.

As I approached the entrance, the darkness cleared a bit, and I could see a little more. The Skoda had turned over. It was on its right side. Jancsi was beneath Imre, who was in the process of climbing out through the door on the top. Jancsi did not move. The Pobjeda had left and was now racing toward Petőfi Bridge. A dripping sound and some moaning were coming from the Skoda, so I ran toward the disabled car. As I did, I heard another car coming. As I looked up, I saw that the Pobjeda had turned around at the Petőfi Bridge and was now racing back toward the university's main entrance.

I jumped behind the trunk of a chestnut tree as the Pobjeda braked to a stop and the goons of the ÁVH jumped out and sprayed the Skoda with more bullets. The flashes of their guns illuminated their faces in the darkness. They were so close that I could see the whites of their eyes. I lifted my submachine gun, rested the muzzle on the tree trunk, aimed, and then tried to pull the trigger, but I could not. I did not know what was happening. I knew they were firing at the Skoda and that I could save Jancsi's life, yet I could not pull the damn trigger! I checked the safety latch, but it was open. It was not that; it was something else.

It was something in me, some hateful, ugly weakness that made me incapable of protecting my friend, of stopping those animals. It was a frightfully terrible moment. It was a moment when you learn something about yourself. A moment that you will hate for the rest of your life. A moment that you will forever remember, one that will keep you up at night for decades. Something that you will be able to correct only in your dreams—in those glorious dreams in which you act like a man, in which you do what any decent human being should and would do—in those dreams from which you wake drenched in sweat and cold from the realization that it was only a dream, that the moment when you should have pulled that trigger has long passed and will never return.

Suddenly the assassins noticed me, and, like a spring hale, the bullets began pouring down all around my chestnut tree. As the bullets hit the pavement, little puffs of dust rose. I was filled with terror. I could not think at all. I was only an observer watching the actions of my own body as it flew over the six- or seven-foot iron fence of the university—boots, gun, and all—and landed on the other side behind the brick base of the fence. (I will never know how I was able to do that. I jumped much higher than ever before, and in full gear.) I peeked out over the low brick wall and saw that the ÁVH murderers were now throwing hand grenades at the entrance. Each time they pulled out the safety latch of a grenade, the igniter spark would illuminate their faces from below. I saw these hate-distorted faces. It seemed that they were not the faces of ÁVH officers, but Satan's own.

Finally, the Pobjeda left. I was still trembling behind the wall. The thousands of students who were sleeping inside the buildings were beginning to wake up, and now there were some lights in the windows. I heard a tremendous rumbling noise. It sounded as if a thousand garbage cans were rolling toward me. As I climbed over the fence, I saw that tanks were coming from the direction of the chemistry building. The road itself was shaking from their thunder. An officer was walking in front of the tanks. Now he started screaming at the top of his lungs: "Stop or I'll shoot to kill!" I had no idea who he was yelling at, but I was relieved, because the yelling was in Hungarian. I finally realized that these were our own tanks. Now I heard footsteps running toward me, two soldiers grabbed me, and I was under arrest. A few minutes later, they realized who I was and let me go.

The soldiers surrounded the Skoda, but I did not want to see it. Instead, I delivered the tranquilizers to Pista. His office door was open now. He was awake and was writing something. When I handed him the sedatives, he gave me a long look and said, "They were after me! Jancsi died because of me! I was supposed to be in that car." I said nothing, but I knew that Jancsi had died because of my inability to kill. After that, he handed me the order to bring blood for the Péterfi Hospital from Vienna. His eyes were bloodshot and his hands were trembling. Kati was trying to make him take some sedatives.

Before we left for Vienna, I had to say farewell to Jancsi. I went looking for him. He was already in the aula. Jancsi Danner's face was calm, serene. The inescapable moment he had talked about, "the inevitable moment of all heroes," had arrived. This tall, blond German-Hungarian from Szeged had played his role well. His blue eyes were now closed. He would not go on any more patrols with me. He would no longer talk about the need for a society that brings the best out of people. His act was over, but the play had to go on.

Gabi, his young bride, did not know it yet. She should not see him like this. Jancsi's body was a mess. We counted twenty-seven bullet holes in it. According to Imre Majoross, the Pobjeda had followed them all the way from the ministry of defense.[1]

We had to build a bier for him. It was about seven in the morning on this Friday, November 2, when we moved a conference table into the middle of the aula, the very place where the Revolution had started. It was there that I first heard Jancsi's voice, when he demanded that the MEFESZ delegate from Szeged be allowed to speak. That moment I will never forget! I remember our scared and deadly silence, the paralysis of our souls, and I remember the arrogance of the DISZ penguins with their red neckties and the lonely voice that changed it all, the trembling voice that dared to say, "Let him speak!"

Jancsi's six-foot, five- or six-inch body was already stiff, yet I had not, I could not, accept that he was gone. Gyurka and Imre were lifting his body at the shoulders, Sándor Varga and I were lifting his feet. As we carried the body, one of his size twelve or thirteen tattered shoes slipped off. I tried to put it back on, but the foot was stiff. Now my denial was shaken; now I was beginning to fear that this was final, that Jancsi was truly dead.

I made a bewildered, delirious effort to put the shoe back on his foot. I was convinced that if I could do that, somehow everything else would fall into place. If I could only put his shoe back, all other things could still be fixed. If I could put it back, his body would not be so stiff, he could still sit up, he could still tell us the outcome of that meeting he had come from, and most importantly, he could still tell us that there was hope, that it was not over. But the foot was too stiff, the shoe could not be put back on, and under the enormous Hungarian flag, which covered the whole bier, one of Jancsi's stiff feet remained covered by only a torn sock.

I must have been shaking, because Gyurka brought me the black officer's raincoat I had left in the MEFESZ office and made me put it on. I also must have looked dazed, because he shook me and slowly asked, "Have you got the orders?" When I nodded, he put his arm over my shoulder and took me to our truck.

The ÁVH and the Russian tanks were gone, the national strike was over, and people were sweeping the streets, filling the bullet holes, and replacing the broken glass in the windows. The capital was getting ready to resume its normal life on the coming Monday. Armed freedom fighters were patrolling the streets and were helping to distribute the food that was brought in by the lorries and trucks of the villagers. The streets of the liberated capital were now flooded with newspapers. They were the first swallows of freedom and democracy. Yet it was hard for me to be happy. Deep down I did know that Jancsi had not died in vain, but it was still hard to truly believe that.

The big bear Gyurka did his best to cheer me up. First, he turned on the radio, which reported that the Soviets had agreed to remove all their troops from Hungary. Because of that, the security council of the United Nations had decided to delay their discussion of the Hungarian situation until Monday, November 5. "You see, things are fine, the Russians are leaving," Gyurka said. When I remained mute, an unusual state in my case, he changed the subject. He told me that he could not fire at human beings, either—that in all wars some 90 percent of all soldiers fire only into the air. The more he talked, the more I knew that if Gyurka had been in my place, Jancsi would be alive, and the murderous careers of the ÁVH assassins would be over. Eventually, he just let me be and suggested that I read the agent albums I had taken from ÁVH headquarters.

I did what he told me. I picked up the first album and started looking at the photographs of the ÁVH informers of Budapest. The names in this volume started with C and went to F. This single volume must have contained some two hundred to three hundred photographs. Under each photo was the usual personal data, followed by a listing of the types of information that spy had already provided. Some entries were underlined and included such things as "Willing to give false witness." A few of the informers were homosexuals, and some were members of the previous ruling class, but there were also alcoholics, gamblers, former Nazis, and a surprisingly large number of average people who were just scared or weak but who had nothing to hide. I quickly read all the names, and to my great relief I found no friend or relative in the volume. Afterward, I felt ashamed that I had thought it possible that I might.[2]

While I read we also listened to Radio Free Europe. We learned that Imre Nagy had fired Peter Koós as Hungary's UN representative, but Koós had refused to step down. Imre Nagy had also asked the United Nations and the leaders of the four great world powers to guarantee Hungary's neutrality. Gyurka was very happy to hear that. "This was the formula the UN used to defend South Korea," he explained. "This is our only security blanket against a new Soviet attack, and it is a good one, too." He had barely finished the sentence when we saw Russian tanks blocking the road in front of us.

We stopped. Assisting the Russians were some Hungarian ÁVH officers. One of them studied my orders to bring blood from Vienna. He slowly read every word of my order, including the imprints of the stamps. When he saw that the chief of police, Sándor Kopácsi, had also authorized our trip, he said, "Yours is the first truck I am letting through, but they might turn you back at the next roadblock, in Budaörs." Then he waved us on. I took the paper back but did not reply. I could not bring myself to talk to a turncoat like that. I could not even imagine how he could look at himself in a mirror.

We were still within the city limits of Budapest. Other than our truck, there was no traffic on the road. The ÁVH man was wearing a warm, quilted jacket of the type worn by the Russian soldiers, called a *pufajka*. The Hungarian ÁVH officers and other renegades who had sided with the enemy were all issued pufajkas by the Russians, who used this as a way of distinguishing their loyal supporters from the rest of us Hungarians. These people we still refer to as the "Pufajkas."[3]

As the ÁVH man had predicted, at Budaörs we came to the second roadblock. Wherever I looked there were Russian tanks. The subservient Pufajkas were tagging behind the Russians like tailless dogs. As they checked our travel permit, the Pufajka in charge gave a subservient smile to a Russian tank commander and tried to make conversation with him as he walked by. The Russian spit on the ground and did not reply. He was an older man; perhaps he remembered their own traitors who worked for Hitler during World War II.

I hated those skunks so much that I had even forgotten to be scared. Gyurka had not. When they finally let us through, I noticed that one cigarette was burning in his mouth while he was taking out another and searching for his matches. I guess that was the first time I smiled on that ugly Friday.

There was no traffic on the road. We were around Tatabánya when we finally saw a bus approaching from the opposite direction. It stopped, and some people got out to talk with us. The bus was carrying a delegation from Győr. They were on their way to Budapest to meet with Imre Nagy. Győr is the center of the northwest region of Hungary, and its Revolutionary Council was in control of the area between Győr and Austria. The delegates were surprised to learn that two circles of tanks surrounded Budapest. They did not know that they had to pass through those roadblocks. With our urging, and after a short debate, they decided to go ahead anyway.

As we reached the outskirts of Győr we came across another road-block. This one was manned by Hungarian freedom fighters. When they saw my tricolor armband, national guard certificate, and travel documents, which were signed by both Police Chief Kopácsi and Colonel Marián, they became very interested. We must have been the first people they had seen from Budapest. They wanted to know everything that had happened in the capital. They wanted to know what we thought, what we had heard. It was not easy to leave them. "You must see our leader, the president of the Transdanubian National Council, Attila Szigethy," said one of them, and he offered to guide us to the city hall.[4]

It was about noon. There was a lot of traffic on the street leading to city hall. I saw a number of foreign license plates. On our way to meet Attila Szigethy, we walked through crowded corridors, we met crews of Western reporters, and we saw a lot of tumult and confusion. In Szigethy's office the people looked tired and unshaved. The conference table was full of empty coffee cups and overflowing ashtrays.

There was no question about who was in charge there. It was self-evident who Attila Szigethy was. He was like Colonel Marián in that he, too, was surrounded by a revolving circle of delegates, messengers, and assistants, but he stood out head and shoulders. He was calm, collected, and organized; he was in full control. He led us into his inner office, looked at our papers, wrote down our names, and asked a lot of questions. He was most interested in the Russian roadblocks, in the number of tanks we had seen, and whether we had noticed any movements of the military. He was also interested to learn whether the tanks we had seen had been the old-style ones that were stationed in Hungary or new ones, which had recently arrived from Ukraine and Romania. We told him as much as we knew, including that some of the tanks appeared to be clean and unused. On a slip of paper he wrote down his telephone number and urged us to give him another report when we were on our way back from Vienna.

As we left Győr, I started reading the other album, the blue one, that I had taken from the ÁVH headquarters. It dealt with an English military attaché. The material was presented in chronological order. The story started in 1949. Its main subject was an English colonel who had been transferred to Budapest in 1949 but had also traveled a lot outside the country.

The colonel's first contact with the ÁVH was made through a former Hungarian aristocrat who easily befriended him because the colonel was a monumental snob. For a year they played tarot and socialized. Then after a year, during one of their tarot games, the aristocrat mentioned that he had lost his Swiss-made wristwatch and could not get a replacement in Hungary. The colonel gladly offered to bring him one from his next trip abroad. The blue-blooded ÁVH informer then discretely slipped the colonel an envelope containing twice the purchase price.

A few months later, another of their tarot partners (also an ÁVH operative) repeated the same exercise, but he asked for two watches, one for himself and one for his wife. Photographs of the watches and the envelopes were pasted in the album right next to the narrative.

According to the blue album, by 1951 the colonel was bringing Swiss watches for whole graduating classes and making more on those transactions than his regular salary. At that point a new tarot partner was introduced to the colonel. He made some vague hints suggesting that the colonel's smuggling activity was not completely unknown to the authorities. The regular tarot game broke up. The ÁVH was watching the colonel to see if he would contact the English Secret Service or if he might harm himself. Other than exhibiting a bit of depression and drinking, the colonel did not do anything else, so in 1952 the Hungarian aristocrat suggested to the colonel that he should hire the aristocrat's cousin as his maid.

By that point the colonel had a pretty good idea of the reason why this cousin wanted to be his maid. Yet he allowed himself to be drawn into a rather well-documented love affair with her, and in exchange for the female tenderness, or because of fear, he did not notice that she was photographing the documents on his desk.

By 1956 there was no more acting. The aristocrat disappeared, and the maid became the boss and threatened or intimidated the colonel into carrying out spying assignments. The colonel contemplated suicide. He was drinking heavily and had fallen into a permanent state of depression. Whenever he was near a nervous breakdown, they would leave him alone for a few weeks. The entries in the album read like the notes of a psychiatrist. The ÁVH was constantly evaluating the likelihood of his emotional collapse and was balancing the consequences of his committing suicide against the value of his services. In the last entry, which was dated in September, 1956, his "handlers" were so worried that they ordered the "maid" to give the colonel some powerful medication.

I was at this point in my reading when Gyurka stopped, because two policemen were waving at us from the middle of the road. Their uniforms seemed sloppy or the wrong size, and they themselves appeared to be rather disoriented. They asked us about our destination, and we learned that they were from Budapest and wanted to visit their relatives in Mosonmagyaróvár. (Even for Hungarians, the name of this border town is a bit long, so it is often referred to as Magyaróvár or just Óvár.) We told them to jump onto the back of the truck and forgot about them.

The roadblock at Óvár was manned by nervous, trigger-happy freedom fighters. Initially we did not know the cause of their frantic state. They explained that on October 26 the local ÁVH border guards had attacked their peaceful demonstration and had murdered close to a hundred unarmed civilians, including women and children. One of the freedom fighters explained, "The ÁVH border guards were up on a balcony and just kept firing and throwing hand grenades onto the square, which was full of demonstrators. Afterwards, we collected one hundred thirteen unexploded hand grenades among the hundreds of casualties on the pavement." Another eyewitness added, "Few people have slept in this town since then. Most families are in mourning, you know."[5]

They took us to the Agricultural Academy. We went in, but the policemen whom we picked up stayed on the truck. The corpses were laid out in the gymnasium, a sickening and shocking sight. The head of the Revolutionary Council was a mustachioed professor. His eyes were red and his trembling fingers were darkened by nicotine. He was near a nervous breakdown. We told him about our trip and about the situation in Budapest, but he did not seem to comprehend. He kept talking about some escaped ÁVH murderers. As we left Óvár, the freedom fighters at the roadblock wrote down our license plate number and the fact that there were four of us in the truck before they let us pass.

It was late afternoon when we reached the border town of Hegyeshalom. On the Hungarian side there were no border guards, and the customs building was empty. So we just drove through. On the Austrian side, I gave my orders to the border guard. He saluted, called over a translator, and shortly thereafter called his superiors. The Austrians had closed the Hungarian border, but the Red Cross had already notified the border command of our coming. Therefore, when a captain showed up, he gave us not only a temporary pass into Austria, but also a map that showed the location of the hospital where the blood was waiting for us.

I had a funny feeling. For the first time in my life I had entered a foreign country. For the first time in my life, I had left my homeland. It was a strange, almost frightening feeling. I kept telling myself that it was only for a few hours.

As we passed into Austria, a remarkable sight emerged. Hundreds of people and vehicles milled around the Austrian side of the closed border. It was like a country fair or an open market. Cars, buses, and trucks were parked not only on the side of the road, but also on the ploughed fields. I saw scouts, priests and nuns, reporters, ambulances, and truckloads of food and medicine intermixed with a lot of reporters and other curious people.

When they heard that our truck was from Budapest, they surrounded it. We could not move. Some wanted to load oranges and chocolates onto our truck, and a group of Dutch students wanted to come back with us to Budapest to help in defending the capital. They did not seem to understand that this was our fight. They did not seem to comprehend why they could not help in it.

A forest ranger in enormous leather breeches covering his pot belly and wearing a Tyrolian hat with a tuft of chamois hair on top of his cheeky and friendly gray head kept pointing at my cockade and saying something like, "Geschenk." I did not understand what he wanted. At that point, from his green hunter's jacket he tore off a hand-carved horn button and handed it to me. Now I understood, so I handed him my tricolor rosette in exchange. There was a sudden silence among the onlookers as that teary-eyed old Austrian, with respectful dignity, pinned on a Hungarian cockade.

It took some time to find the hospital. People were already waiting for us at the door, and when we got there all other activity came to a standstill. Doctors and nurses, elevator operators, and patients were all trying to help load the truck, which was surrounded by a crowd. Strangers were patting my shoulder, and some people cried as they hugged me. No, I did not feel as if I were in a foreign country; I was at home among relatives in Austria.

When we got back to the border, our truck was once again surrounded. They filled the remaining space on the truck with the kinds of fruits I had seldom or never seen. They loaded chocolate bars, candy, colorful boxes, and cans of different shapes and sizes. It seemed as if the contents of a delicatessen had been poured onto our truck. When we were ready to leave, a reporter from *Time* magazine asked if we would take him to Budapest. We agreed. I took one last look at the waving crowd as handkerchiefs fluttered in the air. The captain of the border guards stood at stiff attention as we passed through. And then we were back on Hungarian soil.

CHAPTER 11

Beginning of the End

A T THE ROADBLOCK IN ÓVÁR the leader of the freedom fighters wrote down our license number, checked how many people were on our truck, and disappeared. A few minutes later armed students surrounded our truck, so Gyurka stopped the motor. I got out to find out what was going on. The reporter from *Time* magazine was scribbling furiously in his notebook. I could not even open my mouth when one of the students pointed at my boots and exclaimed, "New officers boots!" Another student pointed at my rubberized black raincoat: "No student has one of these!" I detected hostility and suspicion in the air but did not yet understand the reason for it. After all, I was dressed the same way when we were stopped on our way to Vienna only a few hours before.

Then I saw a car racing toward us. It was still moving when the mustachioed head of the Revolutionary Council jumped out. He was in a frenzy, screaming at the top of his lungs as he approached our truck: "You have smuggled the ÁVH murderers out of the country! You are ÁVH collaborators! You will hang for this!" It was only at that point that we realized what the problem was. We started searching our memories to figure out when had we last seen the two men whom we thought were policeman. We did not even remember if they had gone into Austria with us or not. All we knew was that they had disappeared.

The students let the *Time* reporter go and threw the two of us into the local jail. They told us that a court would decide our fate in the morning. It was dark outside. It was nearing midnight. I was walking up and down in the ten-by-ten-foot cell. Gyurka, this big bear of a man, was peacefully snoring on the floor. "Sleep never hurt anyone; sleep whenever you can" was one of his guiding life principles.

I kept walking up and down most of the night. I listened to the noises of the night: dogs barking, cars arriving or leaving, the inaudible murmur of our guards talking. I could see the first blush of dawn when I heard the phone ringing.

"I am Zoltán Kiss, member of the national guard," said a respectful and resonant voice, and after a pause, "Yes Sir, Mr. Szigethy, they are here. . . . Yes, Mr. Szigethy, they also said something about blood, but my commander thinks that they smuggled ÁVH officers to Austria. . . . No, Mr. Szigethy. . . . Yes, Mr. Szigethy. . . . I will! Right away Sir!" After that I heard footsteps and a door close, and by the time I heard the next telephone ring, I also heard footsteps coming toward our cell.

As the key turned in the lock, Gyurka woke up. His first move, as always, was to search for his cigarettes. The guards returned our papers and added, "Hurry up, so that the ice will not melt in the blood containers!"

"Your lunatic boss should have thought of that sooner," Gyurka grumbled.

It was midmorning on this Saturday, November 3, when we reached the city hall in Győr. The chaos we found was even worse than that of the day before. Two radios, tuned to Kossuth and Radio Free Europe, were blaring simultaneously, while two dozen people were all talking at the same time. We learned that while the Russians had formally agreed to withdraw their troops from Hungary, there were reports that in fact new troops were entering the country. Right now the Russian ambassador, Yuri Andropov, was meeting with Imre Nagy to discuss the details of the withdrawal, Khrushchev was visiting Marshal Tito of Yugoslavia, and the Communist Party chief, János Kádár, had disappeared. Nobody knew where he was.[1]

Szigethy took us into his inner office, where his first question was, "Have you seen troops?"

"No, there are no Russians in that region," I replied naïvely.

"I mean Western troops, Americans, Austrians, anybody!" he said, almost yelling.

"No, only boy scouts, nuns, and reporters," I replied.

Szigethy's neck turned purple and his eyes flashed with outrage. "Those bastards, those heartless, spineless, goddamned bastards!" he hissed through his teeth, then he jumped up and without another word left us.

On the way back, we went in the direction of Komárom, and on that road there were no Russian roadblocks. "I don't know if this means that they are concentrating on the main traffic arteries or they are truly leaving," said Gyurka. It was lunchtime when we arrived at the hospital. They were very glad to see us. We had arrived at the very last minute. They offered us lunch, which Gyurka accepted but I did not because I had stuffed myself with Austrian chocolates during our trip back. So while Gyurka was eating, I grabbed some chocolates and oranges and visited the wounded.

The rooms were overflowing, and the less-seriously wounded were out in the corridors. Those who were conscious gladly accepted the chocolate bars, but some of them did not know what to do with the oranges. They had not seen oranges since the Soviets had occupied Hungary. On one bed a person with a head wound called out in clear American English, "An orange please." He turned out to be the very reporter to whom I had given a tour of the university a week earlier, the fellow who told me, "If it bleeds, it leads."

"Should it be a blood orange?" I asked with my sick sense of humor, but fortunately he did not understand Hungarian, and I did not speak English.

A young farm boy with a leg wound was sitting on the side of his bed. When I offered him a chocolate bar, he did not take it. "Don't you like candy?" I asked.

"Well, it's not that. The point is, you don't want to give me any; I served in the green ÁVH." (The "blue" ÁVH officers were volunteers who made up the political secret police, while the "green" ones were drafted and served as border guards.) I was not prepared for that. Neither did I expect the sorrowful yet accusing expression in his simple peasant eyes. I took the largest chocolate bar and put it on his lap. The farm boy did not return it.

Before going back to the university, we visited Gyurka's family. On the way we had seen a captured Russian tank driven by freedom fighters. Gyurka had slept on the floor of the jail, and I had not washed since collecting the arms in the ÁVH headquarters. That was almost two days before. We were both dirty and needed a bath. When we got to Gyurka's apartment, the family surrounded us, wanting to know everything. Gyurka's beautiful sister, Mária, the ex-wife of Igor Sík, brought us some rum. I had not slept for two days, so the rum knocked me out. They noticed that I was about to fall off my chair and suggested that I take a nap.

Mária took me to the bedroom, turned away while I undressed and slipped under the covers. It seemed that I had not been in a real bed, under clean bedding, for ages. Mária sat down on the side of the bed. She was the loveliest, most alluring women I had ever seen. She noticed my stalk-eyed, devouring expression and responded with a mischievous wink. Then she leaned forward. It was an otherworldly sight. I could not speak, could not even stutter. She leaned even farther. I closed my eyes and felt a soft caressing, a kiss on my forehead, light as air, then she tucked me in, and while she quietly scuttled out, I sank into a deep sleep.

By the time I woke and we left Gyurka's apartment, it was about 6:00 P.M. on this Saturday, November 3. On the way back to the university we passed Corvin Alley. When I got back to the university I found our national guard division at full alert. Our ranks had swelled by the cadets of the Petőfi and Zrinyi Military Academies. There must have been three or four thousand armed students in our buildings. I saw the old faces, the ones I had not seen since our initial march on October 23, two weeks ago. There was Gyuri Egry (Csámpi the Menő); there was Gyuszi Perr with his wife, the blonde little athlete Marika, who was rooting for me at the high-jump competition. There were Laci Zsindely and Attila Lipcsey; they all had come back, and now they were all armed.

In the MEFESZ office, next to Pista Marián, was a new face, that of General Görgényi. He was sent to us by the commander of the Hungarian national guard, General Béla Király. Görgényi looked a bit lost, and we did not understand why we needed him. In fact, we were a bit suspicious of his presence. Pista asked the same questions Attila Szigethy had asked me in Győr: "Did you see Western troops at the border? Were the Russian tanks of the same models that you have seen on the street corners of the city? Did the Russian soldiers look dirty or fresh?" I did not like these questions. I knew what he was driving at, and I could not say anything reassuring. When I told them that we had just unloaded a truckload of candy and citrus fruit in lecture hall KA-51 (where the ÁVH men were kept), Pista remarked, "That will do a lot of good against tanks!"

At about 8:00 P.M. the radio broadcast a proclamation by Cardinal József Mindszenty, who had been freed on November 1: "We are neutral, we have given no cause for the Soviet empire to wage war on us. But, has it not occurred to the Soviet leaders that we will respect them more if they do not shed our blood in an attempt to enslave us?" Although he was right, I did not like the tone of his speech. I felt it was too gloomy. I did not understand why this great cardinal, this saint of a man, was talking in such a pessimistic and skeptical way. After all, the Soviets were about to sign the final agreement concerning their withdrawal. So why the gloom?

A few minutes later, General Király called. He wanted a contingent of one hundred students from among us. We agreed, but that call also bothered me. Why would the commander of the Hungarian national guard need our students as guards? Did he not trust any of his own units? What was the big hurry? Did we not have tank battalions? Did we not have an air force? Were we, the students at this university, the only people he could trust? While General Király was on the line, we asked him about the talks. He sounded, or tried to sound, reassuring. "Our minister of defense, General Pál Maléter, has just left. He will sign the final document, which guarantees the safe departure of all Soviet military forces from Hungarian soil. All the details have already been agreed to, so this will only be a formality, a signing ceremony at the Russian military headquarters in Tököl."

What he said reassured us a bit, but it also made me nervous. Why would the minister of defense go to Tököl? What would happen if the leader of the Hungarian military were needed in the meantime? Why did we not send a politician? Why was this meeting not in the daylight, and why was it to be held in the Russian military barracks? Did such ceremonies not belong in the parliament, in front of the cameras of the international press? We had a lot of questions, a lot of doubt, but we also knew that General Maléter was a brave and competent leader who knew what to do, and it was not for us to question his decisions.

Just as in Győr, now in the MEFESZ office too, all radio stations were tuned in simultaneously. We were listening to Radio Budapest, Radio Free Europe,[2] the BBC, Voice of America, and the short-wave stations, which were reporting troop movements in eastern Hungary. The bits and pieces of the news did not add up to a logical overall picture: the United Nations had delayed the security council meeting on Hungary until Monday, November 5. Hungary was still represented at the UN by a Soviet citizen and KGB agent in spite of his dismissal by Prime Minister Imre Nagy. It seemed that the United Nations still recognized that man as Hungary's representative. The attention of the American people was on their election, on the following day, Tuesday. President Eisenhower was on the campaign trail. The American secretary of state, John Foster Dulles, had been hospitalized. The fighting at the Suez Canal had intensified. It seemed that nobody was in control. God, what chaos!

Each news item sounded like a thud, a hammer stroke driving yet another nail into the coffin of Hungarian freedom. Together they combined into a terrible rattle. It was maddening, infuriating to hear, yet I could not tear myself away. I still hoped for that one sentence that would announce the arrival of some UN observers in Budapest. I was still waiting for the formal recognition of Hungary's neutrality by the great powers. I was waiting, waiting for some sign of human decency.

Instead, at about 11:00 P.M., the radio announced that contact had been lost with our minister of defense, General Pál Maléter. As the news was announced, there was deadly silence in the MEFESZ office. We could not get our breath. We stared into nothingness, our fists clenched, lips quivering. We all knew that the beginning of the end had arrived. We naturally stayed up. From midnight on, every ten minutes or so, we heard the same announcement: "General Maléter is requested to call the prime minister's office immediately!"

That was the worst night of my life. Nobody slept. We were all dazed and overcome by a sense of total abandonment. At about 2:00 A.M., the guards from the KA-51 lecture hall reported that the ÁVH prisoners wanted to go home. "Let them," waved Pista lethargically. At about three o'clock Pista called a meeting. He reported, "It seems that General Maléter has been captured by the Russians. Twenty-six tank battalions, twenty-five hundred tanks, and one thousand other vehicles have entered Hungary from Romania and Ukraine. This is the largest Soviet tank concentration since the German-Soviet confrontation at Kursk. Our airports are surrounded. Any minute now the attack against our capital can start. You know all the details of our defense plans. If you don't feel sorry for your mothers, you can implement it. Remember that you can only die, you cannot win! I am leaving for a last meeting with General Király. Those who decide to go home should leave right away, while the bridges are still open. Those who decide to fight will have plenty of time, because the Russians are coming from the east, so they will first attack Pest. The attack of Buda will come later."

There was stunned silence in the room. We were all thinking the same thing: "Pista is not staying with us?! He is not going to lead our defense? Who will take his place?" We were all pondering those questions, but nobody spoke them out loud. There were no comments, no debate, just silence, desperate and maddening silence, the type of horrifying silence that precedes the worst act that a human being is capable of. As my dazed mind began to clear, as I finally looked around, Pista was already gone.[3]

A few minutes later I saw General Görgényi slowly walking out through the main entrance. He was embarrassed, his briefcase was in his right hand, his eyes stared at the ground, and he did not know what to do with his left hand. He said nothing, and he did not look anybody in the eye. He just walked out, as if this were a movie or something and the show was over. "The skunk!" I said to Gyurka, who was standing next to me, but I heard no reply. I turned to Gyurka, and his eyes, too, were staring down at the floor. He could not, he dared not, look me in the eye, and this idol of mine, this brave and bright bear of a man, just mumbled to nobody in particular, "I am going home, too!"[4]

It was nearly 3:30 A.M. on that dark, ugly Sunday, November 4. The hundred volunteers who would guard General Király were lining up in front of the library. The cadets of the Zrinyi and Petőfi Military Academies and the tank crews from Pilisvörösvár were packing up and walking out. Their equipment stayed, but we did not know how to operate it. László Bónis, an assistant professor of metallurgy, was leading the first group of defenders, who would take up positions on Móricz Square, which was protected by barricades built from paving stones.

The morning was still dark. At that instant I heard the first thunder of the guns from the Pest side of the Danube. It was four or five o'clock. The roar of cannons seemed to be coming from the area of the Kilián Barracks, the Corvin Cinema, and Üllői Street region. "Pista Angyal's coffee kept his fighters awake!" I said to no one in particular. After all, nobody there even knew who Pista Angyal was.

At about five o'clock I heard the voice of Imre Nagy on Radio Budapest: "This is Imre Nagy speaking, the chairman of the council of ministers of Hungary. Today at dawn, Soviet troops attacked our capital with the obvious objective of overthrowing the lawful and democratic government. Our troops are fighting; the government is at its station. I inform the world and my nation of these facts." His announcement was followed by the national anthem. After that, they broadcast the message of the Hungarian Writers' Union. The writers appealed to all intellectuals of the world, begging for military help and for UN observers. These announcements were repeated in four languages, interrupted only by our two national anthems, the *Himnusz* and the *Szózat*, and by Kodály's choral work that has the refrain, "Don't hurt the Magyars!"

I could not stand it. I ran out of the MEFESZ office. I was overpowered by a crying fit, and, like a whipped dog, I retreated into the corner of a semidark corridor. I wanted to throw up. I had lost my interest in life. I was burying my dreams, burying my faith in humanity, burying the person I used to be. I was burying myself.

Like a zombie, for hours I just sat there. The noise, the tramping of footsteps, gradually subsided. Only one radio remained on in a nearby office. It kept repeating the appeal of the Hungarian writers to the world: "Help Hungary! Help Hungary!" it cried into the ether. My throat was dry, my shoulder was hurting from the pull of the submachine gun, tears were streaming from my eyes, and I repeated for the millionth time, "Please God, don't let it be! Don't let them betray us! Please make them help!"

My only contact with life was that radio. While it was on, there was still hope. We still had a voice, a radio. As long as Radio Budapest was on the air, there was hope. Then the radio announcer spoke in Russian, begging the Soviet soldiers not to shoot. My crying face twisted into a grimace. "Not to shoot?" I mumbled, as the windows of the corridor vibrated from the detonations on the other side of the Danube.

Now, suddenly, something changed. I did not know what, but something was different. Something was wrong, dreadfully wrong. Yes! What had happened to the national anthem? I did not hear the national anthem. I jumped up. My legs had gone to sleep, and I almost fell, but I kept running anyway. I reached the office where the radio was. I shook the receiver, thinking it must be a bad battery, but then, over the background noise, I began to hear gunfire. The fight was on for the radio station. Radio Budapest was off the air. That was the last thing I remember.

CHAPTER 12

Lives on the Line

I HAD NOT BEEN ASLEEP, I just passed out. Laci Zsindely found me in the dean's office. He was on his way to the men's room and saw me sitting on the floor, slumped down next to a radio. First I saw his talking face, then I started to hear his voice, and sometime later I began to make sense out of what he was saying: ". . . also at Csepel. They were also beaten back on Üllői Street. The streets of Pest are dotted with burnt-out Russian tanks. Their tanks have also been stopped at Stalin City and in the mining regions of Pécs. According to Radio Free Europe the Congress of American Veterans is demanding that NATO start mobilizing to help us. As of yet, there are no Russians in Buda. The barricades are almost ready on Móricz Square. Every minute, more and more people arrive to man the barricades."

Each news item was a straw to clutch. I wanted to believe that there was still hope. I wanted to do my part, but the first words and the first steps were so hard. If Laci had not been there, I could not have gotten started. Laci had such a warm smile. He knew that we would make it. So I stood up. He was much shorter than I, but somehow he managed to put his arms around my shoulders, and slowly, embracing each other, as if returning from an abyss, we walked back to the MEFESZ office.

The office I returned to was a totally different place. The people who were there were willing to put their lives on the line. We did not need a lot of hot air to communicate. We knew that life was about deeds, not words. There was Gyuri Egry, better known as Csámpi, or Menő. That was the last time I would see him.[1] Gyuszi Perr was there with Marika. They were trying to take more of our tanks to Móricz Square. Fourteen of our tanks were parked next to the library, but with one exception: the rest of the tank crews (from Pilisvörösvár) had disappeared. A single lieutenant was commanding the one remaining tank, which we moved to Móricz Square. His brother had died two weeks before during the first attack. He would fight. Brothers of that sort do fight.

Ede Némethy and Gyurka Burger were listening to short-wave radio broadcasts, while Marika the gymnast left to get some bread. The bread was needed, because Gyuszi's group planned to retreat into the mountains if we failed to hold the square, and Marika wanted to make sure that they would have something to eat. While Marika was gone, I learned that János Kádár had become the Hungarian Quisling and had formed a counterrevolutionary puppet government. The Soviets had given him a radio transmitter in Szolnok, and he was broadcasting his pro-Soviet propaganda from there. This Hungarian Quisling intended to become the new boss of the Hungarian slaves.

To my relief, I also learned that there were no other traitors in Imre Nagy's government. General Király and our one hundred student guards were retreating through the mountains of Transdanubia toward Austria. Imre Nagy and the majority of his cabinet had taken refuge at the Yugoslav Embassy. Cardinal Mindszenty had asked for asylum at the American Embassy, and two brave leaders had not escaped at all but were still at their posts. Sándor Kopácsi was still at police headquarters, and a minister without portfolio (one who does not direct a particular government ministry), István Bibó, was still in the parliament.

While the Soviet tanks were destroying one of Europe's most beautiful capitals, István Bibó was writing a historic document, one that in addition to giving guidance to the Hungarian people and countering Soviet propaganda also outlined a peaceful resolution to the conflict.

Figure 15. István Bibó spent the night in the parliament, where he prepared a historic document, translated it into four languages, and the next morning personally delivered it to four Western embassies. Courtesy *Nemzetôr*

His handwriting was neat, unhurried. When he was done with the Hungarian version, he proceeded meticulously to translate the text into English, French, German, and Spanish. He used his thesaurus to avoid using the same adjective twice. He neatly addressed the four envelopes, packed up his papers, calmly passed the Russian soldiers at the gate, and walked to each of the four embassies. He hand delivered his remarkable document, this confirmation of courage and integrity, this declaration of faith in the international community, in their integrity and sense of justice.

When I heard that most of our tank crews had run off, it occurred to me that Uncle Feri, the husband of my mother's sister, Duduke, was a tank commander in World War II. "Do you think he would be willing to drive some tanks to the square?" asked Laci Zsindely. I had no idea, but I decided to check. So we dropped into the KA-51 lecture hall to pick up some powdered milk from the pile of Austrian gifts and walked over to 1 Béla Bartók Street, where they lived. Duduke was my mother's younger sister. Her baby was only a few weeks old. I was sure she could use the powdered milk.[2]

As we walked through the corridors, I also picked up some blankets left behind by the military cadets. They would come in handy either for us in the hills or for Duduke if they were out of coal and their apartment was cold. As we walked to Bartók Street, I told Laci about Duduke's first baby, which was born some eleven years ago, at the end of the war.

We were in Sopron, and the city was already occupied by the Soviets. Duduke had no milk and could not buy any, because the Russians had commandeered all the cattle and had posted armed guards around the stolen herds. As the baby was slowly starving, Péter and I, ages eleven and nine, decided to steal back some of our milk from the Russians.

We got a white enameled pot, and after dark we took off to find the herd. Around their campfires, the Russian soldiers were drinking vodka while we crept on our bellies toward the herd. This was our first attempt at stealing milk directly from cows. In the tall weeds there was no place to put down the pot, and the cows were kicking and mooing—doing everything except standing still and giving milk. I must admit that our methods of milking were not conventional, and our pulling at their tender teats must have been painful. The end result was a couple of ounces of dirt mixed with milk, and eventually the baby died of malnutrition.

As we walked to Duduke's, we could smell the smoke and hear the unrelenting cannon thunder coming from the Pest side of the river. It was a terrible Sunday! We could also hear a few words from the loudspeaker on Móricz Square, which was broadcasting the transmission of Radio Free Europe. When the pedestrians saw our armbands and the submachine guns on our shoulders, they stared at the ground. There was no more approval or expression of solidarity in their body language. They were just scared.

On the marble stairs in the dignified stair hall of Duduke's house, we ran into scared tenants on their way down. They did not look into our eyes either. They were carrying food and other essentials into the basement. Their eyes blamed us for their predicament.

Even before ringing the bell, I could hear the crying of the baby. Uncle Feri's first words were, "Did anybody see you coming here?" I shook my head and placed the milk powder and the blankets on a side table. The BBC radio was on. It was rebroadcasting the plea of the freedom fighters of Stalin City. They were begging for paratroopers; their ammunition was low, and they were outgunned and outnumbered by the Russians. The appeal ended in English: "For the sake of God, for the sake of freedom and liberty, please help Hungary!"

Nobody said anything yet, but I already knew where we stood. The apartment was filled with terror. They kept staring at our guns. It was obvious that they wished us to leave. I said nothing about our tanks or about the upcoming defense of Móricz Square. I just mumbled something about the milk powder, and we left. As we walked back to the university, the same unrelenting thunder of cannon blasts could still be heard from the Pest side of the river. The intensity of the fighting was even greater now than when we had come. "Pista Angyal's welcoming party!" I pointed toward Üllői Street.

"I'm glad you're in a kidding mood again," said Laci, and he winked at me.

The university was almost empty. We decided to evacuate it and close its gates so that it would not be damaged by the fighting. We walked through all the buildings, turned off all the lights, and locked all the doors. The few people we found—a fireman; two female medical students; Imre Majoross, Jancsi Danner's driver; and a few others—we took to the medical emergency room and told them to wait there until the fighting was over. By the time we got back to the empty MEFESZ office, it was evening.

Radio Budapest had gone silent in the morning, and by now it was in the hands of the traitors. Only BBC, Radio Free Europe, and a few short-wave transmitters were still broadcasting the voices of freedom. Radio Csokonai was still broadcasting from Stalin City, but we could hear the cannon fire in the background as the announcer begged for Western help: "The life of our nation is in the hands of the United Nations. Please save Hungary! Please Help!"

We could still hear the intense fighting from the Pest side of the Danube, but now, suddenly, we could also hear the din of battle from the Buda side, from Móricz Square. We turned off the last lights, locked the main gate, and started toward the square. It was dark. It took us

Figure 16. Getting ready for fighting against the second Soviet assault. Photo by Leslie A. Toth

about an hour to cover the one-mile or so distance to reach the freedom fighters defending the houses of the square. This was because the Soviet tanks were already on the square itself and in the main streets leading to it. Only Gellért Hill and the side streets were still in our hands. My group had to approach the square through the gardens behind the houses on Béla Bartók Street. We were climbing fences and fighting off dogs in the process. As we got closer, the thunder of the cannons got more and more deafening. I had no idea that such loudness even existed.

Between the thundering roars we could still hear the broadcasts of Radio Free Europe amplified through a loudspeaker. At that moment a refined female voice was talking about Eisenhower's chances in the election on Tuesday. "Those damned idiots elected him once because he promised to liberate us. Now they will reelect him because he broke his pledge!" fumed Laci.

We were trying to get to the apartment house where Gyuszi Perr and Marika were fighting. They were on the first floor. First we entered the basement, which had been converted into an air-raid shelter and was full of residents. There was chaos, panic, and confusion. Just a few minutes before, the building superintendent was shot in the stomach as he was assisting the fighters near the entrance. He was lying on his back. There was a rattle in his throat, and he was bleeding profusely. "Would you take him to Orlay Street?" asked somebody, and without waiting for an answer, somebody else was pulling a medic's white smock over my head.

Laci found a short ladder that could be used as a stretcher. We tied the poor man onto it and started out through the gardens, the same way we had come. We were heading toward the office of Dr. Bakay on Orlay Street. It was a long walk and a very hard struggle. The dying man was heavy, the night was dark, and the terrain was impossible. It must have taken an hour to cover this distance of less than a mile. Bakay's office was full of wounded people. We left the poor man on the floor and turned to go back to the square. We brought our ladder-stretcher with us, just in case.

It must have been about midnight when we got back. On the square, all hell had broken loose. Houses were on fire, and muzzle flashes illuminated the sky. The detonations tortured my eardrums and paralyzed my mind. What I felt was more than panic or terror; it felt as if my mind has short-circuited and stopped functioning altogether, that I had turned into a vegetable from these piercing noises and blinding flashes.

The upper floors of the apartment house that Gyuszi Perr and Marika were defending were already ablaze. Cracking and crashing sounds mixed with the thunder of the tank cannons. The front of the building faced the square, and its back was toward Gellért Hill. On the back, or courtyard, side of the burning house an outside corridor ran along the whole length of the building. There I saw Professor Bónis from the metallurgy department on the second floor. He was running from one apartment to the next on that long balcony with his submachine gun at the ready.[3]

Most of the firing was by the Russians. In the center of the square the Soviet tanks stood in a circle, like the pioneers' wagons when attacked by Indians. The freedom fighters fired only intermittently; many of their guns had fallen silent. The tanks, on the other hand, were systematically firing their salvos at each window in which they saw movement or from which they received fire. We ran up to the first-floor apartment where Gyuszi Perr and Marika were fighting with their machine gun. The apartment had received several hits. The wall facing the square was gone, and the floor was knee-deep in debris.

The members of Gyuszi's group occupied several apartments on that floor. Every time the Russian gun barrels turned toward their location, they would run out onto the outside corridor in the back. Gyuszi's machine gun was still operational but was low on ammunition. He was working hard to pierce the gasoline container of the nearest tank, but on these new tanks, the gasoline reservoir was not on the outside but under the armor. Therefore it was next to impossible to puncture it. In spite of that, I could see four or five Soviet tanks that had been destroyed. The one tank that we were able to take to the square had done most of that damage, but now it was silent. Gyuszi's persistent firing at the gas tanks and the Molotov cocktails he lobbed at them afterward had done some damage, too.

Our one tank that had made it to Móricz Square, the one that was driven by the young lieutenant whose brother had died during the first attack, now looked like a pile of junk metal. Both our tank and our one anti-aircraft cannon were facing into Villányi Street's west entrance into the square (see fig. 3). So when the Russians attacked from Fehérvári Street to the south of the square, our fighters' backs became exposed. Still, they stopped the Bartók Street tank column. If we had had just one other tank at the entrance of Fehérvári Street, the outcome could have been different.

There were no Russian infantryman on the square yet; they were waiting next to the tennis courts at the Bottomless Lake. They were waiting for our small-arms fire to subside. Behind all the thunder and chaos, when the noise subsided for a few seconds, we could still hear the broadcasts of Radio Free Europe. It was now Monday morning, November 5, the morning of the day before election day in the United States. The radio was broadcasting a speech by Eisenhower, which he had made four years ago during the previous election campaign, when he announced his "policy of liberation." This policy was our last straw of hope, and we hung onto it. We fought on to give him time to make his move, to support his words with deeds.

Now Gyuszi Perr had noticed the movement of a tank cannon toward the window of our own apartment and yelled, "Escape to the back corridor!" We scrambled out of the room and ran toward the entrance of the apartment on the balcony in the back. When she reached the door, though, Marika turned around and ran back for the bread. "Come back! Leave it!" roared Gyuszi, but it was too late. All we saw was one blinding flash, all we heard was one piercing blast, and a second or two later we saw a puff of smoke and dust billowing out of the apartment door and rolling down the side of the building.

Gyuszi was out of his mind. He was down on all fours, groping and fumbling around, coughing his lungs out. His face was covered with black soot except for the two lines that the streaming tears had washed on his face. We all tried to find Marika. I had covered my mouth with my handkerchief, so I was not coughing too hard. Lacika, also down on all fours, screamed. He had grabbed a piece of red-hot metal, either a piece of the exploded shell or the barrel of Gyuszi's machine gun. As I crawled blindly in the smoke and dust, I almost fell out onto the square, because the front wall of the apartment, the wall facing the square, had completely disappeared, and the smoke was so thick that I could not tell the inside from the outside.

Suddenly there was total silence. We held our coughing, and during this temporary lull we all could hear a slow dripping noise coming from the back of the room. We all crawled into that darkest corner, and then Gyuszi reached into something sticky. As he did, we all heard a pained, animal squeak. It was Marika's leg that he had touched. She was half covered by plaster, her clothing was in shreds, and the wound on her leg was so deep that the knee bone was visible. She was still holding on to the loaf of bread she had gone to save when the tank fired.

The little blonde gymnast was white as a sheet—white as my medic's smock. She was limp and light as we carried her down to the basement. We bandaged her up to stop the bleeding and started out once more with our ladder-stretcher toward the Orlay Street office of Dr. Bakay. Our load was much lighter than during the previous trip. Marika was still holding onto the loaf of bread. We covered her closed eyes so that the flashes of the cannon blasts would not frighten her. Our progress was faster than before. By now we had learned the way, and Marika did not weigh much at all.

Dr. Bakay's office floor was completely covered with the bodies of the wounded. We were stepping over people as we finally found a bit of room in one corridor where we managed to put her down. Gyuszi was talking to the doctor. Marika had lost consciousness. As we waited for Gyuszi, it appeared as if her eyelids moved. I knelt down next to her. Her mouth also moved a tiny bit. I put my ear to her mouth to hear her frail little whisper, "Öcsi, there is some candy in my right pocket; take some."[4]

My heart was in my mouth. I did not know what to say; I did not know what to do. I felt this enormous anger and frustration. It would have felt so good to be able to cry, to weep over my little sister, to cry over our dreams, the dreams of the millions who had dared to give everything they had, who believed—but I could not. I could not because of an anger that was welling up inside me. I wanted to call down the wrath of God on those Red butchers. And I wanted to do the same to the idle bureaucrats of the UN and to the oil-hungry businessman manipulating the Suez crisis. I wanted to curse the rich and heartless leaders of the West and the lying American president. And I wanted to curse myself, most of all myself, for having talked this little girl and so many others into believing that there is justice, that we could win, and that liberty is more precious than life itself, when all I really did was to talk them into committing suicide.

CHAPTER 13

Interrogation

LEAVING BAKAY'S OFFICE, we heard commands being yelled in Russian on Bartók Street. The Russians were close, but they could not see us because the street corner was blocking their view. Now I heard a round of submachine-gun fire, followed by the wails of a male voice. It quickly subsided into a death rattle. We were frozen like four statues in the gateway of the doctor's office on Orlay Street. It was Gyuszi who first regained his composure.

"Let's leave our weapons in these bushes," he said. "Thanks to our white smocks, if we are unarmed, they might not fire, and we might stand a chance." He put down his submachine gun. We did the same and started inching slowly toward the Bartók Street corner. This was the first time in my life that I was glad I had had to endure seven years of compulsory Russian. "Nye stryelyatyes!" "Don't shoot!" I yelled from behind the protection of the corner. We kept yelling for a good five minutes. We also tried to holler more complicated sentences indicating that we were stretcher bearers, or medical orderlies, that we were unarmed, and that they should hold their fire before we emerged from behind the corner.

There was no reply, no response of any kind, so we started shouting again. We stopped periodically, waited for a reply, and when we received none, started again. We heard nothing, received no answer, heard no movement, yet we felt, we knew, that they were right there, just a few yards from us, on the other side of the corner. They were watching and waiting. The windows of the corner store were broken, but the goods were untouched; nothing had been stolen. At other times, that sight would have filled me with pride—pride in my people, pride in the honor of our Revolution—but now I could not have cared less; now my mind was concentrated on survival and nothing else.

Finally, Gyuszi gave a hand signal, and we started slowly forward, with arms lifted high into the air. We walked to the middle of the street. I had already reached the tram rails, and the street was still quiet. The darkness of the night was beginning to lift, and in the first blush of dawn I could see a long row of dark figures on both sides of the street. They were lying on the sidewalks next to the walls of the buildings. I heard an inarticulate command and the steps of a dozen feet running toward us, and then I felt a sharp pain in my back.

I lunged forward and almost fell from the blow. Lacika was next to me. A Russian soldier was pushing him forward with the muzzle of a submachine gun in his back. My heart was in my throat, my eyes were glued to the index finger of Laci's capturer. That finger stayed right on the trigger while he thrust and heaved Laci forward.

The soldier behind me was engulfed in a cloud of rank sweat and vodka fumes. As he shoved me forward I could see his boots and his extra-long overcoat, which had no hemming. It dragged on the pavement. Every time he shoved me forward, he said either "Fascist!" or "Imperialist!" He must have thought I was an Israeli medic and that we were at the Suez Canal. He probably thought the Danube was the Red Sea.

They marched us down Csáky Street and stopped in front of gate four of the university. We waited there. Finally, a Russian officer came. I could hear his swearing from a hundred yards away and could see the drawn pistol in his vehemently gesticulating hand. He kept screaming while he clattered toward us and continued to do so after he arrived.

I did not understand what he was saying, but in his long-winded question I did recognize the names of our prime minister, Imre Nagy, and the Communist puppet who preceded him, Mátyás Rákosi. I finally realized that the officer wanted to know whose side we were on.

The soldier behind me periodically stabbed the sharp muzzle of his gun into my back. The pain was becoming unbearable. My stomach was in my throat and my mouth was dry as I finally stammered out that unspeakably ugly word: "Rákosi." After that, as if to prove that on the road of betrayal, only the first step is difficult, I pulled out my red athlete's certificate, using its color to prove that I was one of them. As I did this, in the depths of my soul I already knew that I would forever be ashamed of this action, and that in my dreams I would keep reliving and correcting that terrible act as long as I lived.

The Russian officer could not have cared less about the color of my athlete's certificate. He wanted to know about the defense of the university and about the resistance he could expect from the buildings on the other side of the gate. When we told him that there would be no resistance at all, that the university had been evacuated, he studied our faces and then decided to enter. He told us to walk slowly in front of them, keeping our hands in the air, while they followed us from the cover of the bushes. We did just that. We walked very slowly. It was daybreak by the time we reached the library. There stood the tanks and the anti-aircraft guns that we had been unable to move. In this semidarkness the guns looked even larger and more menacing than I had remembered.

The officer told us to yell that we were Hungarians and that "they" should not fire. We obeyed, knowing that there was nobody to hear us except for the few people who had stayed in the medical emergency room. As we entered the dark and empty main building, the corridors were full of the guns, blankets, and other belongings of the cadets who had decided to go home instead of fighting. Our hands were still in the air as we marched through those corridors and eventually reached the main aula. All was dark and quiet.

The officer strode into our MEFESZ office, which—it seemed ages ago, but in fact had been only two weeks before—had served as the Communist Party's main office at the university. When he disappeared, the guards lined us up before the door, in single file, and finally allowed us to lower our aching arms. On our left were the offices and on our right stood a row of the busts of the past rectors of the university. I was standing next to the bronze bust of Rector Stocek. By now, there must have been a dozen of us in the line. The Russians found the people in the medical emergency room, and now they, too, stood in the line with us.

We stood in that line for two or three hours on that Tuesday morning, November 6. Finally, at about eight o'clock, a Russian colonel arrived with two assistants. They did not even look at us, but just marched into the MEFESZ office. A few minutes later, I saw that the guards searched the young man at the front of the line and, after that, took him into the office. When I saw that, I reflexively smoothed over my pockets, and as I touched the right side pocket of my corduroy jacket, I felt something hard. It was the little lady's pistol from Czechoslovakia that the police chief Sándor Kopácsi had given me.

Now I was really scared. I had to get rid of it, but how? There was nothing within my reach except Stocek's bronze bust, which was sitting on the marble stand to my right. The guards were already searching the second person in the line, so I did not have much time. I grabbed the pistol in my right hand. It was so small that it practically disappeared in my palm. I waited until the guards started searching the third person, and at that instant I attempted to lift the bust with my left hand.

I leaned against the bust and strained with all my might to lift that chunk of metal. After a second or two, which seemed like an eternity, a small crack appeared at the bottom, and the bust started to tilt slowly backward. Then I pushed even harder, and with superhuman effort I managed to increase the crack a bit more. Suddenly, something let go, and the bust started to tip backward while the crack opened very quickly. I let go with my left hand and slipped the pistol under the bust with my right. Rector Stocek hesitated for a split second and then fell back into his original position. We would have heard a thud if at that instant Laci had not started coughing like a maniac, drowning out the sound made as the bust fell back into place.

As the bust ingested my pistol, I made a solemn promise that in exchange for his assistance, at the first opportunity I would get, I would look up the accomplishments of Rector Stocek and then miss no opportunity to spread the word of his greatness.[1]

It must have been about nine o'clock when it was my turn to be searched. After that they took me into the MEFESZ office, where the Russian colonel sat on Kati Szőke's desk. He was looking through Kati's

Figure 17. The door of the MEFESZ office, where the Russians held the interrogation, is in the center. We were lined up single-file to the left of the door. The bust of President Stocek, under which I hid my pistol, is the first on the left.

papers, the various forms, including the national guard membership cards. He was tall, graying, well informed, and he spoke fluent Hungarian. He knew where he was. He did not talk about the Suez Canal or fascists. The colonel seemed to be shaken by what he had seen on Móricz Square. He kept asking about the defenders: "Were there school girls among them? Did I see that right?" he asked twice, and each time I nodded yes. His eyes were sad; he seemed embarrassed for having fought and killed children.

"We were carrying the wounded," I said, pointing at the blood on my white smock. He did not seem to care about what I had done. He seemed to be thinking about something, staring into the air. So I tried to change the subject. "Why is your pistol-case made of wood?" I asked in a conversational tone. As if I had woken him up, he gave me a surprised look, then took off his belt and showed me. The wooden case could be attached to the butt of the pistol to create a weapon that could be held against the shoulder. "When you are aiming at a target at some distance, this contraption steadies your aim," he told me.

Throughout the "interrogation," the colonel appeared to be absent minded, apologetic, while his two aides (neither of whom spoke any Hungarian) seemed suspicious. They seemed suspicious not of me, but of him. It was obvious that they were fresh troops, while he had been stationed in Hungary for some time.

After the questioning, we were all taken to the KA-51 lecture hall, which they had converted into a temporary prison. That hall had served many functions during the past two weeks. It was there, exactly two weeks ago, that Professor Mutnyánszky, whom we called Mutyi Bácsi, had told us that we had more important things to do than to listen to his lecture on mechanics. It was in this hall that we had kept our ÁVH prisoners, and it was here that we had deposited the gifts of the Hungarian villagers and later those of the Austrians. Here we were again, except this time we were the prisoners.

Laci was sitting on my left. On my right were Ili Tóth and her sister, the two medical students who had stayed in our medical emergency room. The guards were down in the front of the hall near the blackboards. In this lecture hall, with each row of chairs higher than the one in front, we looked down at the guards. They ordered us to sit on the turn-out writing tables that were attached to each chair. That way they could see our hands. There must have been about twenty of us, but our numbers were still increasing as the guards brought in other unarmed people who had been captured on the streets.

At first we were not allowed to speak at all. Later, we noticed that the guards periodically disappeared, and when they returned their mood was happier than when they had left. They must have found a liquor cabinet. The atmosphere was calmer now; we felt relieved. The guards did not look like people who were about to shoot us. Summing up the situation, Laci commented, "Jail or Siberia, yes! Firing squad, no!"

Laci was blond and handsome, my age. We were classmates in the Eötvös High School, and we both were majoring in ship design. Actually, I had picked that major because Laci had selected it, and I wanted to be with him. In high school some called Laci a homosexual because he was always horsing around with his friend Elekes. Those who spread that rumor simply misunderstood his playful love of life and the immense happiness he radiated. To him, life was a big joke, and he did his best to live it lightheartedly.

"Why don't you take off that bloody smock?" Laci asked. He had already taken his off and was sitting in his neat, tailor-made, broad-shouldered sports jacket. The other indispensable component of his teddy-boy uniform was his drainpipe trousers, which were so tight that he had to open zippers to take them off. Laci always paid attention to his appearance. I could not possibly have competed with him. My officer's boots were scuffed now, and my purple corduroy jacket had gotten so dirty that I could stand it up on the floor.

"Why were you crying in the morning?" he asked. At first I did not understand, then I realized that he was talking about yesterday morning, when he had found me on the floor next to the radio.

"I didn't realize I was crying!"

"Yes, you were. You were as white as the wall. Your tears were flowing, and you kept repeating something like, 'Don't let it happen!'"

"Yeah! I remember. After Imre Nagy's speech I lost control; life lost its purpose. But I didn't know I was crying."

"Well you were. It took me some time to cheer you up. You'd better be grateful!"

"OK, I'm grateful. Still, the fact remains that almost everybody ran away when they should have fought. And another fact is that Marika is dying, and we are about to be deported to a cooler climate. In other words, I did have a point."

Laci was trying to reach down to pick up one of those good-smelling oranges that had been left in the hall—the kind individually wrapped in tissue paper—but the screaming of the Russian guard stopped him. When a couple minutes later the guard left, he picked up the orange anyway, started peeling it, and asked, "Have you seen the collection boxes of the Writers' Union? All that paper money! That was some sight!"

"Sure I did. I left one hundred twenty of my one hundred forty forints scholarship in one of them. The remaining twenty forints are still here. I haven't spent a penny during the last two weeks. Nobody would take my money. Not for food, not for anything."

The orange was peeled now. He offered me a grayish, soot-covered slice while shrugging his shoulders to indicate that he had had no opportunity to wash his hands. The orange had an unusual taste. The juices of the fruit waged a futile struggle to overcome the taste of gunpowder, charcoal, and dirt.

"Did you hear the broadcasts of Radio Free Europe on Móricz Square?" Laci asked.

"Well, same as you. A few sentences between the cannon bursts. I did hear about Eisenhower's policy of liberation and the American veterans' vote to help us. That sounds important. I guess they represent all the veterans of the United States. That is something. Do you think they will help?"

Laci was quiet for a moment, his face serious, then he answered, "All I know is that one day they too will need the help of their friends, and God had better make sure that they get no more than the help they are giving us right now. I pray to God for that. I hope that one day they, too, will experience what I feel now, that they will get what they deserve."

At that moment four new soldiers entered the lecture room. They spoke to an elderly fireman among us prisoners; they were looking at his uniform, asking him questions. The old man did not understand a word of what they were saying. I overheard the word *fascist,* and as I did, I also noticed some similarities in the fireman's uniform and that of the German SS. Laci whispered to me, "Hitler wasn't born yet when the fireman of this university were already wearing that uniform. I hope this Mongolian soldier knows that."

Now a Russian officer joined the four soldiers. They said nothing to anyone, but grabbed the fireman and marched him out. There was petrified silence in the lecture room. We held our breath with bad premonition for a few minutes. "Oh, I guess they just moved him to some other jail," said Laci, but immediately after that we heard the burst of machine-gun fire.

"Those goddamned animals, those devils!" growled Laci. I was so shocked that I could not speak for minutes. After our shock and silence melted, I asked him, "If you believe in the devil, do you also believe in God?"

"I don't know. What I do believe, though, is that this little planet is more special than we think. Now that we have conquered nature, now that we are directing our own evolution, now the survival of life is up to us. We probably can't destroy life or nature, but we certainly can destroy ourselves."

Figure 18. The burnt-out apartments of Móricz Square after the fight.
Courtesy *Nemzetôr*

Our discussion went on for a long time. We talked about the devil
and God. We agreed that the devil is hate, and the best way to fight it is
by emphasizing the good in everything and everybody. The morning
turned into afternoon, then evening. I was getting very hungry. Sitting on that hard, turn-out table was painful, but the discomfort was
not the worst. The worst was my hopeless mood. My soul resembled
the burnt-out houses of Móricz Square.

I felt completely exhausted on that Monday night. Sunday night, I
had stayed up carrying the wounded; Saturday night we had all stayed
up listening to Imre Nagy's last words; Friday night, I was in the Óvár
jail; and the night before that, I was up preparing Jancsi Danner's bier.
So as midnight approached, I found it harder and harder to keep my
eyes open.

CHAPTER 14

Home

I FELT A KICK ON MY FOOT. I woke up and looked around as things slowly began to come back to me. Laci was on my left, Ili on my right, but I did not see Gyuszi Perr or Imre Majoross, and it seemed that we were fewer now than a moment ago when I had closed my eyes. Down around the professor's desk, the guards were snoring. Up at the other end of the lecture hall, the entrance door was open. "The guards are dead drunk! This is the time to get out!" whispered Laci.

We rose slowly and tiptoed up to the open door. All we heard was snoring as we quietly made our way through the dark corridor. The night was very dark as we descended into the basement and exited the building through the back door of the gymnasium. There were no Russians to be seen, but we were playing it safe anyway. We stayed in the dark, sneaking from bush to bush. On Budafoki Street, Laci bid us farewell.[1]

Ili and her sister had a rented room nearby. They asked me to walk them home. When I agreed, they hooked into my arms as we strolled through the dark and empty streets in the first glimmer of dawn. In the room I saw only one double bed. "So, how will we do this?" I asked, and they replied in unison, "I will sleep in the easy chair." So I took off my boots and jacket and hit the bed. I do not know what happened next. All I remember is that during the night, when I was turning around, I touched Ili. Her body felt tense, but I could have just imagined that.

In any case, when I woke up the next morning we were all in the same bed, with plenty of space. It was warm and cozy. They had no food, so breakfast was out of the question, and with the girls watching I did not feel like washing myself, so I said a quick farewell and left.[2]

It was midmorning. One could hear bursts of gunfire from the Pest side of the Danube. Here, on the Buda side, all was quiet. It felt strange that the submachine gun was not pulling on my right shoulder. I had gotten so used to the gun that I felt incomplete without it. I still had my tricolored armband. The streets were empty; there was no traffic. It was a workday, but on this day nobody worked.

I walked across the empty Freedom Bridge. The Russian tanks stationed at the bridgehead paid no attention to me. I walked over to the Pest side to visit Ágnes. The burnt-out houses and tanks were still smoking, and unburied corpses were visible everywhere. I saw the remains of a Russian soldier in the hatchway of a burnt-out tank. His clothing had burned away, and his body had shrunk to the size of a child. The Russian tanks were occupying the main avenues but had not entered the side streets. One could not see the Russian soldiers; they felt safer inside their tanks.

While walking on Rákoczy Street I noticed a Russian soldier opening the escape hatch of his tank and sticking his head out. The immediate response was a burst of gunfire from the roof of a burnt-out building. The Russian head disappeared, and the three tanks aimed their cannons at the roof.

Because of the fighting on Rákoczy Street, I crossed over to the next parallel street, Wesselényi Street, and on it I walked toward the Grand Boulevard. As I reached the corner of Akácfa Street, I heard firing, and one of the bullets hit the wall behind me. I suspect that this round of bullets was intended for me. There must have been ÁVH snipers in the area. Now, with the Russian tanks all over, those brave souls once again dared to be sniping at the freedom fighters and the members of the national guard. For a second I considered removing my armband, but I could not make myself do it, so I just proceeded a bit more carefully. I tried to flatten myself against the walls of the buildings. As I advanced on Wesselényi Street and approached the Kertész Street corner, I saw a Russian tank at the Wesselényi Street entrance into the Grand Boulevard. The tank cannon had been lowered and was pointing right into Wesselényi Street.

As I carefully lurked forward, I saw a group of about ten people—unarmed, older workers—protected by the corner of Kertész Street. Apparently they wanted to cross the Boulevard, but could not because of the tank. As I reached them, I heard the siren of an ambulance coming from behind me. As I turned, I saw a minivan with a large Red Cross flag covering its roof. As the driver noticed the tank, the ambulance slowed down.

A blonde nurse was sitting next to the driver. She was leaning forward, staring at the tank. As the ambulance passed us at the Akácfa Street corner, the tank fired. By the time I heard the blast, the Red Cross car had just reached our corner. The explosion was deafening. The left half of the car was crumpled, like a sardine can when hit by a hammer. The driver had disappeared. We stared at the burning wreckage, frozen by shock and fear.

The blond nurse freed herself, then opened the door on the right and tried to stumble out. Now she was on one knee in the middle of the street, facing the tank, about ten or fifteen yards from us, except that we were protected by the corner of the building while she was totally exposed. Now she stood up. She was not more than eighteen. She turned to walk toward the wounded patient in the burning ambulance when the tank machine gun fired. The girl was hit. She lost her balance and fell onto the hood of the burning car. I could hear the burning of her hair, I could see her skin turning darker. I bit my lips. I tasted blood in my mouth.

A bald worker picked up a garbage can and, holding it in front of him, ran out into the street. There was another burst of machine-gun fire, and the next second he was moaning in a pool of blood. The garbage can was full of holes; the bullets had gone through it as if it were made of tinfoil.

Then somebody started pulling on the waterspout running down the side of the building. Our frozen, paralyzed group came to life, and like frenzied lunatics we began tearing at the drain pipe. Our hands

Figure 19. Hiding behind street corners. Courtesy *Nemzetôr*

were bleeding, we pushed and stepped on each other, rust and plaster was falling into our eyes, our clothing was torn, but eventually the pipe began to give, as our frantic efforts paid off. With the ten-yard-long pipe we pulled the girl off the burning car. Her long, blonde hair was gone, her white smock was dark, and so was her skin. Only her open eyes and her teeth were white. It took about half an hour to pull the two dead bodies into the protection of our street corner. The driver and the patient both burned in the car. The tank's machine gun kept firing throughout this ordeal.

Those thirty minutes filled me with such intense hatred that I could have dropped the atomic bomb on Moscow. The people in my group looked like madmen. It took decades to get rid of that terrible hatred, but to forget that girl, to forget the senselessness of a child being roasted like a pig—that I cannot forget and never will.

It took some effort to cross the boulevard, but I finally succeeded. There was nobody in Ágnes's apartment. When I asked the superintendent about her family's whereabouts, he was not communicative at all. It must have been my armband that scared him. The old slave reflexes were already returning. His answers could not have been shorter: "They left for Austria."

"Who are *they?*"

"The boy and the girl."

"Which girl?"

"The blond one."

He walked away, indicating that the discussion was over. So Judit and Gábor had left, and Ágnes was probably still at Lake Balaton.

What should I do now? It was past noon. I was getting very hungry. I also could hear the intense fighting that was still raging around the triangle formed by the Kilián Barracks, Corvin Plaza, and Tüzoltó Street. I started walking in that direction, toward the south. I stayed to the east of the main boulevard, which was bumper to bumper with Russian tanks. It took some effort to cross Rákoczi Street. After that, the thunder intensified. I not only heard the roar of tank cannons but also the scream of mine throwers and the rattle of the Russian aircraft overhead. My progress was slow. I hoped to reach Pista Angyal's group in Tüzoltó Street, but when I got near, I found that crossing Üllői Street was impossible. The street was full of tanks, and they fired at anything that moved. So I stayed in the side streets and eventually reached István Hospital on Nagyvárad Square.

"You cannot enter with arms, you have to leave all your arms here!" said the porter.

"That will be easy, since I have none. Where do I get something to eat?" I asked in return.

"Go to the cafeteria in the basement. They probably have some soup, left over from lunch."

It was 2:00 or 3:00 P.M. on this ugly, ugly day. I got a tray, got my twenty forints ready, and loaded my plate with two bowls of soup and a half-dozen big slices of bread. I had not eaten in nearly two days, so I was ready for a feast.

"How much is that?" I asked the woman cashier.

"It's a lot," she answered, smiling.

"But how much money do I owe you?" I asked again.

"Looking at you, it is I who probably owes you a lot!" she replied, and waved me on.

"I just can't get rid of this twenty-forint bill!" I complained jokingly, and settled down to stuff myself.

The cafeteria was mostly empty. A doctor with black-ringed eyes was drinking espresso at the next table. His hands trembled as he stirred the coffee. Another doctor was copying a list or something, while two nurses were standing in the corner, talking to a cleaning lady. I got down to some serious eating. When I finished the first bowl, I put the second soup plate into the empty one so as not to overadvertise my appetite. The windows were trembling from the detonations, the hospital was overflowing with the wounded, yet the cafeteria was peaceful and my mind was blank. I concentrated on eating.

When I was done with the two bowls of soup, I still had two slices of bread left. I was in the process of stuffing them into the side pocket of my corduroy jacket when I heard a familiar voice: "Is this another test of yours? Are you testing the holding capacity of the human stomach?"

"If it is not the coffee man," I said with a happy grin, looking at Pista Angyal.

"So, how are you progressing with your comparative study of the Jewish-Hungarian and German-Hungarian characters?" he asked. He too was grinning, but I did not answer. Pista looked at me very seriously and asked, "What is it?"

"The test is over. There is no German-Hungarian to compare you with. Jancsi Danner is dead." I was nearly screaming. He put his hand on my shoulder and, after a long, long while, mumbled to no one in particular, "It doesn't look good, does it?"

Pista was with his co-commander, a fellow named Olaf, and a Russian called Vaszil. It was not clear who this Vaszil was, although they seemed to be good friends, and he seemed to be on our side. They asked me about the defense of Móricz Square, and I asked them about their prospects here in the ninth district.

"We are holding our own and are trying to arrange a forty-eight-hour cease-fire with the Russians. They agreed to a meeting and supposedly we will learn the time and place of it at five o'clock this evening. This is why we are here. We are waiting for that call."

"Why can't you call from your garage?" I asked.

"Oh, they have pulverized us with bombs and cannon fire. We have no telephone, no electricity, no water, nothing. They are lobbing grenades at us and are now attacking from the air as well."

"So what is next?" I came to the bottom line.

Pista looked at the floor, then at Olaf, before answering. "The Kilián Barracks is in the process of giving up. Their defenders, the ones with some heart left, are now joining us. Only Corvin Alley, Csepel Island, and Stalin City are still holding out. They, too, are running low on ammunition. The civilians in the ninth district are begging us to give up. This is why we are here. We want to arrange an honorable cease-fire with the Russians. We will try to do that at five o'clock. After that, we'll either talk or fight on, but before either, we will have to get some bread. You are not the only one with a big appetite, you know!"

While Pista, Olaf, and Vaszil were waiting for the telephone call, we talked some more. Pista told me that he had faith in János Kádár. Pista thought that Kádár was a Communist whose quarrel with the Soviets was not so much about their social model as about their totalitarian methods and their occupation of other people's countries. He was op-timistic about the cease-fire and was planning to put up red and black flags next to the Hungarian tricolor on their building. It was nearing five o'clock when I said farewell to them.[3]

Kerepes was twenty kilometers (twelve and a half miles) to the north-east of Budapest. It took me three or four hours to walk home that evening. On Hungária Boulevard some pockets of freedom fighters were still holding out, while others had given up and were on their way home. As I approached the Russian-held airport at Mátyásföld, the road looked like a scene from the Second World War. I had not realized that there were so many tanks in the whole world. Each tank column was a mile long, and they just kept coming, one after the other. Whenever I heard fighting, I detoured into the cornfields and returned to the main road when it seemed to be safe to do so.[4]

Kornél Poppe, our neighbor's son, was also on his way home, so we walked together. There were no Hungarian vehicles on the road. The few pedestrians we met seemed scared when they noticed my armband and did not dare to look me in the eye. Kornél acted as if he did not notice it, but when we got to the outskirts of our village, he decided to take a back road, so I walked home alone. It was dark. As I reached the gate to my house, Bukucs went out of his mind with excitement. He was licking me and climbing all over me while alternately lying on his back and showing his belly. This was his sign of ultimate submission.[5]

Then I heard a suppressed scream and saw Memi running toward me. She was checking me over for wounds when Aptyi arrived. He just took me in his arms and held me. I did not say anything, but after a while, like ice melting or like a volcano building up pressure for eruption, I began to feel an avalanche of emotion that I could no longer control, and I burst into uncontrollable, sobbing and tears.

When we finally straightened out, Aptyi's voice was choked. He turned in the direction I had come from and said, "Well, it's time to go." I had no idea what he meant. Why were we not going into the house? Where were Péter and Andris?[6] We were already out on the road when he explained: "This morning the house was searched by the ÁVH. The Pufajkas were looking for you. So you cannot sleep here."

We were on our way to one of our neighbors, Szabó Bácsi. I would sleep there. They had planned everything. Memi had packed some food, had got me clean underwear, and, without saying it in so many words, let me know that the less time I spent in Kerepes, the better it would be. The Szabós were very nice. They tried very hard not to show that they hated the idea of my being in their house. But it was obvious that they were scared stiff.

My mother, father, and I sat there for a couple of hours, talking without saying anything that the others did not know. We were trying to reassure each other without knowing how that could possibly be done. About midnight, I asked them to go home and told them that I would leave for Budapest early in the morning.

CHAPTER 15

Escaping Hungary

I WOKE TO ANOTHER UGLY DAY. As I dressed, I noticed that my tricolor armband had disappeared. That was my mother's style. It probably was better that way, because I would not have taken it off on my own, and wearing it would have been an invitation to immediate arrest.

It was a long walk back to Budapest. When I reached the city, I could tell from the blasts that Pista Angyal had not gotten his cease-fire from the Russians. The cannon fire and the explosions were unceasing. This was a cloudy day anyway, and the smoke that covered the whole ninth district made it even darker. It was clear that Pista Angyal and the boys at the Corvin were putting up quite a fight.

I let my feet do the thinking, and they got me to gate two of the Technical University. Only when I arrived there did I realize that my home base was gone. Russian soldiers and Pufajkas were standing at the gate. Russian tanks were everywhere. In spite of that, I could not help moving even closer and finally saw a familiar face, that of Zsiga Nagy, one of the MEFESZ leaders of the Agro-Technical University. He was approaching the gate from the opposite direction. His expression was the same as mine. When he got closer, I shook my head and pointed to the other side of the street. He understood and followed me there.

"So, what is happening?" I asked him.

"The Pufajkas paid my parents a visit, and I took off through the back door," he replied.

"Well, that is my story too. So what do we do?"

"Whatever it is, let's do it together," he replied. After that we did a lot of walking. At each street corner, before proceeding, we would stop and check for Russian patrols. Zsiga had heard that the Russians were deporting all young people they caught on the streets.[1] As night fell, we saw a burnt-out bus on Karinthy Street and decided to make it our bedroom. I emptied a couple of garbage cans onto its floor to provide a softer layer. My corduroy jacket acquired yet another layer of dirt, and yet another night passed.

The events of the days that followed are no longer distinct in my mind. They merge together into a couple of weeks of hopeless hiding, depressed wandering. Zsiga and I simply concentrated on avoiding all the places where the Pufajkas might expect us to go.

On each day in the early morning a Russian truck drove down Karinthy Street bringing bread to the troops. It had to make a sharp turn onto Budafoki Street. As it turned, it slowed down. I was a good runner. Even in boots, I could catch it on most mornings. Therefore, on my fast days, I grabbed a loaf of bread and we had something to eat.

As the days passed, we made contact with the remaining centers of resistance. The MEFESZ activity now was directed from the building of the former Piarist Gymnasium on the Pest side of the Danube. We spent a few days there, printing and distributing leaflets calling for a general strike and demanding the withdrawal of Soviet troops. The city was full of graffiti reading "Russians go home!" What we posted in the morning, the Pufajkas ripped down by the afternoon. Gyurka Gömöri was one of the leaders. He wrote several of the handbills.[2]

We also ran into Igor Sík. His father was back as the foreign minister of Kádár's puppet regime and also acted as Hungary's UN representative. Igor was on our side and was still doing his Russian-language short-wave radio broadcasts in which he explained to the fresh troops that they were not at the Suez Canal and that they were not fighting Israelis or Nazis but were oppressing Hungarians.

On Friday, November 9, we held a MEFESZ meeting in the student dormitory on top of Castle Hill (see map). The attendees of the meeting appointed us (Zsiga and me) to maintain contact with the Revolutionary Workers Council of Budapest. When the director of the dormitory, a fellow named Kutassi, heard that we were living in a burnt-out bus, he forged some documents, and for a week or so we had our own beds in his dormitory.

On November 14 I participated in the meeting at United Izzó, which elected Sándor Rácz as the president of all the Revolutionary Workers Councils of Budapest. Sándor was a deeply religious twenty-three-year-old peasant boy. He was also a born leader, patriotic, and brave—and, most importantly, he understood that the job of a real leader was not to follow public opinion but to lead it. He stationed armed guards around the factory. No Russians were allowed in, and none even tried to enter the factory grounds. He ordered a nationwide general strike and started negotiations with the real seat of power in Hungary, the Russian military headquarters. He had a sense of history about him. What impressed me most was his inner strength. He always knew what was right, and if something was right, nothing else mattered to him.[3]

The last meeting of the MEFESZ leadership, which I participated in, was held on Saturday, November 17, on Virányos Street in a former ÁVH cottage that had been temporarily abandoned by its owners. At the meeting we learned that on the previous day several hundred people had been arrested on the Pest side. One of those arrested was my friend Pista Angyal. A participant of the MEFESZ meeting, Béla Jankó, the leader of the Medical University, suggested that we could do more for Hungary by escaping to the West and continuing our efforts abroad. He asked for and received authorization to represent the MEFESZ in exile.[4]

About half the delegates, including myself, voted against leaving Hungary and against disbanding the MEFESZ. The rest felt that resistance was hopeless, MEFESZ activity should be terminated, and we should disband. We debated our immediate plans into the night, and it was well after midnight when we, Zsiga and I, left the meeting. Next day we learned that those who stayed at the cottage were all arrested by the Pufajkas. So, by Sunday, November 18, the majority of the MEFESZ leadership was either in jail or on its way to Austria.

While I was hiding in the student dormitory on András Hess Square,

Cardinal Mindszenty accepted asylum at the American Embassy, and the majority of the legitimate government of Hungary, headed by Imre Nagy, took up asylum at the Yugoslav Embassy in Budapest. On Wednesday, November 21, János Kádár, the head of the Soviet-installed puppet regime, sent a written guarantee to the Yugoslav government that Imre Nagy and his ministers would not be harmed if they left the embassy.

On Thursday, November 22, at 6:30 P.M., a bus was sent by Ferenc Münnich (another Hungarian traitor) to take the Nagy group from the Yugoslav Embassy to their homes. When the group boarded the bus, Soviet military personnel surrounded them, forced the Yugoslavs to leave, and took the members of Hungary's government and their families, including fifteen women and seventeen children, to Romania.[5]

Imre Nagy thus joined his predecessors, Lajos Batthyány, the prime minister who had paid with his life for the Hungarian fight for freedom in 1848, and Pál Teleki, the prime minister who had committed suicide when the Germans forced Hungary to give passage to their troops in 1941.[6]

It was late in the night on Thursday, November 22, when Aptyi finally found me. He had been searching for me all that week. He started looking when Radio Free Europe reported that Hungarian refugees were arriving in Austria. The radio gave the names of some relatives who had already arrived in the West while the fighting was still going on in Budapest. In his search, Aptyi visited our various relatives in the capital, visited the Technical University, and finally decided to check in the student dormitory on Castle Hill.

When he finally found me, he was very worried. He told me that since I had left, the Pufajkas had visited them again in Kerepes and had also tried to find me at the university. "They do not know that you are the Öcsi who worked with Colonel Marián. It also seems that they are preparing some kind of a show trial for the Marián group. There is no question that they are on your trail and that you must escape!"

I must have given him a scared and shocked look, because he turned away, but he repeated it once more: "You must escape!" I had never contradicted my father in my life. It never occurred to me that I ever could, but now I said, "I cannot do that, Aptyi. Please do not make me do that!"

His eyes filled with tears as he said, "I will not survive it if they capture you. You and Péter must escape!"

"But I do not want to live as an alien. I cannot! I just cannot!" I continued pleading. He looked at me for a long time. He was slowly shaking his head, tears flowing on his sunburned cheeks, as finally, with much effort, he said, "Shortly I will tell both of you when and where you should meet."

Friday, November 23, was another dreadful day. I knew that I had to obey my father's orders, yet I was hoping that he would change his mind. I spent the day wandering on the narrow, medieval streets of Castle Hill. There, every stone was a history book and every window a witness to the survival struggle of this orphan island of Hungarians, besieged among Germanic and Slavic seas, eroded by the heaving billows of a tragic history.

When I got back to the dormitory, a message was waiting for me. It was in Aptyi's handwriting. "Péter and I will be waiting for you tomorrow at 9 A.M. at the Kelenföld Railroad Station." My breath failed and my heart stopped. What should I do now? I could not think straight. Perhaps Ágnes could help. Maybe she could give me some advice.

It took me an hour to get to her building. The apartment was empty. She was still not home; nobody was. What should I do? It was late in the afternoon. I had to think. I needed peace and quiet. So I walked into a church. As I wandered inside, a priest stepped out of a confessional and asked, "Do you want to talk?"

I grabbed the opportunity, and he pointed me into the confessional. But we did not communicate. He was an older man, and he wanted me to confess, but I did not want his forgiveness—I wanted his advice. He was a talkative person, and what I was in need of was not a talker, but a listener.

He thought that I came in to confess, but I did not want to talk about my sins. He thought that I was silent because my sins were too great. So he tried to console me: "You know son, if one is defending one's homeland and kills in that process, that person is a soldier and the Church does not condemn soldiers. Freedom fighters are also defending their families against aggressors, and as such, they have no choice." The old man kept talking, and I did not say anything. He eventually absolved and blessed me. I left without having said a word about my problem.

I was awake all night. In the morning of Saturday, November 24, I arrived on time at the Kelenföld railroad station. The sight was

Figure 20. On the road to Austria. Courtesy *Nemzetôr*

reminiscent of Hungarian railroad stations during the war: parting families, crying mothers, grave and morose fathers. Péter was ready; only Aptyi came with him: "It would have been too much for your Mother," he said. I cannot describe our good-bye; there are no words for that. After that, Péter and I hung out of the window for many miles, straining our eyes to see that tiny white spot, my father's waving white handkerchief, which had long disappeared.[7]

The train ride to Óvár was uneventful. Most of the passengers were on their way to Austria. Some still carried their guns. On the train, no Pufajkas and no Russians dared show their faces. They felt safer behind the inch-thick steel plates of their tanks. I do not recall now if the train went only as far as Óvár or if we got off there for some other reason. In any case, we did. The Pufajkas had not arrived yet. Only a few Russian tanks stood on the main square. Their hatchways were closed. They had no contact with the population. The main road leading to Austria was full of refugees.

As the crow flies, we started walking toward the border. We had seen no border guards, no Russians, nothing. We had walked for about ten miles when on the hillside behind us we noticed dark figures running towards us. There must have been a hundred of them. It was early

Figure 21. Even freight cars are full of escaping freedom fighters. Photo by Leslie A. Toth

Saturday evening. This was the area where we expected to come across mine fields (all the western borders of Hungary were mined), yet we started to run toward Austria. As we ran, I looked back and noted that the dark running figures were gaining on us. It was at that point that we both heard sheep bells.

A shepherd boy was running in front, followed by his herd. When he reached us and stopped, so did his herd, and we were surrounded by sheep. The boy told us that during the previous weeks he had given a lot of people directions to Austria, and those people usually left their Hungarian forints with him. "You can't pay with forints in Austria," he said. "On the other hand, I can use them just fine."

So I reached into the outside pocket of my corduroy jacket and gave him the twenty-forint bill that I had not been able to spend for a month—for a glorious and unforgettable month.

On the other side of the border the haystacks smelled of peace. The haycock felt invitingly soft as we settled in for the night, and I slept, hoping that I would never wake up.

Postscript

Those Hungarian students and workers and women and fighting children have done more to close the future of Communism than armies of diplomats. They have exposed the brutal hypocrisy of Communism . . . they have torn its mask off. . . . We owe them pride and praise. For their defeat has been itself a triumph.

—*Archibald MacLeish*

N VIENNA, PÉTER DECIDED that we should go to the United States, which, thanks to a bill introduced by President Eisenhower, gave special permission for 32,000 Hungarian refugees to enter the country.[1] A couple of weeks later we arrived in the United States, carried by a military plane and were taken to Camp Kilmer in New Jersey. By Christmas of 1956 some three hundred Hungarian university students were transferred from the camp to a language school at Bard College, a small and progressive college in New York state affiliated with Columbia University. At Bard we learned little English while managing to teach the professors a lot of Hungarian. We also organized the American equivalent of MEFESZ, which we called AHSA (American-Hungarian Student Association). In December 1956 the AHSA members at Bard College elected me as their president, and in that capacity I visited the United Nations, met Povl Bang-Jensen, lectured, and held meetings with international student leaders, including those of the National Student Association of the United States (NSA).[2]

When the language course at Bard College was over, NSA invited the leaders of our student organization, AHSA, to share their offices in Boston. Besides Péter and me, our initial group included AHSA's unpaid secretary (my future wife), the smart and beautiful Márta Szacsvay; our vice-president, Laci Korbuly; his younger brother Dani; and our secretary general, Feri Gárdonyi.[3] In Boston we worked in various jobs (I was a dishwasher, Márta a waitress), and we spent our free time and money to build our student organization. We published a small newsletter, organized lecture tours about the Revolution, tried to secure scholarships for our student members, and prepared a conference in Chicago for the summer of 1957. To the conference we invited a large number of American political leaders, and in response to our invitations we received a number of supporting statements and salutations, including some from the president and the secretary of state.

When September 1957 arrived, we all had scholarships and went off to our different schools to continue our studies. Márta became a drama student at Skidmore College, Péter went to Oklahoma State University to complete his study of animal husbandry, and I went to Stevens Institute of Technology in New Jersey to complete my first degree as a mechanical engineer specializing in ship design.[4] Stevens was an outstanding engineering school full of caring and friendly people. The individuals who most stand out in my memory are Professor Frederick Bowes and his wife, a painter, who tried to ease my loneliness and poverty by asking me sit for her (while practicing her painting) and paid me for sitting. As a result of her talent, now I can prove that my beautiful corduroy jacket once in fact existed.

I was in school at Stevens when the news arrived that Ilonka Tóth had been hanged, and I was also in school on June 16, 1958, when I learned that the Soviets had executed Imre Nagy and his cabinet ministers. In response to that outrage, we tried to capture the Soviet UN Consulate on Park Avenue in New York City to establish a representation of the Free Hungarian Government there. This representation would have been headed by Anna Kéthly, the only member of the Nagy government who lived on free soil. The police of New York City did not approve of our plans, and I ended up in jail.

During the Christmas break of 1958, even before we graduated, Márta and I were married.[5] Members of the Hungarian student association filled the church of Saint Stephen of Hungary on 82nd Street

Figure 22. I was still wearing my beautiful corduroy jacket in 1957.

in New York City. When it was time for me to kneel, I resisted Father Csaba Kilián's hand pressure on my shoulder. He must have thought that I had some objection against kneeling. In fact, I just did not want all our friends to see the holes in the soles of my shoes.

When I graduated in 1959, Márta was still in school. When I started looking for a job in ship design, I quickly learned that I was a "security risk" (because my parents lived behind the Iron Curtain). So I had to

Figure 23. Márta at our wedding in December, 1958

look for work in a field that did not involve the navy. This in the long run turned out to be a good thing for me, because it gave me an opportunity to look around and pick a newly emerging field. At that time automation, computers, and the whole profession of process control was new, so I picked that. I started to work for Crawford & Russell (later John Brown). The specialty of that engineering design firm was to build plastics plants. Sam Russell, the president, had been FDR's commissioner for developing a synthetic rubber industry during World War II. When the Japanese cut off America's natural rubber supplies, it was Sam's job to invent that industry. He did that in two years. He was a man of vision and action. It was a pleasure to work for him.

My first monthly paycheck (before taxes) was $450, and the rent of our little apartment was $125. The kids came right away: Ádámka (diminutive for Adam) in 1960 and Cica (Hungarian for Kitty, which I often use instead of her real name, Ágnes) in 1961. So we were poor, but that did not prevent us from paying for a $680 airplane ticket for Memi to visit us and later for the other grandparents to do the same, when the Communist puppets finally gave them visas. We were both going to school at night. I was getting my master's degree in thermodynamics and was learning about computers, while Márta was studying costume design and getting her master's in English literature, which later allowed her to teach that subject at the Stamford High School. Naturally, we had no money for baby-sitters, so we had to pick our evening courses so that one of us stayed with the kids while the other was in school. Particularly for Márta this was a very difficult period, because, unless I used the bicycle, she was left without a car, locked up with the kids all day.

By 1961, Sam Russell appointed me, at the age of twenty-five, to head the automation department. So I got myself some serious, black-rimmed eyeglasses (which I did not need), grew a beard, and tried to act respectable, mature, and experienced. But I still did not dare hire engineers who were much older than I. Therefore, as the department grew from three employees to twenty-six in ten years, I ended up hiring some very smart but totally inexperienced kids straight out of school. Sam loved their low salaries, but because of their lack of experience they had to be quickly taught at least the basics of our profession. So I got permission to spend every Friday teaching them the art (not the science) of process control. My Fridays' notes had accumulated on my desk when one day a visiting editor, an old-fashioned Dutch-American man named Nick Groonevelt—who still parted his hair in the middle—asked me about them. When I explained what they were, he asked, "Do you realize that your profession has no handbook yet?"

"Naturally," I responded. "Would I be teaching from these pages if it did?"

Nick knew a good thing when he saw one and talked me into editing these notes into a three-volume handbook (today I am working on the fourth edition of *Instrument Engineers' Handbook*). The handbook set was published in 1969, right after the Soviets suppressed the "Prague Spring." It is for that reason that I dedicated it "To the young people of Hungary and Czechoslovakia." Before publication, I wrote to Edward Teller and asked him to write a preface to it, so that between the dedication, the accents on my name, and his participation, it would be clear to the reader that this was not just a handbook, but a Hungarian contribution to science. Ede Bácsi not only obliged, but spent a whole weekend in the library at Lawrence Livermore Laboratory to learn about my strange and mysterious new field of process control. This was about the same time when another Hungarian refugee of the 1956 Revolution, Andy Grove, formed the Intel Corporation.

In the year 1969, Aptyi died. I was with him and held his hand during the last minutes. The loss I cannot describe. After the funeral, I brought back the family Bible from Hungary. From then on, it became my job to register the births, marriages, and deaths in our growing family. It was then that I stopped thinking of myself as Öcsi and became Béla.

Because of Márta's teaching and the royalties from my books, for the first time in our lives we started to have some extra money. The kids were still rather young and did not mind spending time with us, so instead of buying a house (we were still renting), we purchased a ski condominium in Vermont. That was one of the best investments we ever made. It not only gave us some lasting friendships, and we not only enjoyed the fresh air and the honest people of Vermont every weekend, but we also had an opportunity for long talks in front of the fireplace in those peaceful evenings on Okemo mountain. I got myself a bright yellow parka so the kids could always see where Papa was on the slopes, even in a fog or when it was snowing. In front of the fireplace I embroidered my yellow ski parka with Hungarian folk motifs. Over the years, that yellow ski parka became just as much part of me as was my corduroy jacket during the Revolution. I was wearing it when in 1992, with other Hungarian environmentalists, I tried to stop the construction of the last monument to Stalinist gigantomania, the diversion of the Danube into a concrete-sealed canal at Gabcikovo. I was also wearing it when we celebrated the 150th anniversary of the 1848 Revolution with Governor Pataki in New York City. During the cultural part of the program the governor turned to his son with the comment: "That was your grandfather's favorite song." It was good to hear that. It is always good to see that even in our overly materialistic and somewhat atomized society the old values of respecting tradition and heritage survive.

In the early 1970s the children reached the age to join the Hungarian Scouts, and on every weekend we took them to New York City for their meetings and to attend the Hungarian School. Since we had to be there anyway, Márta started teaching there, and she also prepared a brand-new textbook for teaching Hungarian. I, too, did some teaching and for a few years became the director of that small weekend school. It was about that same time that Nick Groonevelt talked me into editing yet another handbook: the *Environmental Engineers' Handbook*. He argued that if I were able to edit the handbook of one new profession, I should be able to do it for another one as well. I enjoyed working on that three-volume set (it covered air, water, and land pollution) and learned a lot in the process. Today, it has also been published in an electronic format on CD.

In 1975 I finally opened my own consulting firm. It was hard to leave Sam Russell and all the good friends at the office, which I had been bicycling to since 1959. I am still in contact with many of those fine engineers today. After opening my own office, I got very lucky. My first clients included IBM, Hewlett Packard, the National Aeronautics and Space Administration, and the U.S. Department of Energy. At times I was sitting at the same table with Bill Gates, who was pitching his QDOS (Quick and Dirty Operating System), while I presented my "Digital Maid," the home computer that made coffee, opened windows, reported blood pressure, refilled the refrigerator, and much more. For IBM I directed a corporationwide effort to minimize energy consumption, reduce pollution, and increase chip production at fifty-three IBM sites. I also assisted in Jimmy Carter's effort to make the United States energy

Figure 24. With Governor Pataki and son at the Kossuth statue in New York City, March, 1998

independent by designing the plants for converting our abundant coal supplies into synthetic fuel. Unfortunately, President Reagan put an end to that program by deciding that it was easier to send the marines to the Middle East than to build coal conversion plants.

To counterbalance all the good things that happened to me in the United States, I also got some bad news from Hungary. In 1977 I learned that the Soviets, in order to obtain a convenient route for their navy into the heart of Europe, forced Hungary and Czechoslovakia to agree on a project that would take the Danube out of its natural riverbed and reroute it into a concrete-sealed canal on Slovak territory. That project was bound to destroy the unique life forms that had evolved in

Europe's only inland sea delta, the delta of the ancient Pannon Sea, called the Szigetköz. In 1977 I did not take such madness seriously; I did not believe that it could actually materialize.

In the 1980s Márta concluded her teaching career, and we built a studio for her. Ever since, she has been working as a ceramic artist and has created some outstanding objects of beauty. Our children were getting their degrees, Ádámka at Columbia and Yale, Cica at Cornell and the Sorbonne. For me the 1980s was the decade when I got involved (working in Hungary with my good friend from the MEFESZ days, Imre Mécs, whose death sentence was commuted in 1963) in an effort to find the grave of our executed prime minister, Imre Nagy. I also helped the underground democratic press, the young "samizdat" movement, which needed copiers and paper supplies for their publications. The secret police were constantly following me, but I got used to that. Then one day in 1983, when I was having coffee in the dining car of a train, the three familiar faces of my "trailers" showed up again. One of them walked directly into me, and after I regained my balance, I noticed that my coffee tasted strange.

I do not know what happened, but after drinking that coffee I must have acted strangely, because Árpád Göncz (the president of Hungary until recently, then a prominent member of the opposition) drove me to a taxi station to get me back to Budapest. I understand that I made some suicide attempts, and after those I received four electroshock treatments in a hospital. When I recovered from the effects of that strange-tasting coffee, my memory was a mess. As a consequence of not remembering the million specifics of my consulting jobs, I lost some of my clients. This was particularly unfortunate in the case of IBM, because I had designed their headquarters at 590 Madison Avenue in New York as the first "self-heating" building in that city, and I could not even remember my own design.

My recovery, the gradual return of some of my memory, took a long time. In order to make a living, I had to make some changes. One change was the realization that if I could no longer do it, I could still teach it. So I accepted an invitation to become an adjunct professor of process control at Yale University and also gave courses and seminars to other institutions and companies. Even during that difficult period I did not stop my search for the grave of Imre Nagy, and, as a result, on October 9, 1985, I was able to report the location of his grave in an op-ed article in the *Wall Street Journal*. In 1989 Imre Nagy was finally given a formal funeral and was buried in a temporary grave.

In 1985 János Szentágothai, the president of the Hungarian Academy of Science, and Sándor Szalai, the person leading the academy's Danube committee, asked for my help. They felt that the monstrous Danube diversion project could not be stopped without Western help, and believed that I (the editor of the *Environmental Engineers' Handbook*) was the natural person to help them. First I hesitated, but when I learned that even on his deathbed Dr. Szalai was urging his daughters to talk me into facing up to this challenge (which he no longer could—he died from cancer), I got involved. In the years that followed I have spent a great deal of my time (and a fair amount of our savings) in fighting this project of environmental devastation. I organized meetings, lectures, and demonstrations; visited world leaders; and published articles. In that process I also learned a lot about the combined strength of the ultranationalist fanatics of "greater" Slovakia, of cronyism among the former Communists, and of western financial institutions (Austrian and American banks) that were supporting the "concrete lobby" with their loans.

At the time of the collapse of the Soviet empire in 1989, I was positive that we would be among those emigrants who would return to a free Hungary and would help in the rebuilding of our homeland. It did not happen. Part of the reason was that we could not separate ourselves from our children, and the other part was that while I remained 100 percent Hungarian, I also had become 100 percent American. Neither of my loyalties took anything away from the other; they were like the difference between love of one's mother and love of one's wife. Yet becoming a 200-percent person did change something in me. I was no longer an unconditional Hungarian; I could not accept the deals and compromises that were being made.

I felt an outrage when I saw that there would not be even a mini-Nuremberg (probably because of some deal between President Reagan and Premier Gorbachev) and that the guilty would not even be identified. I was equally angry to see that instead of returning private property to the people from whom it was taken, many Communist collaborators managed to "privatize" the national wealth into their own pockets. I just could not stand the idea of a new Hungary built on lies, cover-ups, and theft.

In 1992, on October 23, the Slovak nationalist fanatic Vladimir Meciar blocked the natural flow of our border river, the Danube, and diverted it into Slovak territory. I was there in my yellow ski parka at the head of 647 demonstrators to try to stop the trucks carrying the concrete blocks with which they closed the riverbed, but we failed to stop them. We were dragged away from the trucks and Slovakia got "greater" by murdering a river. After that, I also went to The Hague when the International Court of Justice discussed this case, the first international environmental lawsuit ever. I am still working on this today. I am hopeful that the expansion of the European Union will eventually bring a sense of fairness and environmental consciousness to Slovakia, too. I have prepared a compromise plan that would allow the Gabcikovo Dam to function while returning the Danube to her natural riverbed and allowing the species that evolved in this delta of the ancient Pannon Sea to recover.[6]

In the 1990s our family grew. Ádámka married Jennifer Bitman, and they gave us two grandchildren: Ivan and Katie.[7] In 1998 Cica (Ágnes) married Richard Lawrence and increased the number of our grandchildren to three by the addition of the little blonde Ava.[8] As I am writing these words, I am also thinking of my grandchildren, hoping that one day they might read this memoir.

It was in 1998 that the first sculpture honoring the Revolution was erected in Hungary. It was created by Miklós Meloccó, the son of the reporter János Meloccó, who was hanged because he dared to write about the Communists' drugging of Cardinal Mindszenty. In Miklós Meloccó's sculpture the baby butterfly of liberty is depicted as people are desperately trying to help it to fly. He used real people for his figures: Jancsi Danner is behind the statue, fallen down on the ground, while I am the third from the front on the left side of the sculpture. Another honor that I cherish is the Imre Nagy plaque, which I received from President Árpád Göncz in October, 1999.

Our calendar has entered the third millennium, and the state of Hungary has entered her second. It is a sad new beginning for us Hungarians. It is sad partly because historic Hungary has been split up among nine states, and thus Hungarians have become one of the largest minorities in all of Europe. It is also a sad period because mankind seems to pay attention only to the violent, and the Hungarian minorities are a nonviolent people who believe in democracy and self-determination.

Figure 25. Our family *(left to right)*: Richard Lawrence with Ava, Ivan, Ádám, Jennifer Bitman, me, Márta with Katie, and Ágnes

I do hope that the attitude of the our leaders will change. I hope that the Hungarians of Vojvodina will eventually receive the same protection as did the Albanians of Kosovo. Similarly, I hope that school and church properties will be returned to all Hungarian minorities and that the autonomy of the Hungarian communities of Yugoslavia, Romania, and Slovakia will eventually be restored. But most important, I hope that the European Community will expand into the region so that state borders will become transparent and my divided nation can be at least be culturally reunited. And finally, I hope that now, when a new generation of Hungarian leaders is starting to lay the foundations of Hungary's next millennium, they will rely on the ideals of the 1956 Revolution.

Notes

Prologue

1. Saint Stephen (975–1038), the first king of Hungary (1001–38), founded the
    state of Hungary. He received his crown from Pope Sylvester II, and that
    crown remained as the sacred symbol of Hungarian national existence for a
    millennium. From 1945 the crown was held in Washington and was returned
    to Hungary in 1978 by Cyrus Vance, the secretary of state during the admin-
    istration of Jimmy Carter. That delegation included Csanád Tóth (a former
    president of AHSA and my old friend and schoolmate from Pannonhalma),
    who traveled to Budapest with Mr. Vance.

    In a way, the United States is connected to Saint Stephen because Amerigo
    Vespucci was named after his son, Saint Emeric of Hungary. Therefore, when
    in 1507 the Swiss mapmaker Martin Waldseemueller named the American
    continent after the Italian explorer, he also named it after Saint Emeric of
    Hungary. It is for this reason that in 1999, before his death, Cardinal O'Connor
    proposed that the fifth of November be celebrated as the feast day of Saint
    Emeric of Hungary, the patron of the American continent.

    Another distant connection between Hungary and the United States is
    George Washington's maternal grandmother, Margaret Butler, who was a
    descendent of Saint Margaret of Scotland, who in turn was a descendent of
    Saint Stephen of Hungary.
2. That statement still rings true today, when one reads about Kosovo and
    Bosnia.
3. Some better-known individuals and their contributions: Gábor Dénes (laser
    holograph, the little black bars that are optically read at the check-out
    counters in our stores), Sándor Ferenczi (psychoanalysis), Péter Goldmark
    (color TV), Andy Grove (Intel's microchip), János Harsányi (game theory),
    George Hevesy (tracer isotopes), Theodore von Kármán (supersonic flight and
    guided missiles), John G. Kemény (microcomputing), Arthur Koestler (phi-
    losophy), John Von Neumann (first computer), Tivadar Puskás (telephone
    exchange), Leó Szilárd (first nuclear reactor, and Edward Teller (hydrogen
    bomb).
4. The law he opposed was called "numerus clausus," a kind of affirmative ac-
    tion for the majority, intended to limit the percentage of Jews in higher educa-
    tion to their percentage in the general population.

Chapter 1. Just an Average Day

1. I do not know what the exchange rate of the forint was at the time, but it does not matter, because the prices were artificially fixed. The cost of bread was 3.40 forints a kilo (2.2 pounds), while a good pair of handmade shoes on the black market cost 900 forints.

2. The Közért was a state-owned supermarket chain, the only supermarket chain that existed.

3. Education under the Communists was free, and in addition we received a monthly stipend. The size of the stipend depended on both one's needs and one's performance in school.

4. *Regent* in most nations' vocabulary is a person who rules a kingdom in the absence of the king. In Hungary this term described a ruler who no longer had a kingdom to rule, only some leftover remains of what used to be a kingdom. Miklós Horthy (1868–1957) commanded the Austro-Hungarian fleet in World War I. Horthy became head of state in 1920 and checked two attempts by the Austro-Hungarian Emperor Charles I to regain his throne. Horthy was a nationalist conservative who did not want to become a German ally and whose anti-German premier, Pál Teleki, committed suicide in 1941 over that issue. In October of 1944, the Germans blackmailed the seventy-eight-year-old Horthy with the life of his only living child (three of his four children were already dead) in exchange for his permitting the transfer of power to the Nazis. Later he was arrested by the Germans and taken to Bavaria. He was freed by American troops, was a witness at Nüremberg, and later settled in Portugal, where he died in 1957.

5. József Mindszenty (1892–1975) was bishop when he was arrested for his anti-Nazi views during the German occupation of Hungary in 1944. After the war he was raised to cardinal of Hungary in 1946, but because he opposed not only the Nazis but also the Communists, he was arrested again in 1948. In prison he was drugged and as a result admitted to treason and to illegal monetary transactions that he did not commit. He was freed by the freedom fighters in 1956, and when the Soviets invaded, he took refuge at the U.S. legation of Budapest and stayed there for some fifteen years. In 1971, under pressure from the Pope, he left Hungary, and in 1974 he settled in Vienna, where he died in 1975 at the age of eighty-three.

6. Dóra Néni had three kids just as Memi. Her second son, Miklós, was born the same year as I, and we grew up together. Today he is one of Hungary's best-known sculptors. To honor the Revolution, he created a sculpture that was erected in the city of Szeged.

Chapter 2. Birth of MEFESZ and the Sixteen Points

1. Mátyás Rákosi (1892–1963) was a disciple of Joseph Stalin, an associate of Béla Kun, and the person who designed and implemented the Communist

dictatorship in Hungary. He became premier in 1952 but was forced to resign in August 1956 and fled to the Soviet Union, where it was reported that he died in 1963; the ÁVH was the Communist secret police that served to terrorize the people and to help Rákosi in reaching his goal of destroying all democratic institutions. The ÁVH was the equivalent of the German Gestapo or the Russian KGB.

2. József Szilágyi (1917–58) was a university student who before the war became a member of the Communist Party and was arrested by the Germans because of his antifascist activities. After World War II he joined Imre Nagy's anti-Stalinist faction in the Party and for that reason lost his position of authority in 1949. During those years of disfavor by the Party he obtained an engineering degree. In 1956 he became the director of Imre Nagy's office. After the Revolution he was arrested, separated from the Nagy group, and sentenced to death in May, 1958. The time of his execution is unknown. He was among the 289 people who were hanged after the Revolution.

3. After the Revolution Cholnoky was fired anyway, together with László Gillemot, the other rector of the university.

Chapter 3. My Tricolor Armband

1. Csepel Island is south of Budapest. The Danube splits in two as it reaches it and flows on both sides of this island, which was and still is full of industrial plants. Belojannisz was a major industrial factory named after a Greek Communist leader.

2. In the lobby of IBM's headquarters in Armonk, New York, Neumann is honored as the inventor of the computer. Kármán made his contribution to aerodynamics, particularly to space exploration. They were both members of the Hungarian nobility (barons) and were also Jews.

3. Today, the bust of Ádám Mutnyánszky stands near the university's library.

4. The University was named for József Eötvös (1813–71), a writer and statesman, a reformer, and a Christian liberal. He was minister of education and religious affairs in 1848 and also in 1867. His novel *The Village Notary* exposed corruption in county government and contributed to better government.

5. József Bem was a general in the fight for freedom in 1848. Because he was of Polish origin, we felt that it would be appropriate to meet at his statue.

6. Sándor Petőfi (1823–49) was an exquisite lyric poet. His poetry served as inspiration to the patriots of the 1848 revolution, in which he was killed.

7. The Skoda was a Czech automobile. The few cars that one saw in Hungary were almost all either Skodas or Pobjedas. The Pobjedas were larger, more expensive, and made in the Soviet Union. Few people owned cars or even knew how to drive them. The university owned a couple of cars. They were provided with drivers for the rectors and other officials when needed.

8. The *kuruc* were the soldiers of those insurrectionist armies of Francis II Rákóczi (1676–1735) that fought against Habsburg oppression at the turn of

the seventeenth century (1703). Rákóczi was elected "ruling prince" by the Hungarian Diet in 1704. His armies were defeated by the Austrians, and, in 1711, when he refused to accept the Szatmár Peace Treaty, he fled to Poland and later to France. He finally died in Turkey. Stirring music in his memory was composed by Bihari, Berlioz, and Liszt (Hungarian Rhapsody No. 15).

Lajos Kossuth (1802–94) was a revolutionary hero and a fiery orator whom in 1949 the Hungarian parliament declared to be the president of independent Hungary. In 1849 the joint forces of Austria and Russia crushed the Hungarian armies, and he escaped to Turkey. He lived in exile in England and Italy, visited the United States, and was the second foreigner ever to be invited to address the U.S. Senate. His dream of the Danubian Confederation (the United States of Central Europe) still lives on today and is the basis of the "Visegrád Four" movement. I often visit his statue in New York City on Riverside Avenue at 113th Street.

9. The sixteen point manifesto of hungarian youth:

    1.   We demand the immediate withdrawal of Soviet troops from Hungary in accordance with the peace treaty.

    2.   We demand an election of new leaders of the Hungarian Workers' Party by secret ballot on local, intermediate and central level. The Party Congress should be convened and elect a new Central Committee.

    3.   The Government should be reorganized under the leadership of Comrade Imre Nagy. All guilty leaders of the Stalinist-Rákosi era must be removed from office.

    4.   We demand a public trial of Mihály Farkas and his accomplices. Bring home Rákosi, who is primarily responsible for the crimes of the recent past and for destroying the country, and confront him with a people's tribunal.

    5.   We demand general, secret elections in the country in which several parties may participate with the purpose of electing a new Parliament. We demand the assurance of the right to strike for the workers.

    6.   We demand that Hungarian-Soviet and Hungarian-Yugoslav economic and intellectual relations be revised and reestablished on the basis of political and economic equality and noninterference in each other's internal affairs.

    7.   We demand the reorganzation of Hungarian economic life with the help of our experts. Let them revise our whole economy—based on a planned system—keeping in mind the country's possibilities and the interest of our people.

    8.   Our foreign trade agreements must be made public along with the actual figures of compensation, which in reality can never be paid. We demand open and truthful information about the country's uranium resources, their utilization, and the Russian concession. We demand that Hungary be allowed to sell uranium freely at the world market price for valuable currency.

    9.   We demand the complete revision of norms employed in industry. The salary demands of the workers and intellectuals should be settled promptly and radically. We ask for the establishment of minimum pay for workers.

10. We demand that the compulsory delivery system be put on a new basis and that production be used wisely. We demand equal support for independent farmers.

11. We demand that all political and ecomomic lawsuits be revised by an independent judiciary and all unjustly convicted be freed and rehabilitated. We demand that all prisoners of war and civilians who were dragged away to the Soviet Union be returned immediately, including those who were convicted outside our borders.

12. We demand freedom of thought, speech, and press, free radio and a daily newspaper with large circulation for the MEFESZ (noncommunist youth organization). We demand that the existing "Cadre-list" be made public and destroyed.

13. We demand that the statue of Stalin, the symbol of tyranny and political oppression, be removed and in its place a memorial be erected for the martyrs of the 1948–49 revolution.

14. We wish to replace the present coat of arms, which is alien to the Hungarian people, with the former Kossuth arms. We demand a new uniform for the army following our historic traditions. We demand that there be no work on March 15th, a national holiday, and that there be no school on October 6, a day of national mourning.

15. The students of the Engineering Universtiy of Budapest proclaim solidarity with the youth and workers of Poland in connection with their revolutionary movement.

16. The students of the University of Building Trades set up the local organs of MEFESZ and call together a parliament of youth on Saturday, October 27, when the youth of the entire country will be represented by delegates.

MEFESZ—organization of university students (*Népszava*, October 23, 1956)

Chapter 4. Enough of Listening

1. Ernő Gerő was the head of the Communist Party and an original member of the Rákosi government. He was so hated that even after the Revolution was crushed, the Soviets did not dare to bring him back. He died in Moscow.

2. Ferenc Erdei was an influential Reform Communist; Imre Nagy (1896–1958), an agricultural expert, was the leader of the reform Communists and was particularly trusted by the farmers. As premier in 1953 to 1955, he established a "new course," which deemphasized heavy industry, stopped forced collectivization, and loosened police controls. During the first few days of the Revolution he was surrounded by the secret police and was not properly informed of what was going on. By the beginning of November, 1956, he became a true leader, declared Hungary's neutrality, and terminated her membership in the Warsaw Pact. After the Soviet attack, he took refuge in the Yugoslav embassy. Despite a safe-conduct pledge, the Soviets seized him when he left the embassy. On June 16, 1958, he was hanged and buried in secret. I was one of those who searched for and finally found his grave in 1985.

3. In order to make room for Stalin's monument the Communists tore down a Catholic school named Regnum Marianum. The statue was a hated symbol of Soviet occupation, and after being toppled people spent days to break it into pieces.
4. Gábor Illés was also a Category X student and also lived in the village of Kerepes. His family moved there to save themselves from being deported, which most members of the middle class were if they stayed in the larger cities. After the Revolution, Gábor came to America, married Zsuzsa, became a bank executive and settled in California.

Chapter 5. MEFESZ Headquarters of the Technical University

1. Pál Maléter was born in 1917. In 1940, as a volunteer, he participated in taking back Transylvania from Romania. In 1944 he was wounded and captured on the eastern front, and later he returned to fight the German occupational forces as a partisan commander. After the war he became the commander of the guards of the president of Hungary, Zoltán Tildy. On October 25, 1956, as a major general and tank commander, he was sent to command the Kilián Barracks and to quash the revolt. For two days he fought against the freedom fighters at Corvin Alley, but after meeting and talking to some of his prisoners, he joined the Revolution, and on November 3 he became the minister of defense in the Nagy government. He started the negotiations concerning the withdrawal of the Soviet troops with Soviet General Malinin, and during these negotiations (just before the second Soviet attack on November 4) he was arrested and kidnapped by the KGB's General Serov. He was executed on June 16, 1958.
2. Part of the reason the Soviets withdrew their troops from Budapest at the end of October was that many of their soldiers who were stationed in Hungary for some time had learned the language and sympathized with the local population. Another reason was that the gasoline tanks of the old Soviet tanks stationed in Hungary could be penetrated by handguns, and the leaking gasoline could then be ignited by Molotov cocktails. In contrast, the second invading force did not even know where they were (some believed that they were at the Suez Canal). The gasoline containers of the tanks of this second force were under the armor plate and could not be perforated by light weapons.

Chapter 6. Getting the Arms

1. I found out later that Gyurka (George) Vereczkey was in his fifth year of medical school when he got involved in some anti-Communist activity, was kicked out, and became a driver. I do not know what happened to him after the Revolution.
2. The men at the Zrinyi Barracks were part of the regular army and followed the lead of the regular police in supporting the Revolution. Each military unit

did this in a different way, depending on the local conditions and on the attitude of their officers.

Chapter 7. Hungary's Jews and Germans

1. Molotov was one of the first Communist leaders in Russia. He changed his name to Molotov ("the hammer") to escape the imperial police. After the takeover he became Stalin's vice chairman and negotiated the German-Russian nonaggression pact of 1939 with Hitler. In 1956 he was Russia's foreign minister.
2. The forebears of Sephardic Jews resided on the Iberian peninsula. Sephardic Jews retained many characteristics of the Judeo-Spanish culture.
3. Szabó Bácsi became a legendary figure after just a few days of fighting. He was a natural-born leader—a father figure who led by example. After the second Russian attack on November 4, he was captured, and on January 19, 1957 he was hanged. It was his authentic "working-class credentials" that contributed to him being so hated by the Communists.

Chapter 8. A Barrel of Blood

1. Gamal Abdal Nasser (1918–70) opposed foreign domination of Egypt from a young age. At seventeen he was wounded in an anti-British demonstration and was expelled from school. As a major in the Arab-Israeli war of 1948, he was wounded in action. In 1952 he led the army coup that deposed King Farouk, and in 1954 he became Egypt's premier. In 1956 he was elected as the first president of the Republic of Egypt, and in that capacity he nationalized the Suez Canal. Having been denied passage through the canal, Israel, with French and English air support, invaded Egypt. France and England also sent forces to retake the canal.
   The attendees of the Yalta Conference included the British prime minister, Winston Churchill, the U.S. president, Franklin Delano Roosevelt, and the Soviet premier, Joseph Stalin. The conference was held in the Crimea, USSR, between February 4 and 11, 1945. Many believe that it was at the Yalta Conference where the West accepted Soviet domination over Central and Eastern Europe and thereby gave approval to Communist domination in the region.
2. Jancsi could not have known that on this very day the American secretary of state, John Foster Dulles, handed a formal document to his Soviet counterpart that stated that "the USA has no military allies in Eastern Europe." This in plain language meant that the Soviets could do whatever they felt like in Hungary.
3. After the Revolution, Gábor settled in Philadelphia, and Judit in Munich, Germany.
4. After the Revolution, the Soviets claimed that Western arms, supplies, and agents arrived through the airports of Budapest. Yet the fact is that only Red

Cross aircraft landed in Budapest. The total air traffic during the Revolution consisted of five Yugoslav airplanes and one Swiss airplane, which made several trips to Budapest, while two Polish, two Czech, one Romanian, and one Belgian plane made one single trip each.

5. The Warsaw Pact was the Soviet bloc's equivalent of NATO. The treaty, signed in 1955, was binding for twenty years. Albania withdrew from it in 1968, the year in which Warsaw Pact forces occupied Czechoslovakia. The organization was fully dissolved in June, 1991.

6. There is some controversy concerning the "real" commander of the Corvin Cinema group. While I am not qualified to resolve that debate, I do know that Gergely Pongrátz was certainly among them. After the Revolution he emigrated to the United States, and after 1989 he returned to Hungary. Unfortunately, he has never fully revised his views about General Maléter; he has never forgiven the martyred general for the few days when they were on opposite sides.

7. After the Revolution, Sándor Kopácsi was jailed. General Béla Király escaped from Hungary and after the Revolution became a professor in New York City. He returned to Hungary after the collapse of Communism in 1989.

Chapter 9. Top Secret

1. János Kádár (1912–89) at the age of twenty joined the illegal Communist Party, and, after the Soviets occupied Hungary, he held a variety of high government posts. In 1951 he was arrested for pro-Titoist tendencies, and was jailed until 1954. During the 1956 Revolution he first joined the cabinet of Imre Nagy, but later became a traitor and formed a Soviet-supported countergovernment. In 1958 he tried and executed Imre Nagy, and in 1968 he supported the Soviet invasion of Czechoslovakia. He was ousted in 1988, when another Communist, Miklós Németh, became the premier.

2. I carried that key in my pocket throughout the Revolution and kept it with my other memorabilia until the collapse of the Soviet empire. Today, that key, the original of my order to collect these arms, and other documents are all displayed in the 1956 Museum in Lakitelek, Hungary.

3. The closest political prison to Budapest was the one at Kistarcsa. It was in the center of the village next to Kerepes, where we lived. Next to this prison I used to sell the wild mushrooms I picked in the woods, because the open-air market was right next to the prison's tall walls.

Chapter 10. Jancsi's Murder

1. After the Revolution, Dr. Gabriella Somkuty never married and played a key role in keeping the memory of Jancsi alive. Partially as a result of her efforts, both the Technical University of Budapest and the city of Szeged have honored Jancsi with memorial tablets.

2. As of 2000 (ten years after the collapse of the Soviet empire), none of this information has been made public, neither the list of spies nor their reports to the ÁVH leadership. This is in stark contrast with the "cleansing process" that followed World War II. In the case of the activities of the Communist secret police, the secrecy and cover-up is continuing. Some say that this has to do with some secret agreement that was reached between President Reagan and Soviet President Mikhail Gorbachev, aimed at avoiding reprisals. All I know is that in my own case, when I was finally able to obtain the contents of my secret police files, all 104 spy reports were dated after 1980; there was nothing in my folder dated before that. On the reports that were included in the file, the names of the people who provided the information had been removed. All reports of the preceding years had either "disappeared" or were still being held back. This Hungarian practice differs from that of Germany, where the reports of both the Nazi Gestapo and the Communist Stasi spies were made public, and the informers themselves were identified and required to make a public apology if they wanted to hold government jobs. In Hungary, no apologies have been heard to date.

3. It is a strange phenomenon of the present political situation in Hungary that the most senior leader of the Communist Party's successor party (called the MSZP, an abbreviation for Hungarian Socialist Party) is Gyula Horn, who is a former Pufajka. It is also telling that the average Hungarian is under the impression that Horn joined the Pufajkas in response to the murder of his brother Géza by freedom fighters. A review of the facts reveals that Horn's brother died in a car accident late in December 1956, well after the second Soviet attack. Still, the Communists were able to spread such false rumors, which the public accepted as fact. Most other leaders of the MSZP, like Nemeth Miklos, were too young in 1956 to join the Pufajkas.

4. Győr is halfway between Budapest and Vienna on the Slovak border at the confluence of the Rába and Danube rivers. It is an industrial city, a railroad hub, and a river port with a population of over 100,000; after the Revolution, Attila Szigethy was captured and committed suicide in jail.

5. At the time we visited Magyaróvár we saw more than fifty dead bodies. Later, that number climbed. It took forty-three years to bring a lawsuit against the commander of the Hungarian ÁVH border guards, István Dudás, who on October 26, 1956, ordered his troops to fire into the crowd of over one thousand demonstrators. During the trial Dudás claimed that he did "not have the strength to answer any questions." It is interesting to note that ten years after the collapse of Communism in Hungary, Dudás is still free and we still do not know who gave the order for Dudás to fire. Even after 1989, the democratic governments did not make the secret police files public.

It is also interesting to note that although after World War II the Hungarian Nazi collaborators were immediately punished or at least were not allowed to hold government jobs, after the collapse of Communism not a single former Communist leader has been jailed or prosecuted. Actually, the overwhelming majority have kept their privileged jobs and have taken advantage of the "privatization" process to get rich. As of this year (2000), the largest news- paper, the national radio, and most of the media in Hungary is still in the hands of the former Communists, and the value of the real-estate possessions of their party, the MSZP, is twenty-fold the combined value of all the posses- sions of the other five parties in the Hungarian parliament. On top of that, they pay no real-estate taxes at all.

Chapter 11. Beginning of the End

1. Yuri Vladimirovich Andropov (1914–84) was the ambassador to Hungary and played a major role in crushing the Revolution. Later he directed the ideological campaign against the Chinese Communists. In 1967 he was ap- pointed to head the KGB. In 1982 he became the secretary of the Communist Party and later the premier of the USSR. He maintained a repressive hard-line policy against dissidents.

   Nikita Sergeyevich Khrushchev (1894–1971) was premier of the USSR and first secretary of the Communist Party of the Soviet Union (1953–64). He was born into a Ukrainian peasant family. In 1938, as first secretary of the Ukrai- nian Communist Party, he carried out Stalin's ruthless purges, and after Stalin's death in 1953, he replaced Malenkov as first secretary of the party. In 1956 he orchestrated the lies that prevented the United Nations from acting in time to protect Hungary and gave the false impression to the government of Imre Nagy that the Russians were leaving, when in fact they were entering with new equipment. As a reward for such "leadership," in 1958 he replaced Bulganin as the Soviet premier and became the undisputed leader of both the Communist Party and the Soviet state.

   Josif Broz Tito (1892–1980) was the son of a Croatian blacksmith. In World War I, he was a soldier in the Austro-Hungarian army and as such was captured and turned into a Communist by the Russians. In Croatia, he was imprisoned as a union organizer (1929–34) and by 1941 he emerged as the leader of the partisan resistance in Yugoslavia. In 1945, supported by the United States, USSR, and Great Britain, he became the head of the Yugoslav government. As dictator, in 1946 he jailed Archbishop Stepinac but later tried to give the appearance of a nonaligned leader. In 1956 he first gave refuge to the members of the government of Imre Nagy but later turned them over to the Soviets, who hanged them.

2. The role of Radio Free Europe in the Revolution is still somewhat murky. Some believe that less blood would have been shed if they had not given so much emphasis to Eisenhower's "policy of liberation" and just reported the facts. Others argue that we, the listeners of RFE, were reading too much into their reports—that in fact we took routine propaganda slogans for promises of help and for encouragement to fight. Besides radio broadcasts, RFE also sent in leaflets by balloons and books by regular mail. All of this activity

added up in our minds to an indication that America was our ally and would help if help was essential.

3. Colonel Marián did not take part in the defense of Buda. Still, after the Revolution he was sentenced to life imprisonment; he served over six years of that sentence. He was pardoned as part of a general amnesty in 1963. To this day he is a close and respected friend of mine.

4. That was the last time I saw Gyurka. In 1995 I did meet a young man with the last name Vereczkey, but he was no relation. I have no idea what has happened to Gyurka.

Chapter 12. Lives on the Line

1. After the Revolution Egry became the director of a chemical plant in Peru. He brought up his sons, Lehel, Ákos, and Levente, as loyal Hungarians. He died in 1994.

2. For decades, in my mind, the age of this baby, Andrea, was a gauge of the years passed since 1956. In my mind her age was the length of Communism's death struggle after it was mortally wounded on the streets of Budapest. Unfortunately, Andrea did not live to see this end. She took her own life before the red monster expired.

3. After the Revolution Professor Bónis became a professor at MIT, and today he is known for being a major supporter and sponsor of the Boston Opera.

4. This was the last time I saw Marika. I do not know whether she survived that awful leg wound, but her last sentence I will treasure forever. In the early 1990s I did hear from Gyuszi Perr. He was flying over my city of Stamford, Connecticut, and was calling from his company's airplane, that of the Cummings Engine Company of Columbus, Ohio.

Chapter 13. Interrogation

1. Forty-four years have passed since then, and I still hope that one of these days I will fulfill that promise. In the mid-1980s I lifted that statue once again to show the pistol to my daughter, Ágnes. At that time it was still there.

Chapter 14. Home

1. This was the last time I saw Laci until very recently. In the 1970s I heard that he had become an airline pilot in Switzerland. In the last decade a cousin of his married a nephew of mine, and in 1997 we finally met again at a New Year's party. He has not changed.

2. This was the last time I saw the Tóth girls, although decades later, when I was teaching at Yale, a student from Hungary asked me if I was the same Béla Lipták his aunts talked about.

3. This was the last time I saw István Angyal. He was captured on November 16, 1956, was sentenced to death, and was held in the same cell with Imre Mécs (my friend from the Technical University who was also sentenced to be hanged, but survived). In prison Angyal wrote, "The Hungarians fought and died for world freedom in 1848, and we are following in their footsteps today. This fight of ours can determine the future of all mankind. It is an honor to be the son of such a nation. I am happy that I was born to be a Hungarian, and if I could relive my life, I would want to live it exactly as I did." When Pista was being taken to the gallows on December 1, 1958, he tore his photograph from his identity card and on the back of that passport-sized picture wrote in pencil, "Long live free Hungary!" He handed the photo to Imre Mécs.

4. Later I read in the papers that the Soviets used 2,600 tanks during this second invasion.

5. This was the last time I saw Bukucs, my loyal dog and good friend, with whom I spent many happy days in the woods. After my departure, he refused to eat and died.

6. My younger brother, Andris, was sixteen during the Revolution. As I visited Kerepes only twice during that one-month period, I saw very little of him. Later, I learned that with his classmates he was involved in the removal of a large red star from one of the buildings of Budapest and while doing that, a friend of his fell to his death.

    After the Revolution he completed his schooling (Ph.D. in mechanical engineering) and married Zsóka Wekerle, the charming blond daughter of the secretary of Imre Nagy. He became the technical director of the central heating system of Budapest and in that capacity felt that he had to become a member of the Party. Zsóka and Andris had two lovely daughters, Noéme and Timea, and today are the happy grandparents of four grandchildren in free Hungary.

Chapter 15. Escaping Hungary

1. During the Revolution, it is estimated that a total of about 15,000 Hungarians participated in the actual fighting, of whom 2,700 were killed. Reprisals after the Revolution included hanging (289 victims), jailing, and deportation within Hungary. In addition, some 40,000 ended up in the Soviet Republic of Kazakhstan and have not been repatriated to date.

2. Thirty years later I ran into Gyurka Gömöri at Cambridge University in England, where he was teaching Polish literature.

3. Later, as in the case of General Maléter, Sándor Rácz was also arrested during a trick meeting and was sentenced to life imprisonment. In 1999 he received from the president of Hungary, Árpád Göncz, the Imre Nagy memorial plaque in recognition of his actions in 1956. (I received the same recognition.) Sándor lives in Hungary, stayed away from politics, and enjoys the well-deserved respect of the nation.

4. Later, Béla Jankó became the first international president of the Union of Free Hungarian Students (UFHS) in Geneva, Switzerland. The Hungarian students who came to the United States also formed an organization, the American-Hungarian Student Association (AHSA), at Bard College, and in December, 1956, I was elected the first president, with the task of extending our membership to all U.S. universities.

5. The Soviets chose Romania partly because it was one of their most reliable satellites, but also because after World War I, Romania doubled her size at the expense of Hungary, which resulted in anti-Hungarian sentiments there. (We hate whom we hurt.) After capturing the legitimate Hungarian government and after a long interrogation period, a show trial followed. All members of the government maintained their innocence and bravely accused the Soviets of aggression against a neutral nation. One of the ministers, Géza Losonczy, was murdered in jail by force feeding (food was pumped into his punctured lungs). József Szilágyi was hanged in April, 1958, and Imre Nagy, Pál Maléter, and Miklós Gimes followed him to the gallows on June 16, 1958. The other members of the government received lesser sentences and were eventually released, in 1963.

6. When in April, 1849, the Hungarian parliament declared that Hungary was an independent republic, Lajos Batthyány became the premiere and Louis Kossuth the president. Hungary surrendered at Világos to the combined military forces of Russia and Austria. After the surrender, the Austrians hanged Prime Minister Batthyány.

   Pál Teleki (1879–1941) was Hungary's prime minister when, early in 1941, it became evident that Hungary would be forced by Germany to invade Yugoslavia. He knew that this tragic first step would lead to Hungary's entering World War II on the wrong side. After exploring all possible alternatives and after finding no way out, he shot himself.

7. The entries in our family Bible are mostly of births, weddings, and funerals. There is one exception, which reads, "My two little boys, Péterke and Öcsike— after fighting to the end in the heroic freedom-fight of 1956—on the 24th of November, had no choice but to escape the Russian reign of terror and fled to Austria."

Postscript

1. After the 1956 Hungarian Revolution more than a quarter million people escaped from Hungary. Taking into account the forty thousand who were deported to the Soviet Union and the nearly three thousand killed in the fighting, the state of Hungary lost nearly 3 percent of her population.

2. Povl Bang-Jensen was a Senior Political Officer at the UN who was found dead in Alley Pond Park in New York City after he burned the list of Hungarian witnesses who testified before the UN's "Special Committee on the Problem of Hungary." He resisted the pressure of his superiors to turn over this list, because, as the UN officer with the responsibility for screening and selecting

potential witnesses, he had promised witnesses that they could testify anonymously in order to protect their relatives who still resided in Hungary.

On January 3, 2001, his son, Per Bang-Jensen, wrote:

My father's reasons for burning the list were somewhat more complex. It was not just that he wanted to protect the witnesses' families in Hungary. He, on behalf of the UN, had made a promise to potential witnesses that they could testify anonymously. He believed that the UN could not legally or morally change this promise retroactively. I should add that over the years I have found it interesting, but not surprising, that the event to which most people refer when capsulizing my father's life is the burning of the list of the names of witnesses. I think that this in some way was a relatively easy decision for my father, since he believed he really had no choice.

I believe my father's greater personal challenge was regarding the UN Report on the Hungarian Revolution. The original justiffcation for having these Reports was that since the UN was not able to stop the Soviet invasion or to make them withdraw, it was important for the UN to document what happened so the Soviets would pay a price in the courts of public opinion throughout the world. This perhaps would also serve as a deterrent to some potential aggressor nations in the future. Unfortunately, some at the UN thought that the report should be critical, but not be too critical of the Soviets.

My father thought the report should be very comprehensive, even when it meant that it would be specifically critical of the Soviets or Kádár's government. He thought that the Report should, for example, include (1) accurate information on Kádár's support and involvement in the early decisions of the Nagy government, (2) details of the specific actions of the Soviet military during the Revolution, and (3) evidence despite soviet denials that Hungarians were being deported to prisons or work camps in the Soviet Union and elsewhere in Eastern Europe. In spite of these and other problems, my father thought the inital Report was a relatively good initial report.

However, after the issuance of the initial Report, when others thought that it was in the UN's best long-term interest to put the Hungarian matter behind them, he tried in mid-1957 to get the UN to write Supplemental Reports (as envisioned in the Special Committee's charter) as a means to expand the initial Report and to ensure that the full and accurate facts regarding the Revolution and the on-going repression after the Revolution were made known. He believed that Supplemental Reports with the resulting continuance of international attention would be a means to help protect the lives of those imprisoned after the Hungarian Revolution. Sadly, in spite of considerable information regarding arrests, trials, and executions that continued to be smuggled out of Hungary at great risk, the UN did not issue a Supplemental Report until after the June 1958 executions of Imre Nagy, Pal Maleter, and their associates.

3. Laci Korbuly is now a respected architect and an active participant in Jimmy Carter's Habitat for Humanity project. Feri Gárdonyi recently died; he was an accomplished film producer in Mexico.

4. Péter completed his degree in animal husbandry and for a while experimented with both regular and self-employment. He got married and was divorced twice, then became a hippie, experimented with drugs and, later, also with homelessness. He is the father of two lovely grown children: Aron, who has just returned form the Peace Corps in Uzbekistan, and Caitlin, who has just graduated as a teacher from college. Today, Péter is nearly blind and back in Hungary, living on his social security income. My younger brother, Andris, is helping him.

5. Márta's father's family left Transylvania and came to Hungary when that ancient Hungarian land was given to Romania in 1920. She grew up in Budapest until she was deported to a small village with all her family in the early 1950s. This occurred partly because my father-in-law was a professional soldier but mostly because their apartment was needed for some Communist Party officials.

   Márta graduated from Skidmore with a degree in theatrical scene design while carrying our son Ádám. Next year our daughter, Ágnes, was born and she was locked up with them in our tiny apartment. When in 1975 I decided to open my own office, she pitched in to help with the initial expenses by becoming an English teacher in the local high school. Later, she became a ceramic artist. She started with ceramic sculptures and went through many phases. Today her specialty is to blend the forms and colors of ceramics with driftwood. This gives us the excuse to search for driftwood in some wonderfully secluded places and allows Márta to create marvelous pieces. One even appeared in the *New York Times.* Today, her studio and kiln are next to my office, so that our dogs can have convenient access to both of us.

6. In 1997 I was in The Hague trying to influence the decision makers to return the Danube into her natural riverbed and explaining that a compromise plan (CP) existed, which would allow us to convert the whole region into a three-nation nature-protection park. The court decided not to support any specific plan and asked the parties (Hungary and Slovakia) to try to negotiate a settlement between themselves.

   Today, we are trying to put pressure on the Hungarian government (through lawsuits and other means) to bring the case back to The Hague for a second round and a final decision. This they are hesitant to do, because their primary concern is to be allowed into the European Union, and good, tension-free relations with their neighbors is an essential prerequisite of that. We, the environmental nongovernmental organizations, on the other hand, are arguing that the four hundred unique species of the Szigetköz (this former delta of the ancient Pannon sea, the only inland sea delta of Europe) must not be sacrificed to any short-range or practical consideration. I am also convinced that implementing the CP would allow us to maintain good relations with Slovakia while protecting the environment. Concerning this broad issue of river protection, on May 13, 2000, I wrote the following letter to the *New York Times:*

To the Editor

Vice President Gore campaigning near the Snake River dams referred to the conflict between farming interests and the preservation of salmon. This conflict does not need to exist. When dams are replaced by Parshall straits the water level is kept high while the riverbed is kept open and the salmon are therefore free to travel.

This is also the solution proposed by the Compromise Plan for the controversial Gabcikovo dam on the Danube.

Béla Lipták
Stamford, CT

7. Today Ádám is a senior counselor in the legal department of the *New York Times,* while Jenny works as a veterinarian in an animal hospital in New York. Their son, Ivan, is showing artistic talent, while Katie, their daughter, has such a logical and systematic mind that she will most likely end up an engineer or a scientist. Theirs is a happy family, which I love to visit not only because of the obvious reasons but also because they live in Manhattan next to Kossuth's monument on 113th Street, and that is a special place for me.

8. Ágnes is the president-owner of one of the best decorative painting companies in New York, where, in the southern tip of Manhattan, Richard also operates his own firm named Mediterranean Imports. Richard has also obtained dual citizenship for my blond little granddaughter, Ava, who, thanks to the efforts of Ágnes and her Hungarian babysitter, Edith, is just beginning to speak both English and Hungarian. Ava is full of energy, always happy; it is a pleasure to visit them, particularly, because she calls me Papa. Her optimistic, cheerful personality reminds me of my mother, Memi.

Index

Academy of Dramatic Arts, 40
accident with rifle, 52
Ádámka (son, diminutive for Adam).
    See Lipták, Ádám or Adam
agent albums, 108, 116
Ágnes, 16; and corduroy jacket, 21; at
    Lake Balaton, 83; cannot find, 53;
    her letter, 95; left for Lake Balaton,
    57; movie missed, 23-33
Agricultural Academy of Magyaróvár,
    120
Agricultural University of Gödöllő, 34
Agricultural University of Keszthely, 60
airports occupied, 97
air traffic during the revolt, 184
Akácfa Street, 152
Alkotmány Street, 46
ambulance fired at, 153
American election: day before, 139; day
    of, 142
American Hungarian Student Associa-
    tion (AHSA), 189; formation at Bard
    College, 167; moving to Boston, 168
András Hess Square: hiding in the
    dormitorium, 161
Andrea (Duduke's daughter), 188
Andris (younger brother). See Lipták,
    Dr. András
Andropov, Juri (ambassador to Hun-
    gary), 124, 187
Angyal, István or Pista, 70; arrested,
    161; being Hungarian and Jewish,
    77; hanged, 189; captured on Nov.
    16, 157; meeting him, 71; our long
    talk, 79–81; photo, 72; with Olaf
    and Vaszil, 156; "We have won," 84
anti-Jewish Laws, 10; numerus clausus,
    179

anti-Semitism, 5; incident on Bartók
    Street, 67-68
applause, 27
Aptyi (father), arrest 12; background,
    8; he finds me, 162; his last minutes,
    172; lifting Russian soldier, 11;
    personality, 9; takes me to the
    Szabós, 158; walking home after the
    attack, 157; "you must escape," 162;
    wrote in the Bible, 190
armed patrols, 72
arm-in-arm, 39
arms, getting, 66
arrested by my own, 114, 123
Astoria restaurant, 61
attack by secret police, 175
aula of the Technical University, 25; not
    a soul, 55; waiting as a prisoner, 144
Austria, bringing blood from, 121
autonomy for Hungarian minorities,
    177
ÁVH (Hungarian communist secret
    police), 7, 181; agent albums, 116;
    "blue" and "green," 125; aristocrat
    informer, 119; captain from
    Kistarcsa, 108; collecting the weap-
    ons at headquarters, 104; disinte-
    grated, 82; escaping through attic,
    109; execution, 101; fake identity
    cards, 109; firing at the radio, 48;
    identity of spies not released, 185;
    lawsuit against István Dudás, 186;
    prisoners in KA-51, 93; prisoners go
    home, 128; Pufajkas, 117; seeking
    protection, 88; smuggling murder-
    ers, 123; snipers, 152; Szabad Nép
    building, 53; throwing hand gre-
    nades, 113

bácsi, 10
Bácsi, Jani (coach), 16
Bácsi, Petik, 73
Bácsi, Szabó (legendary reader of Széna
    Square), 184; four eggs, 85; his
    headquarters, 84
Bakay, Dr.: his office, 138; Marika on
    the floor, 140
Bakonyi, Aladár (Tibi's father), 21
Bakonyi, Tibi (friend), 21
Báli, Sándor, 98
Bang-Jensen, Per (son of Povl), 190
Bang-Jensen, Povl, 167, 190
barbiturates in the sausage, 57
Bard College, 189; arrival, 167
Baross, Gábor (minister), 7
Baross Square, 17, 52
barrel of blood, 99
barricades on Gellért Square, 53
Bartók, Béla (composer), 4
Bartók Street, 67; getting captured, 142
Bástya movie house, 23
Batthyány, Lajos (1848 prime minister),
    190; hanged, 162
BBC Radio, 10
begging for paratroopers, 136
Békéscsaba (town), 7
Béla Bartók Street, 16
Belojannisz factory, 37, 98, 181
Bem, József (Polish general), 41, 181
Bem Square, 43-44
Benes, Eduard (Czech politician), 5
Benke, Valéria, 48
Bible, family, 190
Bibó, István (member of free govern-
    ment), 188; writes a historic docu-
    ment, 133; photo, 134
bier for Jancsi, 115
Bitman, Dr. Jennifer (daughter-in-law),
    177, 192; photo, 178
blood: from Austria, 121; in a barrel, 99
bombing the Suez Canal, 98
Bónis, László (professor): fighting on
    Móricz Square, 129; in the burning

building, 138; supporter of Boston
    Opera, 188
book-burning, 13
Bosnian wars, 5
Bottomless Lake, Soviet infantry, 139
Bowes, Professor Frederick, 168; wife
    painted my portrait, 169
Britain stabs us in the back, 91
Bródy Street, 48
Budafoki Street, 151; stealing bread,
    160
Budaörs (town): roadblock, 117
Budapest: map, 18
Bukucs (my dog), 19, 34, 157, 189
Bundi (Saint Bernard dog), 11-12
burned-out apartments on Móricz
    Square, 150
burned-out Russian tanks, 60; with
    corpse in hatchway, 152
bust of Rector Stocek, 145
Butler, Margaret, 179

Camp Kilmer, 167
Carpathian Mountains, 4
Carter, President Jimmy, 179; energy
    independence project, 173
Castle Hill Dormitory, 161
casualty figures, 189
Category X (middle class), 13
Charles IV (last king of Hungary), 8
child roasted by tank, 154
Cholnoky, Tibor (university president),
    26, 31, 181; refuses printing de-
    mands, 33
Christmas Eve, 9
Cica (daughter). *See* Lipták, Ágnes
city at peace, 86
Clemenceau, Georges, 5
Cliff Chapel, 24
cobblestone barricades, 53
cockade for horn button, 121
coffee, strange-tasting, 175
collection box for the victims, 62
Communist crest, cutting out, 44

Communist Party: bureaucracy, 13; headquarters, 101; leaders, not one jailed or persecuted, 120; power in today's Hungary, 186; Youth Organization (DISZ), 26
Communist secret police, cover-up, 185
communist zoo or capitalist jungle, 59
"Comrades!," 46
concrete lobby, 176
confession, 163
Congress of American Veterans, 132
corduroy jacket, 20; could stand up on its own, 82, 148; first blood, 52; painting of, 169; pistol in pocket, 145
corpse on street corner, 61
corpses in the gymnasium, 120
Corvin Alley: freedom fighters, 83; holding out, 157
cover-up of ÁVH spies continues, 185
crates jump, 76
Crawford & Russell, 171
Csáky Street, being captured, 143
Csepel Island, 34, 181; holding out against second attack, 157
Csömör (village), 14
csukas (shoes), 20
Czechoslovakia, 56

Danner, János or Jancsi, 185; armored car of Imre Nagy, 86; at the gate, 36; in the meeting, 27-31; shoes, 114, 115; loudspeaker, 41; meeting at ministry of defense, 110; MEFESZ office, 63; military department, 55; murder of, 112; on religion, 89; on sculpture of 1956, 177
Danube River: Compromise Plan, 177; diversion into Slovakia, 177; fight to restore river's environment, 176; three-nation nature-protection park, 191
Danubian Confederation, 5, 182
David, Francis, 4

Deák Square, 69
defense triangle, 84
delegate from Szeged, 28
delegation arrested at radio, 48
demands, fourteen, 33; read to family, 34
demonstration: arm-in-arm, 39; printing call for, 34
deportations, 69; of Jews, 6; of Márta's family, 191; of middle class, 12; after the Revolution, 189; to Kazahstan, 189
Diet of Torda, 4
DISZ (Communist Youth Organization), 26
Dohány Street, 75
domestic agents, 107
Dóra Néni (wife of János Meloccó), 22
Dorog (mining town) 36
Döbrentei Square, 44
dual monarchy, 8
Dudás, István (ÁVH commander), 186
Duduke (Memi's younger sister): her apartment house, 56; the starving of her baby, 11, 56; powdered milk for the new baby, 135
Dulles, John Foster: betrayal of, 184; gives green light to Soviets, 184; hospitalized, 128
Dutch student volunteers, 121

Egry, Gyuri (the Menő) 23; armed, 126; class leader, 39; death in Peru, 188; defending Móricz Square, 132; volunteer, 93
Eichmann (Gestapo chief): deports a relative, 10; expelled from capital, 7
Eisenhower, President, 19; admits 32,000 Hungarian refuges, 167; policy of self-liberation, 35, 92
Elizabeth Bridge, 44
Emke restaurant, 60
Emperor Charles I, 8
English spy, 118
environmental devastation, 176

Environmental Engineers' Handbook, 173;
   role in Danube environment, 176
Eötvös High School, 13, 147
Eötvös, József (writer), 181
Eötvös University, 40
Erdei, Ferenc, 46, 182
escaping: freedom fighters on the train,
   165; from Hungary, 159; from jail,
   151; photo, 164
Europe's largest minority, 6
execution of fireman, 149

fake ÁVH identity cards, 109
Fazekas, György, 98
Ferencváros (district), 16
fighting started at radio, 50
fireman among prisoners, 148
first gunfire, 48
first truck to get through, 117
flag of the Revolution, 75
food for Budapest, 59
forced assimilation, 73
formal order, 104
fourteen demands (points), 33-34
Ferdinand, Archduke Francis, 5, 24
Freedom Bridge, 16, 44
freedom of religion, 4
freedom fighters of Corvin Alley, 83
free food from villages, 61
Free Radio Kossuth, 97
FRESCO, 192
Furkó Puszta (family ranch), 9
Future Engineer, 39

Gabányi, Laci (student flagbearer), 41
Gabcikovo (dam on Danube), 173;
   Compromise Plan, 191
Gábor (Ágnes' brother), 95, 184
Gabriella or Gabi (Jancsi Danner's
   bride), 55, 65
Gáli, József, 80
Gárdonyi, Feri (AHSA student leader),
   168; died in Mexico, 190
Gates, Bill, 173

Gellért Hill, 24
Gellért Spa, 15
Gellért Square, 41; Jancsi's murder, 112
General Bem's Square, 43-44
general strike, 161
German occupation, 10
German-Russian nonaggression pact,
   183
Gerő, Ernő (Communist Party Secre-
   tary), 46, 182; fired, 58
Gillemot, László (university president),
   26, 31, 181; at gate, 37
Gimes, Miklós (member of Nagy gov-
   ernment): hanged, 190
God and life's purpose, 149
Golden Bull, 4
goods untouched in windowless dis-
   play, 61
Gömöri, Gyurka (student leader), 160;
   at Cambridge, 189
Göncz, Árpád (former president of
   Hungary), 189; gets me to hospital,
   175; Imre Nagy plaque, 177
Görgényi, General, 126; leaves us with-
   out a commander, 129
Gorbachev-Reagan agreement, 176,
   185
grandfather and Jews, 69
Greater Romania, 6
Greater Serbia, 5
Groonevelt, Nick (publisher), 172
Grove, Andy (inventor), 172
guards get drunk, 147
guerilla leader, 84
guns in the gymnasium, 71
Győr (city), 186; delegation to meet
   Imre Nagy, 117

Habsburgs (or Hapsburgs), 4
Hague: Danube Lawsuit, 177; Compro-
   mise Plan, 191
hangings, 189
Haynal Clinic, 52
Hegyeshalom, 120

"Help Hungary!," 130
Hero's Square (Hősök Tere), 48
high-jump competition, 16
Himnusz (national anthem), 12; at
    Parliament, 47; on Nov. 4, 130
Horn, Géza, death of, 186
Horn, Gyula (former Pufajkas), 186
Horthy, Miklós: arrest by SS, 6, 21;
    background, 180; German black-
    mail, 180
hospital in Austria, 121
house searched by ÁVH, 158
Hungária Boulevard, 157
Hungarian Academy of Science, 176
Hungarian autonomy, 177
Hungarian cockade on Tyrolian hat,
    121
Hungarian Jewry, assimilation, 5
Hungarian neutrality, 103
Hungarian refugees: in United States,
    167; worldwide, 190
Hungarian Revolution of 1848, 30
Hungarians as largest minority in
    Europe, 177
Hungarian School in New York, 173
Hungarian Scouts, 173
Hungarian tanks, 49
Hungarian Writers Union: appeal for
    UN observers, 130; collection box, 63
Hungary: lost 3 percent of population
    in 1956, 190; protects communist
    spies, 186

IBM Headquarters, 175
identity cards, fake ÁVH, 109
Illés, Gábor, 49, 182
imprisonment, 143
independent student organization, 29
industry, employee ownership of, 99
Instrument Engineers' Handbook, 172
Interior Ministry: collecting the weap-
    ons, 104; the siege, 105
International Court of Justice: Danube
    Lawsuit, 177; Compromise Plan, 191

interrogation, 142; in MEFESZ office,
    145
Israel: attack on Egypt, 91
István Hospital, 155

jailed: in Magyaróvár, 124; in New
    York, 169
jampec (teddy-boy) pants, 21
Jankó, Béla (MEFESZ leader), 161;
    Union of Free Hungarian Students
    (UFHS), 161
Jankovich, István (professor), 31; Topo-
    lino, 4
jazz band, 13
Judaism: being a Hungarian Jew, 80
Judit (Ágnes' sister), 95, 184

KA-51 lecture hall, 38; ÁVH prisoners,
    84; as a prisoner, 147
Kabars, 73
Kádár (Csermanek), János, 103, 185;
    disappears, 124; forms counterrevo-
    lutionary government, 133; gives
    false guarantee of safety to Imre
    Nagy, 162
Karinthy Street, 160
Károly barracks, 51
Kelenföld Railroad Station, 163
Kerepes (my village), 12, 34; after the
    first attack, 57; the last visit, 158;
    walking home after Nov. 2, 157
Kassa or Kosic (town), 56
Kertész Street, 153
Kéthly, Anna (member of free govern-
    ment), 169
Khrushchev, Nikita Sergeyevich, 15,
    187; visit to Marshal Tito, 124
Kiefer, Nándi (friend), 42
Kilián Barracks, 57; commander Pál
    Maléter, 60, 84; meeting of armed
    forces, 99
Kilián, Father Csaba, 169
King Farouk, 184
Kinizsi sports field, 16

Király, Béla (general), 100, 185; commander of national guard, 126;
wants a contingent from us, 127
Kiss, Tamás, 28, 181
Kistarcsa (village with concentration
camp), 108
Komárom (city), 125
Koós (Konduktorov), Péter (UN repre-
sentative) 104; refuses to step down,
116
Kopácsi, Ibolya (wife of police chief),
70, 79
Kopácsi, Sándor (head of free police of
capital), 43, 185; alone in his office,
69; commands the national guard,
94, 100; joins the Revolution, 60;
police supplies arms, 52
Korbuly, Laci (friend): AHSA vice-
president, 168; Habitat for Human-
ity, 190
Kosice or Kassa (town), 56
Kossuth and the Blessed Virgin, 69
Kossuth, Lajos or Louis (president of
Hungary, 1848-49), 5, 182
Kossuth's Song, 46
Koszorús, Ferenc (colonel), 6
Közért (general store), 17
Kuczka, Péter (writer), 30
Kun, Béla, 6, 180
kuruc soldiers, 44, 181

Lawrence, Ava (granddaughter), 177,
192; photo, 178
Lawrence, Richard (son-in-law), 177,
192; photo, 178
Lipcsey, Attila (student friend), 22;
armed, 126; volunteers to fight, 93
Lipták, Ádám or Adam (son), 171, 191;
graduation, 175; marriage and
children, 177; photo, 178; profession, 192
Lipták, Ágnes (daughter), 145, 171;
graduation, 175; marriage and child,
177; photo, 178; profession, 192

Lipták, Dr. András (younger brother,
Andris), 8, 14, 19, 20, 189
Liptak, Áron or Aron (Péter's son), 191
Lipták, Béla (author): as a child, 10;
could not fire gun, 113; hiding at the
Szabós, 158; hiding pistol under
bust, 145; painting of, 169; photo
in 1990, 101; worst night of life,
128. See also Ösci
Lipták, Béla, Sr. (father), 8. See also Aptyi
Liptak, Caitlin (Péter's daughter), 191
Liptak, Ivan (grandson), 177, 192;
photo, 178
Liptak, Katie (granddaughter), 177,
192; photo, 178
Lipták, Márta Szacsvay (wife, now
often called "nagymama"): AHSA
secretary, 168; ceramic artist, 191;
drama student at Skidmore College,
168; studio, 175; masters in English,
171; photo, 178; prepared text and
teached in Hungarian School, 173;
wedding, 170
Lipták, Dr. Pál (grandfather), 7, 10, 12;
and Jews, 69
Lipták, Péter (older brother), 8, 14, 19;
alerts the university of Gödöllő, 35;
at the radio, 50; escaping together,
165; move to Boston, 168; return to
Hungary, 191
Litván, József, 10
Losonczy, Géza (member of free government): murdered in jail, 190
loudspeaker car, 86
loyalties, dual, 176
Lutheran High School, 12
lynching, 101

MacLeish, Archibald (American poet),
167
Magyaróvár (city of ÁVH massacre),
120; walking to Austria, 165
Majoross, Imre (driver), 42, 64; his
escape, 113; murder of Jancsi, 112

Maléter, Pál (general), 60, 183; captured, 129; commander of Kilián Barracks, 84; confrontation with Pongrácz, 100; contact lost at Soviet headquarters, 128; hanged, 190; leaves for signing Soviet withdrawal agreement, 127
mankind's purpose, 90
march on the radio, 49
Marián, István (colonel), 31; hiding, 56; his past, 64; "Jancsi died because of me," 114; life imprisonment, 187; moves to MEFESZ office, 64; nervous breakdown, 110; quits, 129, "we will march in daylight," 32
Mária (Gyurka Vereczkey's sister), 126
Marika (bride of Gyuszi Perr), 17, 188; armed, 126; and bread, 133, 139; wounded, 140; on Móricz Square, 137; "take some candy," 140
Marshall Plan, 35
Martyrs of the Revolution, 3
Marxism-Leninism University, 40
Masaryk, Thomas (Czech politician), 5
massacres by ÁVH: at Magyaróvár, 120; at Parliament, 62
Matthias Corvinus (king), 4
Meciar, Vladimir (Slovak nationalist), 177
Mécs, Imre or Imi (student, friend), 30; photo, 101; searching for the grave of Imre Nagy, 175
Mediterranean Imports, 192
MEFESZ (free student organization): "Allow me to speak," 28; formation, 29; headquarter office, 58, 63; interrogation by Russians in MEFESZ office, 145–47; meeting at Castle Hill, 161; Szeged's representative Tamás Kiss, 26; the last meeting, 161
Meloccó, János (diplomat, editor, family friend), 12, 22; writing about Cardinal Mindszenty, 177

Meloccó, Miklós (sculptor, friend), 180; 1956 sculpture, 177
melon farmer, 73
Memi (born Margit Dieballa, my mother), 8; after our defeat, 157; in Cliff Chapel, 24; visits us in America, 171
Menő (Gyuri Egry), 23; death in Peru, 188; defending Móricz Square, 133; on my right, 42
minefields, 165
Military Department, 31; officers hiding, 55
milk stealing, 57
Mindszenty, Cardinal Jósef: arrest of, 7, 12; asylum at American Embassy, 133, 162, 180; background, 180; drugging, 22; freed, 98; his trial, 22; photo, 99; proclamation, 127
Molotov (Soviet foreign minister), 183
Molotov cocktails, 183; making them, 78; used in Móricz Square, 139
Móricz Circus (Square), 54; barricades ready, 132; burned out apartments, 150; carrying the wounded, 138; defenders of, 129; defending the apartment house, 138; getting captured, 142; Gyuszi Perr and Marika, 137; Radio Free Europe transmission by loudspeaker, 137; superintendent wounded, 138; tank aims at our apartment, 139; the fighting starts, 136; we can move only one tank, 133
Mosonmagyaróvár (city), 120
MSZP (Hungarian Socialist Party), 185; its real estate possessions, 186
multiparty system reestablished, 91
Museum Boulevard, Russian tanks, 53
"Mustache, the." See Pongrácz, Gergely
Mutnyánszky, Ádám or Mutyi Bácsi (professor), 37, 181; "go my sons," 39; prisoner in his lecture room, 147
Münnich, Ferenc (Communist leader): role in betraying Imre Nagy, 162

Nagy, Imre (premier of free government), 7; abolishes the one-party system, 96; asks for protection of neutrality, 116; asylum at Yugoslav Embassy, 133, 162; forms new government, 78; hanged, 190; in Parliament, 83; life story, 182; meeting with Andropov, 124; named prime minister, 58; neutrality declared, 103; plaque, 177; Soviet attack announced, 130; speech at Parliament, 46; taken to Romania, 162; terminates Warsaw Pact membership, 103

Nagy, Zsiga (student), 159; hiding together, 160

Nagyaptyi (grandfather). *See* Lipták, Dr. Pál

Nagymemi (grandmother), 19; her apartment house, 11

Nagyvárad Square, 155

Nasser, Gamal Abdal, 184

national anthem. *See* Himnusz

National Guard, 67; defense strategy, 84; division at full alert, 126; forming the regiment, 70

National Student Association of the United States (NSA), 167

Nemcsik, Bandi (student activist), 30

Nemes, Kati (professor), 33

Németh, Miklós, 185, 186

Némethy, Ede, 30, 33

néni, 10

neutrality, 98; Imre Nagy asks for guarantee, 116

newspapers appear, 115

New York Times, letter to, 191–92

1956 Museum in Lakitelek, Hungary, 185

nonstop elevator, 106

normal life returns, 115

North Koreans, 13

November (activity by date): Nov. 1 (Thu.), 103-10; Nov. 2 (Fri.), 111-24; Nov. 3 (Sat.), 124-28; Nov. 4 (Sun.), 128-41; Nov. 5 (Mon.), 142-50; Nov. 6 (Tue.), 151-58; Nov. 7 (Wed.), 159-60; Nov. 8 (Thu.), 160; Nov. 9 (Fri.), 161; Nov. 10-22, 162; Nov. 23 (Fri.), 163; Nov. 24 (Sat.), 164

numerus clausus, 179

nurse burned, 153

O'Connor, Cardinal, 179

October (activity by date): Oct. 21 (Sun.), 15-20; Oct. 22 (Mon.), 20-35; Oct. 23 (Tue.), 36-50; Oct. 24 (Wed.), 51-57; Oct. 25 (Thu.), 58-65; Oct. 26 (Fri.), 66-73, Oct. 27 (Sat.), 74-81; Oct. 28 (Sun.), 82-90; Oct. 29 (Mon.), 91-96; Oct. 30 (Tue.), 96-97; Oct. 31 (Wed.), 97-102

Olaf, 100

on the road to Austria, 164

oranges in KA-51

Orbán, Party Secretary, 26

Ordassy, Éva, 21

Orlay Street: Dr. Bakay's office, 138; getting captured, 142

Óvár (city), 120; walking to Austria, 165

Öcsi (author's nickname), 3, 8; cover name to protect from ÁVH works, 162. *See also* Lipták, Béla

Pannonhalma (benedictine high school), 12

Pannonia (Roman province), 4

Pannon Sea, 15, 175; delta of, 191

Pataki, Governor George, 173; photo of, 174

pater-noster, 106; destroyed, 109

patrol with Jancsi Danner, 88

penguins (DISZ functionaries), 27

permit number three, 83

Perr, Gyuszi (Marika's fiancee; friend), 17, 188; announcement of demonstration, 34; armed, 126; defending

Móricz Square, 133; machine gun, 138; trying to find Marika, 140
Péterfy Hospital, 71; call for blood, 99
Petőfi battalion, 84
Petőfi Bridge, 81; the Pobjeda with the assassins, 113
Petőfi Military Academy, 67, 96; cadets join us, 126; cadets leave before fight, 129
Petőfi, Sándor (poet), 181; poem, 44
Petőfi Statue, 43
Piarist Gymnasium (high school), 12; new MEFESZ center, 160
Pilisvörösvár (town), 76; tank crews leave before the fight, 129
Piros, László (Communist minister), 42
pistol from Kopácsi, 70; hiding under Stocek's bust, 145
Pobjeda (car), 181; murder of Jancsi, 112
Pointcar, Raymond, 5
police headquarters, 69
police station on Baross Square, 53
policy of self-liberation, 91; rebroadcast on Móricz Square, 139; role of Radio Free Europe, 187
Polish solidarity march, 40, 43
Pongrácz, Gergely (guerilla leader, "the Mustache"), 100, 185; photo, 101
Pope Sylvester II, 179
Poppe, Kornél (neighbor's son), 157
pornographic magazines, 107
Poznan (city in Poland), 7, 23; surrounded, on strike, 29-30
prisoner: in Magyaróvár, 124; in Budapest, 144; in New York, 169
produce from villages, 94
provocation (anti-Semitic), 67
Pufajkas, 117, 186

racist fanatics, 67
Rácz, Sándor, 98; elected president of Workers Council, 161; received life sentence, 189

radio broadcasts in Russian, 97
radio building, 48
Radio Budapest goes silent, 131
Radio Csokonai, 136
Radio Free Europe (RFE), 57, 91; balloons, 187; role in the Revolution, 187
Rákóczy Street, 34; Stalin's monument on pavement, 53; Russian tanks firing, 152; untouched stores, 60
Rákoczy, Francis II (leader of 1703 uprising), 4, 44; ruling prince, 182
Rákosi, Mátyás (Stalin's Hungarian puppet), 7, 180
Rapavy, József (neighbor), 59
Reagan-Gorbachev agreement, 176, 185
Red Cross ambulance fired at, 153
red star on the Parliament, 46
regaining self-respect, 43
Regnum Marianum (Catholic school), 182
reindeer-drawn sled, 9
reporter looking for blood, 93; with head wound, 125
Revolution: number killed, 189; sculpture commemorating, by Miklós Meloccó, 177
Revolutionary Councils, 74
Revolutionary Workers' Councils, 98, 161
riding boots, 88
rifle: accident, 52; grimy, 51; my first, 50
roadblock: at Győr, 118; outside Budapest 117
Romania (Soviet ally): doubled her size at the expense of Hungary, 190; jails the arrested members of the Imre Nagy government, 162
Roosevelt Square, 75
Ruggyanta factory, 52
Russell, Sam (president of C&R), 171
Russian colonel stationed in Hungary, 147

Russian families removed from Hungary, 97
Russian language broadcasts, 88
Russian occupation, 11
Russian soldiers, 124; being captured by, 143; sympathizing with Hungary, 183
Russian soldiers on Béla Bartók Street, 143
Russian tanks, 77, 139; at Wesselényi Street, 153; blocking the road, 116; commander speaks Hungarian, 61; fire on ÁVH, 62; firing at ambulance, 153; in Dohány Street, 75; killing nurse, 153; on Museum Boulevard, 53; photo, 154; second invasion, 129
"Russkis go home!," 31, 46

Sabbattarians (Széklers of Jewish religion), 73
Saint Emeric of Hungary, 179
Saint Gellért Mountain, 15
Saint Gellért Square, 41; building barricades, 53; Jancsi's murder, 112
Saint Margaret Bridge, 45
Saint Margaret of Scotland, 179
Saint Stephen (king), 4, 179
Saint Stephen of Hungary Church, 168
sanctuary for Jews, 6
sandals: disintegrating, 69; reattached with wire, 88
Sándor, Iván (editor of The Engineer of the Future), 33, 39
Satan's face, 113
scholarship, 15
searched by Russians, 145
second attack: begins, 130; invasion force, 183; just before American election, 128; photo of fighters, 137; twenty-five hundred tanks, 129
secret police (ÁVH), 7; attack in 1983, 175
security risk, 169

self-heating building, 175
self-liberation policy, 91
self-propelled waste basket, 77
Sephardic Jews, 80, 184
short-wave radio transmitter, 86
Sík, Endre (Communist ambassador to Moscow) 67; back as Kádár's UN ambassador, 160
Sík Igor (Endre's son), 67; Russian language broadcasts, 88, 160
Sík, Sándor (poet), 67
sixteen points (demands), 44, 182-83
skiing in Vermont, 172
Skoda (make of car), 42, 181; murder of Jancsi, 112; turned over, 113
smuggling watches, 119
society, ideal, 59
Somkuty, Gabriella (Jancsi Danner's bride), 65, 185; Jancsi's bier, 114
Sopron (city), 69
Sopron University, 64
Soroksár Street, 50
South Korea "formula," 116
Soviet UN Consulate, attempt to capture, 169
Soviets agree to leave, 116
spirit of buildings, 56
spy albums, 108; English military attache, 118
Stalin's Monument, 48, 182; head on Rákóczy Street, 54
Stalin City (Dunapentele): freedom fighters, 136; holding out against the second attack, 157
stealing milk from Russians, 57, 135
Stevens Institute of Technology, 168
stipend, 19, 23; deposited in collection box, 63; left with shepherd at border, 166
Stricker, Katalin, 51
Stocek (rector), 145; his bust (photo), 146
stolen horse and carriage, 11
stores, untouched goods in, 143
strike proclamation, 48

student from Szeged, 26
students from Poland, 29
Suez Canal, bombing of, 98
Suez Canal war, 91; oil-hungry busi-
nessman, 141; Russians think they
are at Suez Canal, 143
suicide contemplated by spy, 119
superintendent wounded, 138
Szabad Ifjúság, 31
Szabad Nép (Communist Party paper),
47; fight at headquarters, 53
Szabó, Iván, 30; loudspeaker, 41
Szacsvay, Márta (wife). *See* Lipták,
Márta Szacsvay
Szalai, Sándor, 176
Szatmár Peace Treaty, 182
Széchenyi Chain Bridge, 44; bringing
weapons, 75
Székely (Szekler or Siculi), 73
Széll, Sándor, 45
Széna Square, 84
Szentágothai, János, 176
Szigethy, Attila (president of
Transdanubian Revolutionary
Council), 82; his suicide, 186; meet-
ing him, 118; rescues us, 124
Szigetköz, 175
Szikra publishing house, 48
Szilágyi, József (director of Imre Nagy's
office), 30; hanged, 181, 190
Szilárd, Leó (scientist), 39
Szőke, Kati (professor), 33; at gate, 36;
in MEFESZ office, 64

tanks: cannot kill ideals, 90; firing at
ambulance (photo), 153; from
Pilisvörösvár, 76; killing nurse, 153;
new ones from Ukraine and Romania, 118; on observation duty, 78;
second invasion, 129; tanks in a
circle, 138; trapping them, 84; Uncle
Feri, 134; we are the target, 139; with
our flag, 75; we have only one, 133
tarots, 22

teaching: at Yale University, 175; process control, 171
tearing down the waterspout, 153
Technical University of Budapest, 13,
22; entering as prisoner of Russians,
144; formulating the sixteen points,
30; locking up before the fight, 136;
MEFESZ headquarters, 58; Russian
soldiers and Pufajkas at the gates, 159
Technical University of Miskolc, 13
Teleki, Pál (anti-Nazi prime minister),
6, 190; suicide, 180
Teller, Edward (scientist), 39; preface to
my handbook, 172
Tétényi Clinic, 110
Tildy, Zoltán (ex-president), 183
Tisza, István (prime minister), 5
Tito, Marshal Josif Broz, 124, 187
Topolino, 44
"top secret," 107
torches made of *Szabad Nép*, 47
Torda Diet, 4
Tóth, Csanád (friend), 179
Tóth, Ili (student friend), 65, 74; escape,
151; prisoner, 147; overnight visit,
152, 188
Tóth, Ilonka (young doctor), hanged, 169
Tököl (Soviet headquarters): Maléter
visits to sign agreement, 127
Török, Laci (student friend), 13
200-percent person, 176
tranquilizer for Marián, 110
Transdanubian Revolutionary Council,
118
Transylvania, 4; Székelys, 73
Trianon Treaty, 5,6
Tüzoló Street garage, 71, 77; István
Angyal captured on Nov. 16; in the
basement, 78; holding out against
second attack, 157

Üllői Street, 52, 74
Uncle Feri, 56; asking him to move our
tanks, 134

Uncle Szabó, 85
Union of Free Hungarian Students,
    161, 189
Unitarian Church, 4
United Izzó (factory), armed worker
    guards, 161
United Nations: delays discussion of
    Hungary, 116; my visit, 167
University of Gödöllő, 37
University of Sopron, 64

Vance, Cyrus (secretary of state), 179
Varga, Sándor (student), 64, 66
Vereczkey, Gyurka (driver, friend), 64,
    183; does not stay to fight, 129; his
    family, 71; sleeps in jail, 124; smacks
    the anti-Semite, 67
Veres, Péter (president of Writers'
    Union), 44
victory in the air, 82
Világos (theater where the combined
    forces of Austria and Russia de-
    feated the Hungarian freedom fight-
    ers in 1849), 190
Villányi Street defense, 139
Viola Street, 77
Visegrád Four, 182
visiting universities on Pest, 40
Vojvodina, 177
volunteers to guard General Király, 129
von Kármán, Theodore (scientist), 39,
    181
von Neumann, John (scientist), 12, 39,
    181
Völgy Street military laboratory, 86

Waldseemueller, Martin (mapmaker),
    179
Wallenberg, Raul, 7

Wall Street Journal, op-ed article, 176
Wars of Independence: 1703-11, 4;
    1848-49, 5
Warsaw Pact, 7, 184; leaving the pact,
    98
Warsaw surrounded by tanks, 30
Washington, George, 179
weapons delivery, 75
weapons from ÁVH headquarters, 109
wedding, 170
Wekerle, Zsóka (Andris' wife), 189
Wesselényi Street, 152
Wigner, Eugene (scientist), 12, 39
Wittner, Mária, 51
Wilson, President Woodrow, 5
Women of Selistye, The, 19, 23
wooden pistol case, 146
World Wars I and II, 5, 6
wounded, 125; carrying, 146
Writers' Union's collection box, 62

X Category (middle class), 13

Yale University, 175
Yalta Treaty, 35; betrayal repeated, 91;
    Soviet domination approved, 184
yellow star, 69
Yugoslavia, 56

Zádor, Pali (student), 63
Zrinyi Barracks, 74, 183
Zrinyi Military Academy, 70; cadets
    join us, 126; cadets leave before
    fight, 129
Zsindely, Laci (friend and classmate),
    27; armed, 126; finds me, 132; in
    captivity, 148; naval architecture,
    38; pilot, 188; volunteers to fight, 93
Zsuzsa with submachine gun, 49

Eastern European Studies

Stjepan G. Meštrović, Series Editor

Cigar, Norman. *Genocide in Bosnia: The Policy of "Ethnic Cleansing."* 1995.

Cohen, Philip J. *Serbia's Secret War: Propaganda and the Deceit of History.* 1996.

Gachechiladze, Revaz. *The New Georgia: Space, Society, Politics.* 1996.

Gibbs, Joseph. *Gorbachev's Glasnost: The Soviet Media in the First Phase of Perestroika.* 1999.

Knezys, Stasys, and Romanas Sedlickas. *The War in Chechnya.* 1999.

Meštrović, Stjepan G., ed. *The Conceit of Innocence: Losing the Conscience of the West in the War against Bosnia.* 1997.

Polokhalo, Volodymyr, ed. *The Political Analysis of Postcommunism: Understanding Postcommunist Ukraine.* 1997.

Quinn, Frederick. *Democracy at Dawn: Notes from Poland and Points East.* 1997.

Savage, Ania. *Return to Ukraine.* 2000.

Shlapentokh, Vladimir, Christopher Vanderpool, and Boris Doktorov, eds. *The New Elite in Post-Communist Eastern Europe.* 1999.

Tasovac, Ivo. *American Foreign Policy and Yugoslavia, 1939–1941.* 1999.

Teglas, Csaba. *Budapest Exit: A Memoir of Fascism, Communism, and Freedom.* 1998.

BÉLA LIPTÁK immigrated to the United States after the events detailed in this book. He holds a bachelor's degree from Stevens Institute of Technology and a master's from the City College of New York. He now makes his home in Stamford, Connecticut.

ISBN 1-58544-120-1

9 781585 441204

90000